A HYMN TO HIM

A HYMN TO HIM

THE LYRICS OF

ALAN JAY LERNER

LIMELIGHT EDITIONS
LE
Books of the Performing Arts

First published in the United States in 1987 by
Limelight Editions,
118 East 30th Street,
New York 10016

Introduction and notes © Benny Green 1987
Other copyright holders are acknowledged on page 315

Designed by Craig Dodd

ISBN 0-87910-109-1

Printed and bound in Great Britain
by Billings and Sons Limited, Worcester

☆ CONTENTS ☆

'Musicals have to have very strong bones, because there's an awful lot of nonsense going on. Something has to hold the roof up.'
Alan Jay Lerner

☆ INTRODUCTION ☆

The art of putting words to music is so riddled with imprecision that it cannot even agree on its own terminology. Ira Gershwin, that most erudite of all practitioners, confessed in his writings on the subject that although throughout his life he had been described as a lyricist, he was very much afraid that so far as purists like himself were concerned, the term was a solecism, and that the true word was 'lyrist'. He also acknowledged that lyrist, for all its correctitude, was a lost cause, defeated by the world's refusal to deploy it. Lyrist, then, is correct but spurned, lyricist wrong but familiar. For those who feel uncomfortable in the face of controversy, there is always solace to be found in the evasions of 'lyric writer'. But whatever the term, Alan Jay Lerner certainly ranks among the six greatest toilers in the field. As to the worth of that eminence, Lerner himself was given to whimsical disparagement, on one occasion telling a New York audience that although lyric writing was an art form, 'It's only a minor one, somewhere a little above photography and woodcarving.' But that was only the comically false humility of a highly sophisticated man who knew it would amuse the informed audience he was addressing, which it did. So far from being a casual, slapdash sort of business performed by cigar-chewing philistines in bowler hats and utterly lacking in real creativity or literary finesse, writing words to music was, for Alan Lerner, as it was for Cole Porter, Lorenz Hart, Noël Coward, Ira Gershwin and Johnny Mercer, a process so subtle, so intricate, so demanding, so severe in its exercise of the art of concision, that he was, on more than one occasion, known to have agonized for a week over a single line, and not always to his own satisfaction (see 'Wouldn't it be Luverly?'). This fierce dedication to the Flaubertian ideal of *le mot juste* might surprise those who have never had dinner with a good lyricist, but certainly there was no more fanatically dedicated servant of the art of the lyrist, or lyric writer, or lyricist, than Alan Lerner.

And yet, in the everyday sense in which the term is applied, Alan Lerner was not a songwriter at all. He would often make this point, especially when some well-meaning entrepreneur invited him to write a song for some momentarily prestigious event, a theme song, perhaps, for a series, or a title song for a picture. Alan's answer was always the same. He wouldn't do it. He couldn't do it. He never had been able to do it. He never would be. He was, from start to finish, a dramatist who wrote part of his plays in rhyme. The distinction is profound, even though unnoticed by most of those who professed to understand the nature of Lerner's work. (He once said, 'Over the years I've been constantly amazed at the number of people who think, for instance, that Lerner and Loewe wrote the music and somebody, the actors perhaps, made up the lyrics as they went along.') Before he could begin to conceive even the vaguest shadow of a shape of a lyric, he had to be intimately familiar, it would seem, with the singer's past life, present predicament, future prospects. He had to know what tensions lay behind the scene and which factors had brought them about, what the character was wearing and what the nature of the backdrop. After all, how can it be possible to put words into a person's mouth without some knowledge of that person's likely vocabulary? Lerner's Guinevere says 'ergo' instead of 'therefore', and would, no doubt, in defining her station in life, have talked of being fortunate; Alfred Doolittle on the same theme refers to his 'bloomin' luck'. The point is almost too obvious to need making, yet is overlooked consistently in assessments of versifiers labouring in the musical theatre. Professor Higgins displays in his songs a correctitude verging on the pedantic which becomes his professorial pretensions; the lady in *Love Life* defines her dream man as 'Mister Right' and babbles of cocktail shakers and Tyrone Power; when the minstrel chorus in *1600 Pennsylvania Avenue* explain why the poor get poorer they sing 'Cuz Dey's Dum'.

The classic definition of a song in a musical production is of a set of verses put to music which serves as a device for thrusting the action of the plot forward. The lyrics do not describe or embellish the action. They *are* the action. If they are not, there is no point in using a song at that juncture at all. When Henry Higgins admits that he has grown accustomed to Eliza's face, the confession comes as a revelation to him if not to us. It is not an amplification of what has been said or will be said. A song lyric is part of the dialogue; the phrase 'I've grown accustomed to her face' is not just a paraphrase of but also a replacement for the moment in *Pygmalion* when Higgins tells Eliza, 'I have grown accustomed to your voice and appearance,' which is excised from the text of *My Fair Lady* because there is no further need for it now that the identical sentiment has been expressed in song. Therein lies the essence of the art of adaptation. Merely to insert songs would be to elongate the evening to an insufferable length, calling to mind the remark of a New York critic, 'I quite liked the first two years of Act One.' Lerner's consummate skill as an adapter lay in his ability to strip down the text and repair the damage so skilfully with his lyrics that the seams become invisible.

Of course he acknowledged readily enough that there were some lyric writers with the ability to knock off something brilliant or moving without foreknowledge of any personality or dramatic context. He revered the best of these men, referred to them as songwriters, and, intending that definition to indicate high praise, once told me he believed the greatest American songwriter of the twentieth century was Johnny Mercer, because Mercer could conjure an 'Early Autumn' or a 'Goody Goody' literally out of thin air. It comes back to me how he gave a laugh of delight when I told him of the music hall writer of Max Beerbohm's recollections who, on being asked by a County Court judge how much he earned each year, replied without hesitation, 'Three hundred and sixty five pounds,' and on being asked to explain the exactitude of his figures, said, 'I write a song a day and I receive one pound for each song.' That was what you called a songwriter. Lerner belonged to the other group, the versifying dramatists whose place was neither in Tin Pan Alley nor the halfway house of Hollywood, but in the living theatre. In his autobiography (*On the Street Where I Live*, 1979) he has hardly begun before he defines his own status:

I am a librettist. However, whenever I fill out a form which asks that I identify my profession I do not say I am a librettist, I say 'playwright-lyricist'. Until a few years ago, it was not even proper to say 'lyricist' because there was no such word in the dictionary. A man who wrote words for a song was officially called a lyrist. Popular usage finally defeated tradition and lyricist became accepted. Amen. One of the reasons I dislike the word librettist is best illustrated by a famous Mrs Malaprop of New York who years ago, when asked where she had been the night before, said, 'To the opera.' Asked what she had seen, she replied, 'It was some Italian opera called *Libretto.*' A librettist has always seemed to me someone associated with opera and operetta and who specialized in unintelligibility and anonymity. Nevertheless, that is what I am. A librettist.

In the light of this definition of himself, Lerner is disclosed not as an artist who was first inspired by the popular jingles of the day, but as a member of the theatre audience, in which regard he was singularly fortunate in his choice of parents. His mother had in her teens aspired in a genteel sort of way to a vocal career and at one time had as her accompanist the mother of Richard Rodgers. His father, by all accounts an extraordinary man, seems to have inspired his son without actually performing any practicalities as a mentor. A dentist manqué, the old boy built up a successful chain of stores and, by the time his son was old enough to notice, was indulging his two great loves, prizefighting and love itself. With regard to women, Lerner opens his autobiography with a sentence which contrives in only twenty-three words to make a lengthy quote from the Gershwins, imply the state of the family fortunes and make the whimsical confession that the marriage of his parents had collapsed:

My Pappy was rich and my Ma was good-lookin', but by the time I was born my father no longer thought so.

Lerner writes: 'My father's influence on me was indelible and my love for him as alive as it was on the day he died in 1954, but there were many issues where we parted company. Principally there were politics and women.' Two other aspects of Lerner senior which had relevance to his son's attitudes were his atheism and his wit, which at times coalesced to produce a memorable phrase. Two days before his death he confirmed to his son his adamant atheism. By now a veteran of a different kind of theatre from the one to which his son aspired, and about to undergo his forty-ninth bout of surgery, he filled in the form sanctioning the next operation and wrote underneath, 'When it gets to fifty, sell.'

Alan recalls that, although he started studying the piano at the age of five, had resolved on a career in the theatre by the time he was twelve and was already writing songs in his early teens, his father 'paid no attention'. What he did do was to express his reverence for the English language by shipping his children to England to learn it, and never failing to apply to their range of knowledge the most stringent tests and measurements. Not very long after Alan had won a Drama Critics Award for his work on *Brigadoon*, he received a note from his father, whose struggle with cancer had finally deprived him of the power of speech:

Alan – I have counted the words you have used this weekend and you have an active vocabulary of 297 words. I don't see how you can make a career as a writer with an active vocabulary of 297 words. However, I believe you have talent and if you would like to return to school and study, I would be more than happy to subsidize you.

But both of them knew that there was a sense in which Alan had never left school, never stopped studying. His alma mater was Broadway, his campus the theatres and rehearsal rooms, his fellow-students the performers and technicians who made the productions possible. In this most demanding of all universities, Alan worked tirelessly all his life, never deterred by failure, never rendered complacent by success, never disillusioned by the numberless hordes of jackasses with which the administrative ranks of the entertainment world are staffed. After *Brigadoon* had been acclaimed, a friend said to

Lerner senior on the beach in Florida that Alan 'is certainly a lucky boy', to which the old man scribbled the reply, 'Yes, it's a funny thing about Alan. The harder he works the luckier he gets.' And Lerner adds his own postscript: 'I know the story is true because the man sent me the slip of paper.' Apparently not till the very end of his life did the old man come close to expressing his pride and admiration. One day, when the son was wheeling the father's bed into the operating room, the patient handed him a note which said, 'I suppose you're wondering why I want to live.' Alan read the note and nodded. The second note read, 'Because I want to see what happens to you.' The sad irony was that Lerner senior never did find out. He died one month before his son started to write *My Fair Lady*.

He bequeathed to his son among other things a love of England and the English which animated every word he ever wrote and was the inspiration for his finest work. In his indispensable history of his craft, *The Musical Theatre, a Celebration*, published posthumously in 1986, he prefaces his tribute to W.S. Gilbert with these sentiments:

It is my biased opinion that the British society is the most civilized on the planet Earth. One of the most prominent reasons for the civility of the English is their possession of that most precious of all human traits – a sense of humour. The French may be witty, but there is no appreciation of civilized silliness. Lots of aphorisms but no giggles. George Bernard Shaw, for instance, who although born in Ireland spent more than seventy years of his creative life in England, is the only major humorist who ever lived who was not bitter.

The passage tells us as much about Lerner as it does about Shaw. Of all the men I ever knew, Lerner was the one who exulted most in the entertaining absurdities of anecdotal recollection. His hero Shaw once told Florence Farr: 'It is by jingling the bells of a jester's cap that I, like Heine, have made people listen to me. All genuinely intellectual work is humorous.' The remark is doubly significant in the context of Lerner's career because, as well as proclaiming the golden rule of the librettist, it nods obliquely in the direction of one of Lerner's much-loved mentors, as we shall see. Lerner's history of musical comedy is that very rare thing, an erudite work shaking with silent laughter. The prose is crisp, the thinking crystalline, the verdicts judicious. But bubbling away underneath the scholarship are the springs of comedy, bestowing on even the harshest judgements the benison of charitable good humour. In conveying to posterity, for instance, the fact that the voice of Gertrude Lawrence was perhaps less spectacular than her power over audiences, he quotes one of his collaborators, the Berlin émigré Kurt Weill: 'She had the greatest range between C and C sharp of anyone I ever knew.' And this from the gifted lyricist Howard Dietz on the theme of Sigmund Romberg's tendency to lean a little too heavily at times on Tchaikovsky and company: 'I don't like composers who think. It gets in the way of their plagiarism.' But Dietz could turn a pretty compliment too. When Alan sent Dietz his introduction to Dietz's autobiography, he received this response:

Dear Alan,
    When I received your introduction to my book I was in the hospital.
    When I finished reading the introduction I went home.
                                        As ever, Howard

In discussing some of the dramaturgic follies of 1931 Alan recalls that the shortest run of the year, a calamity called *The Singing Rabbi*, opened on the Thursday and never saw Monday. He adds: 'I do not know if they gave a performance on Saturday.' And in recalling the problems of piecing together his early musical *The Day Before Spring*, he tells how the choreographer asked Fritz Loewe to compose twelve minutes of ballet music depicting Paris at five o'clock in the morning. Fritz then locked himself away for a week, wrote the music and then invited the choreographer to hear it. When the recital was over the choreographer complained, 'It sounds more like six in the morning,' to which Fritz replied, 'Yes, I see what you mean. Come back next week.' When the second recital took place the choreographer said, 'Just right,' and that was that. Lerner confesses he thought they were both mad. I recall one blissful Sunday lunch in the hospitality lounge of a London television company. Lerner, Andre Previn and myself were to appear on a show to do with the popular arts and had, as always, been called hours too soon. So we beguiled the time by amusing each other. Lerner knew of my appetite for the comically absurd, and told of an episode in the later, decrepit years in Hollywood of John Barrymore. It was at a stage in his career when the great actor was no longer able to remember even the briefest snatches of dialogue, a handicap he was bravely attempting to overcome with the device of the cue-card. One day they were shooting a scene in which Barrymore, alone in his room, opens the door to a stranger and asks, 'Yes?' Fearful that he would forget what to say once he opened the door, he had arrived at the studio armed with a huge sheet of cardboard on which was scrawled the word 'Yes'. At first the director indulged Barrymore's whim, but at last, after several unsuccessful attempts to locate the sheet of cardboard in a place where Barrymore could see it but where it was out of camera range, he asked Barrymore if he was quite sure he needed the card. 'Certainly I need it,' Barrymore is purported to have replied. 'Without the card I might open the door and say "No" – and then where would we be?' But the stories Alan liked best of all were those in which the goons from Front Office were done down by the witty artist, for which reason he delighted in the tale of how in 1944 the impresario Billy Rose commissioned Igor Stravinsky to write a fifteen-minute ballet for the Broadway production *Seven Lively Arts*. After the opening in Philadelphia, Rose sent Stravinsky a telegram:

Your music great success stop could be sensational success if you would authorize Robert Russell Bennett retouch orchestrations stop Russell orchestrates even the work of Cole Porter stop.

Stravinsky wired back:

Satisfied with great success.

Of all the wits and jokers who crossed Alan's path, the most resourceful and entertaining seems to have been Fritz Loewe, Alan's longest-standing partner. Alan once started telling me of a few of Fritz's extra-cultural exploits, and was so funny on the theme that I finally stopped him and asked why he hadn't written it all down, guessing even before I asked the question what the answer would be. By this time Loewe was a semi-invalid in splendid retirement; sure enough, Alan explained that some of the stories, for instance the one about Fritz and the lady critic from Boston, could not be made public until after Fritz had gone. Nobody, least of all Alan himself, suspected that Fritz, fourteen years the older of the two and in a frail physical condition, would survive the longer.

The two men had come together in the oddest of ways, through the vicissitudes of fortune both of them had suffered in the boxing ring. As a child Alan had often accompanied his father to Madison Square Garden on Friday nights to watch the fights. The experience gave him such an appetite for the Noble Art that while at Harvard he strove to get into the college boxing team. One day an opponent caught him with a left hook so potent that it damaged his sight permanently. After several operations he emerged with only one good eye, a disability which, it seems to me, he masked from the world with complete success. Once or twice in my association with Alan, when the word was about that some charlatan of a director was giving him a hard time in the revival of one of his works, I wondered to myself why Harvard's ex-featherweight prospect did not succumb to the temptation to give the fool a shot in the head and quieten down his pretensions. But Alan was far too much of a gentleman ever to have done such a thing, more's the pity.

Fritz Loewe's boxing career was much more spectacular and actually reached the professional arena. Nothing Alan ever told me about anything or anybody astonished me more than his statement that Fritz had once stepped into the same ring as Tony Canzoneri. For the benefit of the insular and the uncultured, I had better explain that Tony Canzoneri was to the feather- and lightweight divisions what someone like Vincent Youmans or Arthur Schwartz would be to the art of composing melodies. Canzoneri was an Italian-American artist who came out of New York City to win world titles in the early 1930s in the most brilliant and ruthless fashion. It has been a source of incredulous astonishment to a great many people that the composer of such felicities as 'The Heather on the Hill' and 'How to Handle a Woman' should have been a professional fighter. That he had once dared to challenge the great Canzoneri was much more incredible. 'What happened when they met?' I asked Alan, hardly daring to hear the answer. 'Well,' said Alan, 'if Fritz had stopped Canzoneri I wouldn't have written *My Fair Lady*. Fritz had a strategy for the Canzoneri fight, to box on the retreat and keep out of Canzoneri's reach. He was convinced he could have danced all night. Canzoneri's reach turned out to be just a little longer than Fritz had figured. Fritz was stopped in the first, and the musical profession gained a new recruit.' I have pondered that story ever since, hoping fervently that Canzoneri, a great professional, might have been able to find consolation for his eventual dethronement by Barney Ross in the thought that at any rate Ross could never claim to have ko'd the composer of 'On the Street Where You Live'.

And so, whatever posterity may find to say about the partnership of Lerner and Loewe, it will certainly have to concede that this was the most accomplished songwriting team, pugilistically speaking, in the history of the American theatre. It will also take note of Lerner's description of how his father utilized his own love of boxing to practise the Noble Art of Self-Indulgence, and how, through a careless miscalculation regarding the latest boxing information, he crashed to matrimonial disaster. Sometimes when Lerner senior said he was off to the Friday night fights, he was not being strictly accurate; as his son put it: 'On many occasions his taste for combat drew him to other, more quilted arenas.' Alan continues:

In those days people worked on Saturdays and one Saturday morning, my father later told me, as he was preparing to go to the office, two things happened that had never happened during his entire married life. The first was that while he was dressing my mother woke up. The second was that as she opened her eyes she said: 'Who won the fight?' Alas, that Friday happened to have been one of the nights my father's ringside seat was empty. I do not remember who fought in the main bout, but we will call them Smith and Jones. My father, taking a chance, said, 'Smith'. My mother turned over and went back to sleep. My father went into the dining-room and opened the *New York Times* at the sports page. Jones had won.

That both Alan's parentage and his professional partnership should have been so profoundly affected by a sport which figures nowhere in his collected works will bemuse as well as amuse many of his admirers, but I can assure them that Alan's interest in and admiration of the great gladiators of his boyhood never left him; as proof of his enduring loyalty I can cite his exasperation when the English edition of his autobiography, which mentions the fights between Joe Louis and Max Schmeling, referred to the challenger as Schmelling and then unbelievably compounded the error in the index by omitting all reference to Louis and listing instead a mysterious figment of the indexer's imagination called 'Schmelling, Louis'. Whether he retained much interest in the techniques of the latterday champions I couldn't say, but I suspect that, like most of us, the real giants for him were those of his childhood. I never quite reconciled myself to the streak of controlled pugnacity which must once have been visible in the temperament of one of Harvard's up-and-coming nine-stoners, for Alan was of all things sweet and gentle in his worldly relationships. Yet there must once have been a time when hitting people was a prime interest in his life. Were there moments, I wonder, when the two partners, the sucker for a left hook and the sacrificial offering to Mr Canzoneri, ever beguiled the hours between shows by boxing a few rounds? I doubt it. Both of them were pianists, and a pianist must always care for his hands.

It would perhaps be taking discretion to absurd lengths to attempt an introduction to the works of Alan Lerner without referring to his relationships with women. He was famous as one of the most-married gifted men in the Western world, but I always felt that his private life was his private business and that nobody had any right to pry or publicize his fortunes in this area. But I can report that Alan seemed to have a delightful sense of the unorthodoxy of his situation sometimes and expressed it with memorable whimsicality. The first time I ever met him he was staying with his then wife at the Berkeley Hotel in London. I forget now who arranged our meeting or on what pretext, but whatever the circumstances, there is always a great difficulty on these occasions in breaking the ice. I, a local nobody, find myself alone in the room with one of the world's greatest practitioners of his art. We have never met. He knows nothing about me. What am I to say? I have faced the dilemma a hundred times, with every sort of celebrity from Orson Welles to Frank Sinatra to Compton Mackenzie to Harold Wilson, but never was I disarmed so humorously or so painlessly as on my meeting with Alan. He emerged from the bedroom, extended his hand and said, 'I believe you know my father-in-law', a remark of such stupefying incongruity that I backed into an armchair and started laughing. We both knew that I was by some years the younger man, and yet, with this eccentric opening gambit, Alan was placing himself on the side of youth, prepared for an encounter with a member of the older generation. The facts were that someone had briefed him about my jazz background, and that he had inferred from what was told to him that I must at some time have come across the very famous jazz piano player whose daughter was now Mrs Lerner. Not only was she younger than Alan, but so was her father, and when I asked Alan what the piano player had thought about it all, he told me that the initial impulse had been to go out and find a child-bride of his own. By this time we were laughing at and with each other like old friends, and it had been all his own work, the first of many small kindnesses and courtesies he was to show to me.

My only other recollection of any observation by him on the vexed question of the battle of the sexes takes me back to an afternoon when we had been discussing the details of a recital we were to give, together with Elaine Stritch, for an arts festival, the idea being that my dissertations on the art of the theatre lyric should be interrupted periodically by Alan and Elaine, who would recite words without music. The fate of the eventual recital falls outside the bounds of this narrative, but on the afternoon when Alan and I met to find out what he might care to select for recitation from his own works, he was pressed for time because of rehearsals at the Adelphi Theatre for a revival of *My Fair Lady*. After displaying great patience for an hour or so, he then announced his imminent departure for the theatre, inviting me to share his taxi. Along Knightsbridge we found ourselves trapped in a spectacular traffic jam, at which point Alan suddenly took to chatting about matrimony in general and his own experiences in particular. I sensed that he might not altogether be content with his current arrangements, and that his present preoccupation was very much with Eliza Doolittle, but his talk was so amusing and so utterly lacking in any taint of self-pity that I was not sure whether to commiserate or laugh. Suddenly we found ourselves inching through the afternoon traffic of the Strand and approaching the end of the journey, at which point he cut off his ruminations and announced his final conclusions on this most insoluble of problems. 'What can you do with them?' he asked, and then, glancing at me with just a shade of uncertainty, as though fearing I might find him guilty of self-idolatry, he quoted his own wonderful words, 'Their heads are full of cotton, hay and rags.' And then he darted out of the taxi leaving me laughing on the pavement and asking myself if he had ever thought of playing the role of Henry Higgins. That evening, the London papers carried the story of his engagement to the beautiful singer-actress playing the role of Eliza, Liz Robertson. After that, judging from his demeanour whenever I saw him, I deduced that he had found the perfect partner at last.

There remains one dominant part of his make-up which he never mentioned in his conversation but which time and again inspires his most moving work. Like his father, Alan was what might be called a secular Jew, a man born into the religion who never practised its rituals. In his autobiography he describes the following incident:

Two days before his death, my father looked up from his hospital bed and wrote to my younger brother, Bob: 'What religion are your children?' Bob replied good-humouredly: 'I don't know. Whatever church is on the corner I'll send them to.' My father nodded approvingly and wrote: 'It's all a lot of apple sauce.'

But if Alan was not religious in the conventional way, he was certainly sustained by what could be called a supernatural belief. He was convinced that none of us dies in the accepted sense:

Nothing, outside of the theatre, has intrigued me and sustained my unflagging interest more than the occult, extrasensory perception, reincarnation and all that is called metaphysical until it is understood and becomes physical.

And on the night when he was honoured by a one-man show in New York, he told his audience at the outset, 'Fundamentally I suppose I'm more interested in the dreams of

Man, which are eternal, than in the temporary perversions of those dreams called reality.' At this point we are not a million miles from the belief in the Life Force which so animated Alan's great intellectual hero Bernard Shaw, nor are we very distanced from Shaw's remark about all serious work being humorous and the invoking of the art of Heinrich Heine. By one of those coincidences which Alan would insist were not coincidences at all but conjunctions of sympathetical spirits, Heine too figures in Alan's pantheon, in the following curious way.

Unlike some lyric writers in the musical theatre, Alan was a great historian of the genre. The last book he published was proof of his knowledge of the songwriting past of America, and it was proof too of his belief in the importance of song-with-words to all of us. The closing words of his history of the musical are these:

In the musical 42 Street, the director of the play says, in an ecstatic moment, 'The two most glorious words in the English language, musical comedy.' Quite right.

It follows that any man who contributed to that much-loved form would have been among Alan's heroes, and that he should have seen the rest of the world through the prism of the musical stage. In composing his introduction to Howard Dietz's book, he bemoans the passing of the Age of Giants, in all things, not just the theatre. This is how he sums up the world leaders of the early 1970s:

Compared to Churchill and De Gaulle, Wilson and Heath are 'rep' and Pompidou is an understudy who can barely keep the curtain up. Next to Roosevelt or even Kennedy, Nixon is the Chicago company (of the Capone era at that), and in Russia they have to have two fellows alternating in the same part.

And then, having had his fun at the expense of the panjandrums, he comes to the real heroes, and in a sense lays down the terms of his credo:

In the 1930s, when I was at school I was induced into trance by the pipes playing 'Dancing in the Dark', 'Just One of Those Things', 'Where or When' and 'Embraceable You'. To me, an exotic aphrodisiac was a pair of great legs on a girl in the front line. And the gurus who led me on to the next plane of happiness had nice Occidental names like Gershwin, Rodgers, Porter, Hart, Berlin, Dietz and Schwartz. I knew every song and every lyric they wrote, including the verse and second chorus.

Notice that Alan has taken double care to place Lorenz Hart among the great masters of his chosen art, by naming not only the writer but the title of one of his loveliest and metaphysically profound ballads. Lerner had a special place in his heart for Lorenz Hart. The two men were friends in the last years of Hart's tragic life, and the older man never failed to encourage and advise the apprentice. And then, having described the sad end of this great man, a direct descendent of Shaw's hero Heine, Alan writes:

I believe in reincarnation, and I pray the next time he returns he is six feet tall and that he will be repaid in kind for the joy he gave and never shared.

Alan was one of the most gifted, most dedicated and charming men I ever knew. He was always the lyricist, never the bore about lyrics. One night, in the car park of the Chichester Festival Theatre, a small group of us were chatting idly about the musical we had just seen, when one of the company happened to make a flattering remark about the polysyllabic vanities which feature in the talk-song of Henry Higgins. I think it may have been the passage which runs: 'Exasperating, irritating, vacillating, calculating, agitating, maddening and infuriating.' Alan listened to the recitation and then, turning to give me a sidelong conspiratorial glance, said, 'They're the easy ones. It's the short ones that give the trouble.' It was his glance to me, in the half-light of the swirling car headlights around us, which I shall always treasure as yet another of his little compliments to somebody who was after all no more than a passing acquaintance. I shall miss his presence in London. Even after long spells without meeting, his proximity seemed to make the theatre a more interesting place. I shall miss his 'Dear boy' as he greeted you, and the full-hearted boyish laughter which followed the recitation of one of his absurdly true stories. If his conviction regarding the paranormal possibilities of the human race turn out to have been an inspired guess, then I venture to suggest that even as I type these words, he is off in some cool corner of paradise arguing his case before a jury consisting in its entirety of Bernard Shaw, and insisting that it was right and proper for Eliza to get her Henry Higgins in the end. In the meantime, we have his lyrics to console us. I am perfectly well aware that in the introductory note to his autobiography, Alan wrote: 'Lyrics, no less than music, are written to be heard. A lyric without its musical clothes is a scrawny creature and should never be allowed to parade naked across the printed page.' And having said that, Alan ended the book with thirty-nine of his own lyrics. I rest my case.

Benny Green
London, 1987

☆ WHAT'S UP? ☆

Nothing much is remembered of this show except that it constituted the Broadway début of Lerner and Loewe. It opened on 11 November 1943 and ran for only sixty-three performances, thanks partly to the reputation of its leading man, Jimmy Savo. Kinkle's *Encyclopaedia of Popular Music and Jazz* lists three items from the show which registered at the time, 'My Last Love', 'You've Got a Hold on Me', and 'Joshua'. The publishing records at Chappell's list a fourth tune, 'You Wash, I'll Dry', but the files have disclosed only three survivors among these four items. One man who would not have been very concerned by the oblivion to which the show was consigned was Lerner himself, who, in exaggerating the débâcle years later, wrote that it was 'an ill-advised little effort which lasted about a week'. Its failure must have been even more difficult for Loewe than for Lerner, who was at least young enough to be undeterred by failure. Loewe, in contrast, was by now beginning to amass an impressive record of failure. After a brilliant career as a child prodigy in his native Vienna, Loewe, the son of a famous tenor singer in operetta, had written a million seller when he was fifteen. It was called 'Katrina' and it was his last material success for a long time. In 1924 he came to America, failed to make any impression on the world of music, and drifted into cattle punching, gold-mining, then into the prize ring and after that a spell as a riding instructor, all of them occupations which read well in retrospect but which are pure hell at the time. His hopes must have been riding on *What's Up?*, but its life totalled only eight weeks.

My Last Love

My last love didn't touch my heart this way.
My last love wasn't on my mind all day.
I felt no yearning
Deep inside me burning,
But this time I'm learning,
What it is that love can do.

My last love never danced with me all night.
My last love never held my hand so tight.
But that's a past love,
Very much out-classed love,
And I hope my last love
Will be you,
My you.

You Wash and I'll Dry

All that glitters isn't always gold
There's no guarantee romance will hold.
Ev'ry infant knows it,
Nevada clearly shows it,
That heated love can easily grow cold.

The failures say that Cupid missed 'em.
That isn't so,
They simply had no system.

We'll ride on the beam,
Make a good team,
Now that we've decided,
You wash and I'll dry.

We'll each own a share,
Laughter and care
Will be well divided,
You wash and I'll dry.

There'll be no Reno if, baby,
We know the way to do a good job
On ev'ry prob-
lem.

So, sign on the line,
Ev'ry thing's fine,
We're a clinch for heaven,
You wash and I'll dry.

You've Got a Hold on Me

You've got a hold on me.
You've got that magic hold on me.
When I'm alone now,
I wonder
What is this power
I'm under.

You cast a spell on me
That moment heaven fell on me.
You've got a hold on me.
What can I do,
But always hold on to you.

☆ THE DAY BEFORE SPRING ☆

With this show, a musical play whose realism was tempered with typical Lerneresque fantasy, the partnership of Lerner and Loewe began to get under way. The show opened on 22 November 1945, starring Irene Manning and Bill Johnson, was reasonably well received, especially for its featuring of dream ballets within the context of the action, and ran for 165 performances, which was certainly a respectable run, although Lerner later defined it as 'a succès d'estime, meaning a success that runs out of steam'. His aim at the time was to write lyrics which combined the wit of Lorenz Hart with the poetic drama of Hammerstein. The partial extent to which he succeeded may be gathered from the lyrics of the show which have survived.

The Day Before Spring

Weary, my heart was weary,
Alone and dreary,
The day before spring.

The winds of winter
Had kept me waiting
Alone and waiting
The day before spring.

Then music burst from the heavens above,
Angels began to sing,
Spring came the day I found you,
And I forgot
The day before spring.

You Haven't Changed At All

HE

Who would ever dream
The remote extreme
You'd be lovely as you were?
Not an optimist or idealist
Would have had the thought occur.

You haven't changed at all,
Though it's been a while,
You're as I recall,
The thought of how you spoke,
And in the long ago
You awoke,
Then, when you said 'Hello'.

You haven't lost your touch,
Haven't changed the smile
That I loved so much.
The seasons change and Maytime fades
Into the fall,
But you, you haven't changed at all.

SHE

You haven't changed at all,
Every word you say
I can still recall.
The funny way your eyes look
When you hold my hand,
And that sly look
I still understand.
You haven't changed a line,
You still have a way
That I can't define.
The world may change
And kingdoms rise to power and fall,
But you, haven't changed at all.

HE

I haven't changed at all.

SHE

I still feel the same.

HE

I'm still at your call.

BOTH

The years may pass and oceans keep us far apart
But I'll never change my heart.

A Jug of Wine

Could we find a world of strange delight?
Like the world I dreamed the other night?

A jug of wine, a loaf of bread and thou – baby!
I dreamed we sat beneath a scented bough – baby!
My heart beat so!
      (D'ya hear it beat?)
I'm all aglow
      (D'ya mind the heat?)

Tonight I know
That I'm complete-
Ly yours alone.

A nightingale made music in a tree – baby!
And heaven seemed to smile on you and me – baby!
But I woke up,
And all broke up;
My jug of wine, my loaf of bread and thou – baby!

A jug of wine, a loaf of bread and thou – baby!
You stared at me the way you're staring now – baby!
Your eyes ashine;
      (And what a pair)
Your face near mine;
      (Oh, keep it there!)
And you declare
You're mine alone.

The fragrance of gardenia filled your hair – baby!
The yellow dust of moonlight lit the air – baby!
But I woke up,
And all broke up;
My jug of wine, my loaf of bread and wow! – baby!

God's Green World

If you want to go
Down to Mexico
Go, my child.

If you want to fly
Down to Uruguay
Fly, my child.

If you want to be
Down in Tennessee,
Take a flyer.

You won't see the world
Sitting home and curled
By the fire.

Out in God's Green World you'll find
All the joy your heart has designed,
There's a ship waiting down at the shore;
There's a highway not far from your door;
And a world all around to explore – just waiting!

Under God's Blue Heaven above
Lies the dream you dreamed ever of;
There's a wonderful wish to be made;
And a glorious song to be played;
And it's all waiting yonder in God's Green World!

Out in God's Green World you'll find
All the joy your heart has in mind.
There's the tang of a fresh autumn breeze;
And the sighing of leaves on the trees;
All of nature is trying to please, so
Take it all in while you're young; then out of
God's deep night you'll hear
Some one call your name very clear,
And as sure as the tang of the breeze,
And as sure as the leaves on the trees,
It is love coming for you from God's Green World.

I Love You This Morning

I love you this morning!
My heart sings: What a day!
I love you this morning;
Love the glow in your cheek,
And the blush when you speak,
And the way that you say
I love you this morning!
My heart sings: All is right!
I love you this morning!
More and more ev'ry way,
For I love you today
Even more than I did last night.

I love you this morning!
My heart sings: What a day!
I love you this morning!
Love the bounce in your walk,
And the zing when you talk,
And the way that you say
I love you this morning!
My heart sings: All is right!
I love you this morning!
More and more ev'ry way,
For I love you today,
Even more than I did last night.

This Is My Holiday

This is the spring that never came;
This is the fire once more aflame;
This is the dawn that slipped away;
This is my holiday!

I see the blue Elysian sky;
I'll touch the clouds that whisper by;
I'll find the dream that went astray;
This is my holiday!

I'll drink from a fountain
Wine sparkling with May.
Here high on a mountain
I've journeyed to stay.

This is the love I've waited for;
I heard the song of evermore;
And now at last I'm on my way;
This is my holiday!

Gone is the life I have known;
Shadows and mem'ries have flown;
And now I'm free to love and roam,
And call the far off hills my home.
Life was a yawn and a sigh;
Gay and alive now am I.
I see the sun – the sun at last;
Here is the spring I thought was past;
Here is the dawn that slipped away;
This is my holiday!

I see the blue Elysian sky;
I'll touch the clouds that whisper by;
I'll find the dream that went astray;
This is my holiday!

I'll drink from a fountain
Wine sparkling with May.
Here high on a mountain
I've journeyed to stay.

This is the love I've waited for;
I heard the song of evermore;
And now at last I'm on my way;
This is my holiday.

My Love is a Married Man

My lonely bitter heart has needed him to make it sweeter;
He came he saw he conquered and then sic transit Peter.
And now I shouldn't cry, I should be brave instead;
But bravery is cold in bed.

My love is a married man;
I'm a marital also-ran;
Though I love him so,
Does he love me? No!
I'll never enter his life
Because he's true to his wife.
My love is a married man.

How often I dream and plan
That he'd climb on my caravan.
I'm a childish dope;
Will it happen? Nope!
He's not that kind of married man.

My dreams abundant
Are redundant
And they fall very short.
The ship I hoped for,
Sat and moped for,
Docked in someone else's port.

He's gold I can never pan;
He's the ember I'll never fan:
And I know it well;
But, oh what the – tell
Me what to do with a married man.

The man I could love I found;
But the man is by contract bound;
He is six feet of
Concentrated love.

He knows how deeply I care,
And he has manhood to spare,
But he won't spread himself around.

The man who controls my heart
Has a conjugal counterpart.
And her dinner meals
Are enough, he feels;
He'll never have to go à la carte.

I'd like a nest in
Some clandestine
Hide-away on a hill.
Though passion sweep me,
Heaven keep me,
For I know he never will.

Now I'm back where I began;
All alone on my divan.
And if I am chaste,
It can all be traced
Right to the love of a married man.

My love has a loving bride.
What he wants she can well provide.
Though I missed my aim,
I am not to blame;
For who could ever foresee
That such a thing there could be
As a husband who's satisfied?

My love has an easy way;
He's amusing and wise and gay.
We could have such fun;
Clean or maybe 'un'.
But he won't ever come out and play.
    His wife is lucky;
    But I'm plucky.
    For remorse I'll never beg.
    I wish her health and
    Joy and wealth and
    Truly hope she breaks a leg.
Some day I will wed some man;
Settle down on the Morris Plan.
But we'll have no heirs
For I'll sleep downstairs
And all because of that married man.

☆ BRIGADOON ☆

Apart from being the first of the Lerner-Loewe musicals to achieve world fame, *Brigadoon* is the most instructive of their works in that the details of its pre-production trials and tribulations have been amply documented. The plot was not one calculated to inspire potential backers, for it was pure J. M. Barrie, and Barrie, then as always, was something of an acquired taste. Brigadoon is a Scots highland village which comes to life only for one day every century. In its one day of life in the twentieth century, it is visited by two Americans, one of whom falls for a local girl. When he learns about the spectral life to which he will be condemning himself if he stays with the girl, he runs home to New York. His love, however, proves stronger than logic, and he ends by returning to the village. Both the words and the music cunningly reflect the Scots flavour of the theme.

For a long period after they had written it, Lerner and Loewe felt they might never see it produced. It was first offered to the Theatre Guild, whose administrators, deeply involved in discovering American history as taught in *Oklahoma!* and *Carousel*, said they might be interested if the locale could be switched from Scotland to America. 'Somehow,' writes Lerner, 'we did not know how to do that.' It was then offered to John C. Wilson, then to George Abbott, then to Herman Shumlin, then to Rodgers and Hammerstein, all of whom turned it down. Finally Billy Rose agreed to produce it, but only on his own terms. Rose, a small big-mouth whose contributions to the evolution of Western art included a lyric called 'Does the Spearmint Lose Its Flavour on the Bedpost Overnight?', was difficult from the very first meeting, attempting to establish his bona fides by making remarks to the two writers like 'Never argue with a man who has more money than you have'. Among the terms Rose laid down was that he would have the power to call in other writers and composers, that Fritz Loewe, an expert vocal arranger, would be disbarred from orchestrating the vocal score, and that he, Billy Rose, would have sole right of casting. Lerner and Loewe then attempted to discuss these conditions and were told, 'Sign or else.' They then broke off negotiations with Rose. Lerner says of this episode, 'The contract that he wished us to sign negated Abraham Lincoln's Emancipation Proclamation that freed the slaves.'

At which point there entered the lives of Lerner and Loewe one of the most remarkable women in the history of American theatre. Cheryl Crawford was born into a God-fearing middle-class family in Akron, Ohio in 1902, and attended Smith College, where she read Plato and Nietzsche, lost her religious faith and replaced it with an idealism for the theatre. Against her family's advice, she went to New York after graduation and lived the conventional life of the unconventional, subsidizing herself by constantly winning at poker and selling the other players home-made booze. She then drifted into the Theatre Guild, and in her third year with that idealistic organization, was asked to take a *Porgy and Bess* company to London, where C. B. Cochran was to present Gershwin's opera at His Majesty's Theatre. On opening night, when Miss Crawford saw that the programme listed Cochran as the producer, with no mention of the Theatre Guild, she refused to allow the cast to begin the performance until Cochran had made a speech of apology before the curtain. The start was delayed for twenty-five minutes while the two rivals played their game of bluff, except that Miss Crawford was in deadly earnest. No apology, no show. At last Cochran ate his slice of humble pie, the performance began and for the rest of the run the two enemies never spoke to each other. In time Miss Crawford moved on from the Guild to Lee Strasberg's Group Theatre, another organization fuelled on idealism. Miss Crawford stayed till 1937, at which point the Group disintegrated and she became an independent producer.

Not till 1942 did she become involved in what might loosely be called musical comedy, when she brought together Ogden Nash, Kurt Weill, S. J. Perelman and Marlene Dietrich in an adaptation of F. Anstey's supernatural comedy of Victorian London, *The Tinted Venus*. (Miss Dietrich subsequently backed down and was replaced by Mary Martin. The show became a hit under the title of *One Touch of Venus*.) By now Miss Crawford was making money, but the flame of idealism still burned brightly; when producing *Anna Lucasta* she cut her cook Rosa in on the deal. (Rosa ended up four thousand dollars to the good, but went on cooking.) In retrospect it seems that her entire past career had been preparing her for the romantic idealism and Scots whimsy of *Brigadoon*. It may even be that her attraction to the show had something to do with the fact that it reminded her of one of her very first independent productions, Barrie's *A Kiss for Cinderella*.

Years of cheese-paring on costs made Miss Crawford the perfect producer of a show which could find no backers. Having read the play and heard the music, she calculated that it would cost $200,000 to bring it to New York. (This was in 1947, when par for the course would have been something closer to $300,000.) Lerner's details contradict Miss Crawford's. He says that the show was budgeted at $150,000, but whatever the figure, all parties are agreed on how the money was found. Lerner recalls:

Fritz and I gave fifty-eight performances, sometimes three a day, to raise the money. The last audition was three days after the show was in rehearsal.

Having raised the money, Miss Crawford now proceeded to display a frugality in spending it which was perfectly in the spirit of some of the characters in Lerner's libretto. Years after the event, she was interviewed by the European correspondent of *The New Yorker*, Janet Flanner, who described how *Brigadoon*'s budget was disbursed:

Most musicals involve at least eight costume changes for the female chorus. All *Brigadoon*'s girls except the dancers are rigged up with a basic skirt and blouse over which tartan kilts, scarves, aprons and the like are draped to effect changes. There was big talk of importing costly tartan kilts from Scotland; Miss Crawford bought her tartans at Gimbel's and Bloomingdale's, and the only imported items were a couple of dozen pairs of tartan stockings. The sets consisted of romantic canvas drops instead of realistic wooden constructions; in a household, this would be the difference, roughly, between paying for a nice new curtain to divide a room and paying for a new wall.

The Boston reviews were poor, audience reaction excellent. In Philadelphia the reviews were excellent, audiences ecstatic. By the time the show opened at the Ziegfeld Theatre in New York, on 13 March 1947, the box-office advance topped half a million dollars. The critical reactions read less like reviews than the idle daydreams of some frustrated author:

To the growing list of major achievements on the musical stage, add one, *Brigadoon*. This excursion into an imagined Scottish village is an orchestration of the theatre's myriad arts, like a singing storybook for an idealized country fair long ago. *New York Times*.

Brigadoon is a work of imagination and beauty. *Daily News*.

A musical fantasy of rare delight and distinction. A jubilant and brilliantly integrated show, a scintillating song-and-dance fantasy that has given theatre-goers reason to toss tam-o-shanters in the air. *Herald Tribune*.

Brigadoon an enormous hit. Best Musical Play of the season. *Sun*.

Brigadoon is an absolute enchantment, tender, exciting, fantastic and real, stirring and soothing. *World Telegram*.

But Miss Crawford's work as an idealist was not yet done. The minimum weekly wage at the time for a chorus girl was fifty dollars. Miss Crawford paid sixty-five. When the minimum was raised to sixty, she paid eighty. She also dipped into her own profits to pay for the medical insurance of the entire cast, each member of which also received a fortnight's holiday with pay. It is also striking that support for *Brigadoon* was so predominantly female. Seventeen of the show's thirty-eight angels were women, who were repaid their investment within sixteen weeks. Once the show went into profit, forty thousand dollars a month went to its backers. The most revealing aspect of all this is that Miss Crawford, a bookish lady with a hunger for romantic poetry and the more reflective philosophers, turned to her favourite authors in moments of trial and distributed them with reckless profligacy once the trial became transformed into a triumph. At the last dress rehearsal in the Boston try-out, she absented herself, hiring a taxi to drive her to Walden Pond, where she purchased an ancient pamphlet written by Ralph Waldo Emerson. The following day, she insulated herself from the tensions of the Boston opening by retiring to the office and reading the pamphlet. The following Christmas, finding herself with profits from the show beyond even her idealistic hopes, she sent Alan Lerner, among other things, a copy of Ben Jonson's poems, a folio of Giotto prints, an Elizabethan reader, a study of Herman Melville, two novels by Christopher Isherwood and a book by Freud. (Alan got off lightly. When Mary Martin toured with *One Touch of Venus*, Miss Crawford presented her with a trunk containing two Bernhardt biographies, several volumes of Shaw, a treatise on Duse, a book about the Moscow Art Theatre and assorted essays on the art of acting. Miss Martin later claimed it took her two years to work through the contents of the trunk.)

There is a curious postscript to the history of *Brigadoon*. After the show had opened, the garrulous critic George Jean Nathan publicly accused Lerner of having stolen his plot from a German tale called *Germelshausen*, by a Herr Gerstacker. Not till thirty years had passed did the explanation for this extraordinary behaviour of Nathan's come to the surface. It seems that when Nathan went to see the show he emulated its hero and fell in love with the leading lady, Patricia Hughes. What followed is described by Lerner:

Nathan developed a high-school crush on her, invited her frequently to supper and sent her all his books, each inscribed with an adolescent expression of endearment. One weekend he called to ask her out and discovered she was visiting me in the country, not for artistic reasons. This so enraged him that he devoted his entire next week's column to how I had stolen the plot of *Brigadoon* and *The Day Before Spring*. His attacks continued for three weeks with such venom that the *New York Times* called and offered me space to answer him, which I did, labelling the whole accusation as rubbish and documenting the developments of each play into the final product. Nathan took my article, deleted a sentence here and a word there until it seemed as if I had confessed to plagiarism, and then published it in his annual year book of the theatre.

Nathan's libido notwithstanding, *Brigadoon* won the award for the best musical of the year, and Brooks Atkinson in his Sunday column in the *New York Times* reported that Nathan believed that the plot had been pilfered 'from some ancient Icelandic legend that only Mr Nathan was old enough to remember'.

The arguments about the origins of *Brigadoon* have long since been forgotten, and Mr Nathan's theory well and truly exploded. To impartial onlooker, it seems certain that the truth of the matter is contained in Lerner's claim to have been inspired to write the play by his affection for the works of J. M. Barrie. Those of us who, in remembering that Barrie had been born and raised in a sleepy Scots village called Kirremuir, take note of the rhythms and assonances of that name and the name of Lerner's village, will no doubt be pardoned for digesting the bones of the controversy and asking, 'Nathan who?'

Brigadoon

Brigadoon, Brigadoon,
Blooming under sable skies,
Brigadoon, Brigadoon,
There my heart for ever lies.
Let the world grow cold around us;
Let the heavens cry above!
Brigadoon, Brigadoon,
In the valley there'll be love.

I'll Go Home with Bonnie Jean.

I used to be a rovin' lad.
A rovin' an' wanderin' life I had.
On any lass I'd frown
Who would try to tie me down
But then one day I saw a maid
Who held out her hand an' I stayed an' stayed.
An' now, across the green,
I'll go home with bonnie Jean.

Go home, go home, go home with bonnie Jean!
Go home, go home, I'll go home with bonnie Jean!

I used to have a hundred friends;
But when ye are wedded the friendship ends.
They never come to call,
So farewell to one an' all.
Farewell to all the lads I knew;
I'll see them again when they're married too.
For soon, across the green,
I'll go home with bonnie Jean.

Go home, go home, go home with bonnie Jean!
Go home, go home, I'll go home with bonnie Jean!

In Aberdeen I used to know
A lass with an air an' her name was Jo;
An' ev'ry night at ten
I would meet her in the glen.
But now I'll not see her again;
Especially not in the glen at ten.
For now, across the green,
I'll go home with bonnie Jean.

Go home, go home, go home with bonnie Jean!
Go home, go home, I'll go home with bonnie Jean!

Hello to married men I've known.
I'll soon have a wife an' leave yours alone,
A bonnie wife indeed,
An' she'll be all I'll ever need.

With bonnie Jean my days will fly.
An' love her I will till the day I die.
That's why, across the green,
I'll go home with bonnie Jean.

Go home, go home, go home with bonnie Jean!
Go home, go home, I'll go home with bonnie Jean!

Waitin' for my Dearie

Many a lassie as everyone knows 'll
Try to be married before twenty-five.
So she'll agree to most any proposal,
All he must be is a man an' alive.

I hold a dream an' there's no compromisin';
I know there's one certain laddie for me.
One day he'll come walkin' o'er the horizon;
But should he not then an old maid I'll be.

Foolish ye may say.
Foolish I will stay.

Waitin' for my dearie,
An' happy am I
To hold my heart till he comes strollin' by.

When he comes, my dearie,
One look an' I'll know
That he's the dearie I've been wantin' so.

Though I'll live forty lives
Till the day he arrives
I'll not ever, ever grieve.
For my hopes will be high
That he'll come strollin' by;
For ye see, I believe

That there's a laddie weary
An' wanderin' free
Who's waitin' for his dearie;
Me!

Almost Like Being in Love

Maybe the sun gave me the pow'r,
For I could swim Loch Lomond
And he home in
Half an hour.
Maybe the air gave me the drive,
For I'm aglow and alive!

What a day this has been!
What a rare mood I'm in!
Why, it's . . . almost like being in love!

There's a smile on my face
For the whole human race!
Why, it's . . . almost like being in love!

All the music of life seems to be
Like a bell that is ringin' for me!

And from the way that I feel
When that bell starts to peal,
I would swear I was falling,
I could swear I was falling,
It's almost like being in love.

There But For You Go I

This is hard to say,
But as I wandered through the lea
I felt for just a fleeting moment
That I suddenly was free
Of being lonely;
Then I closed my eyes and saw
The very reason why.

I saw a man with his head bowed low.
His heart had no place to go.
I looked and I thought to myself with a sigh:
There but for you go I.

I saw a man walking by the sea.
Alone with the tide was he.
I looked and I thought as I watched him go by:
There but for you go I.

Lonely men around me,
Trying not to cry.
Till the day you found me
There among them was I.

I saw a man who had never known
A love that was all his own.
I thought as I thanked all the stars in the sky:
There but for you go I.

From This Day On

You and the world we knew
Will glow till my life is through;
For you're part of me
From this day on.

And
Someday if I should love,
It's you I'll be dreaming of;
For you're all I'll see
From this day on.

These hurried hours were all the life we could share.
Still I will go with not a tear, just a prayer.

That
When we are far apart
You'll find something from your heart
Has gone! Gone with me
From this day on.

Through all the years to come
An' through all the tears to come
I know I'll be yours
From this day on.

The Love of my Life

At sixteen years I was blue an' sad.
Then Father said I should find a lad.
So I set out to become a wife,
An' found the real love of my life.

His name it was Chris an' the last was MacGill.
I met him one night pickin' flow'rs on the hill.
He had lots of charm an' a certain kind o' touch,
An' a certain kind of eagerness that pleased me very much.
So there 'neath the moon where romance often springs,
I gave him my heart – and a few other things.
I don't know how long that I stayed up on the hill
But the moon had disappeared an' so had Christopher MacGill.

So I went home an' I thought I'd die;
Till Father said: Make another try.
So out I went to become a wife,
An' found the real love of my life.

He came from the low lands, the low lands said he;
I saw him an' knew he was perfect for me.
Jus' one thing that puzzled me an' it always will,
Was he told me he had heard about me from his friend MacGill.
We quick fell in love an' went down by the creek;
The next day he said he'd be back in a week.
An' I thought he would, for now how was I to know
That of all the low land laddies there was never one as low!

I told my father the awful truth.
He said: What difference? ye've got your youth.
So out I went mad to be a wife,
An' found the real love of my life.

Oh, he was a poet, a rhymer was he,
He read me some verse he had written for me.
He said they would move me these poems from his pen;
An' how right he was because they moved me right into the glen.
We stayed till the dawn came an' lightened the sky.
Then I shook his hand an' I bid him goodbye.
I never went back for what I had heard was true;
That a poet only writes about the things he cannot do.

My pa said: Look out for men who think.
Ye'll be more certain with men who drink.
So out I went to become a wife,
An' found the real love of my life.

Oh, he was a soldier, a fine Highland son.
He told me about all the battles he'd won.
He wasted his time tellin' me about his might,
For one look at him decided me to not put up a fight.
We skirmished for hours that night in the glen,
An' I found the sword has more might than the pen.
But when I was drowsin' I snored to my dismay,
An' he thought it was a bugle an' got up and marched away.

Now Pa said: Daughter, there must be one,
Someone who's true or too old to run.
So I'm still lookin' to be a wife,
An' find the real love of my life.

My Mother's Weddin' Day

Now if ye think this weddin' day went jus' a bit amiss,
Then I will tell ye 'bout a weddin' far more daft than this.
The lad involved turned out to be no other but my pa.
An' by the strangest bit o' luck, the woman was my ma!

MacGregor, MacKenna, MacGowan, MacGraw,
MacVitie, MacNeil an' MacRae;
Ay, all of the folk in the village were there
At my mother's weddin' day.
For Pa had asked his friend MacPhee,
An' Mac had come with May MacGee,
An' May invited ninety-three
To my mother's weddin' day.
Then up the road came Ed MacKeen
With half the town of Aberdeen.

Ay, ev'ryone was on the scene
At her mother's weddin' day.

At quarter to five everybody was there
A-waitin' around in the room,
MacVocker, MacDougall, MacDuff an' MacCoy,
Everybody but the groom.
An' as the hours turtled by
The men got feelin' kind o' dry
An' thought they'd take a bip o' rye
While a-waitin' for the groom.
An' while the men were dippin' in
The ladies started on the gin.

An' soon the room began to spin
At her mother's weddin' day.

Then all of a sudden the liquor was gone;
The gin an' the whiskey an' all.
An' all of a sudden the weddin' affair
Had become a bonnie brawl.
For Pete MacGraw an' Joe MacPhee
Began to fight for May MacGee,
While May MacGee an' Sam Mackee
Were a-wooin' in the hall.
So cold an' stiff was John MacVay
They used 'im for a servin' tray.

For ev'ryone was blithe an' gay
At her mother's weddin' day.

MacDuff an' MacVitie were playin' a game
An' usin' MacCoy for the ball.
MacKenna was eatin' the bridal bouquet
An' MacNeil hung on the wall.
When finally my father came,
His eyes were red, his nose aflame;
He dinna even know his name:
He was the drunkest of them all.

The people were lyin' all over the room,
A-lookin' as if they were dead.
But mother uncovered the minister quick,
And she told 'im: Go ahead.
So Pa kneeled down on Bill MacRae,
An' mother kneeled on Jock MacKay;
The preacher stood on John MacVay;
An' that's how my ma was wed.
It was a sight beyond compare.
I ought to know for I was there.

There never was a day as rare
As her mother's weddin' day!

Come to me, Bend to me

Because they told me
I can't behold ye
Till weddin' music starts playin',
To ease my longin'
There's nothing wrong in
Me standin' out here an' sayin':

Come to me, bend to me, kiss me good day!
Darlin', my darlin', 'tis all I can say:
Jus' come to me, bend to me, kiss me good day!
Gie me your lips an' don't take them away!

Come, dearie, near me
So ye can hear me,
I've got to whisper this softly.
For though I'm burnin'
To shout my yearnin'
The words come tiptoein' off me.

Come to me, bend to me, kiss me good day!
Darlin', my darlin', 'tis all I can say:
Jus' come to me, bend to me, kiss me good day!
Gie me your lips an' don't take them away!

The Heather on the Hill

Can't we two go walkin' together,
Out beyond the valley of trees,
Out where there's a hillside of heather
Curtseyin' gently in the breeze?
That's what I'd like to do:
See the heather – but with you.

The mist of May is in the gloamin',
And all the clouds are holdin' still.
So take my hand and let's go roamin'
Through the heather on the hill.

The mornin' dew is blinkin' yonder;
There's lazy music in the rill;
And all I want to do is wander
Through the heather on the hill.

There may be other days as rich and rare;
There may be other springs as full and fair;
But they won't be the same – they'll come and go;
For this I know:

That when the mist is in the gloamin',
And all the clouds are holdin' still,
If you're not there I won't go roamin'
Through the heather on the hill,
The heather on the hill.

☆ LOVE LIFE ☆

Neither in his autobiography nor in his history of the musical does Lerner give any indications as to how he came to be working with Kurt Weill on *Love Life*, which opened in New York on 7 October 1948 and enjoyed a respectable run of 252 performances. The only clue to this departure from the alliance with Loewe is found in a biography of Weill by Ronald Sanders, which explains it in the following way. After the closure of his show with the poet Langston Hughes, *Street Scene*, Weill began to search for new partners. After abortive attempts to work with William Saroyan and Herman Wouk, Weill

was approached by Cheryl Crawford, fresh from her success as the producer of *Brigadoon*. There had been a bit of a falling out between that show's librettist, Alan Jay Lerner, and its composer, Frederick Loewe, and she proposed that Lerner and Weill get together and do a show.

What caused the falling out, and how it was patched up, remains unspoken, but Lerner, knowing that Weill's feelings about the American republic were as strongly patriotic as his own, concocted an original plot in which the history of the United States is seen through the lives of the hero and heroine, a married couple who remain ageless throughout the long years of American history. The working title for their show was 'A Dish for the Gods', and the hope was that Gertrude Lawrence would star. Weill had already written a Broadway score for Miss Lawrence, *Lady in the Dark* (1941), with lyrics by Ira Gershwin, an experience which had left him with a deep admiration for Miss Lawrence tempered by a musician's nagging doubts, which he expressed to Lerner as follows: 'She had the greatest range between C and C sharp of anyone I ever knew.' Miss Lawrence eventually declined the offer to play in the Lerner-Weill musical, and approaches were made to Mary Martin and Ginger Rogers, both of whom refused. The role was eventually accepted by Nanette Fabray.

The specialized nature of the project dictated the style of the songs and their relationship to each other. For instance, the idyll of 'Here I'll Stay' represents rural Connecticut in 1791, with the married couple running their farm, selling home-made furniture and generally jogging along in a modest, comfortable sort of way. But this way of life is doomed, as the ethics of modern big business begin to obtrude; the next song is 'Progress', a vaudeville soft-shoe number which proclaims the loss of Eden and the beginning of the neurotic pursuit of money. After this jokey hymn of disillusion, we see our couple embracing their bucolic paradise for the last time, in 'Green up Time'. Again the pastoral mood is shattered by a vaudeville routine, this time a ragtime quartet called 'Economics'. All in all, it was one of the most ambitious musicals in terms of thematic intent which Broadway had ever seen, and this may have had something to do with its narrowly missing genuine popularity.

At the opening, according to Lerner, 'the audience stood and cheered and the press was very mixed indeed'. The consensus of opinion indicates that *Love Life* was slightly too self-consciously intellectual, a shade pretentious; even Miss Crawford, always a devotee of Lerner's writing, conceded that the script had shortcomings, and that this had its effect on Weill's music: 'Because Kurt's music served the style of the writing, it didn't have the warmth of his best ballads.' However, it should be noted that these sentiments are expressed in a book on Weill's career, not Lerner's, and that Lerner, when he participated in our evening of songs without music made a point of reciting 'Economics', which he performed with the wistfulness of someone bidding farewell to a much-loved child. *Love Life* ran for 252 performances and quietly faded. By the time it closed, Weill was within a year of death and Lerner and Loewe were discussing their next collaboration.

Progress

One time this was a very quiet planet.
The reason was nobody was around.
But then one day, Jehovah, who began it,
Got bored and clamped a couple on the ground.

And right away when man and woman came here
They took a peak and nature took its course.
He said 'I love you' and she answered 'Same here';
And love became the greatest human force.

And from then and through the ages
It was love, love, love!
From the peasant to the sages
It was love, love, love!
   Man and woman did discover
   When they set out to explore
   All the world loves a lover
   But a lover loves it more.
Everybody was devoted to it;
Love, love, love!
Until they all were bloated with it;
Love, love, love, love, love, love, love, love!

For suddenly the mind of man was changing;
He started moving on in greater haste.
And perspectives took a drastic re-arranging,
For love and home had fin'lly been replaced.

They discovered something better than affection,
Far more rugged than a hug-ud ever be,
And they started in a happier direction,
Leaving love beneath the good old apple tree.

What is this thing
That's better than spring?
What thing is this
That's greater than a kiss?

What is the 'X'
That's bigger than sex?
What could it be?
What could it be?
What could it be?

It's Progress!
Where ev'ry man can be a king,
Why, next to Progress
Love's a juvenile thing.
Yes, with Progress
Your chance to hit the top is great.
One year you may need a loan
And the following year you own
New York State.

Yes, it's Progress!
    Now that's the life for you.
Where you can make a pile a day,
    Oh, it's incred' what you can do.
Why, next to Progress –
    You don't need brains at all;
Love is dull as croquet.
    Just a helluva lot of gall.
Yes, with Progress –
    A Tom, or Dick, or Hank –
Why, there's a world to make and hold –
    Might any day buy up a bank.
You start a clerk underneath
And the following day your teeth
Are all gold.

One day the prices
Begin to soar!
You made a living,
Now you need more.
You're getting frantic;
You're running short!
You have a fam'ly
You must support,
And when you think it'll never stop,
There is a sudden awful drop!
It's a panic!
It's a recession!
It's a Depression!
It's a Crash!
It's –

Progress!
The greatest thing there'll ever be!
Why next to Progress
Love's a cup of warm tea,
Yes, it's Progress!
Where any cluck can make a buck,
You buy a few shares of stock
And the following day –

The markets crumble!
The prices crack!
And down you tumble
Upon your back!
You're over-extended,
You have no slack!
It can't be mended.
You can't turn back!
And you're out in a growing mob
Without a dime, without a job!
It's a panic!
It's a recession!
It's a Depression!
It's a CRASH!
It's –

Progress!
Where ev'ry man can own the skies!
To win with Progress
Just industrialize.
Yes, it's Progress!
The only way to happiness.
No greater love could there be
Than for P-R-O-G-R-E-
Double S!

Here I'll Stay

If I've no will to go from home;
Or have no urge the seas to roam;
Or turn my back on a distant star
And never burn to wander far;
It's not because of fear.
It's because my goal is clear.

There's a far land, I'm told,
Where I'll find a field of gold,
But here I'll stay with you.

And they say there's an isle deep with clover
Where your heart wears a smile all day through.
But I know well they're wrong and I know where I belong,
And here I'll stay with you.

For that land is a sandy illusion;
It's the theme of a dream gone astray,
And the world others woo
I can find loving you,
And so here I'll stay.

This is the Life

This is the life, the life for me!
This is the way that life should be!
I'm free!

I can be as sloppy as I damn well please.
I can sprawl on the bed at my leisure and ease.
I can throw my ashes all around the floor.
I can read at night! I can even snore!
The closet's mine, ev'ry hanger there,
No more loaded hooks do I
Ever share.
The tub is mine! The sink is mine!
The chair is mine! The room is mine!
Yes siree, this is the life, the life for me!
I'm free!

Sure I miss the kids I guess.
I miss them more than I could ever say.
But I'm told that time will make it less
And I'll grow used to having them away.

Outside of that, I'm glad I am alone.
This is the sweetest thing I have known.
No more the troubled over-anxious thought
About her mood, or what she's thinking of.

No more the hopeless feeling I am caught,
Yes, there is peace in having not to love!
Yes, there is peace if hearing no one sigh!
Yes, there is peace, and that's the reason why

This is the life, the life for me!
This the way it ought to be!
I'm free!

　　(Picks up phone on table – speaks)

Room service!

continued . . .

(Sings)

It's great when you're hungry
To phone below,
And not have to wait
Until your wife –

(Into phone)

Hello?
Oh, this is Samuel Cooper
In seven twenty-eight.
I'd like to order dinner
Before it is too late.
I'll have shrimps and steak,
Make it medium well.
And the richest dessert
In the whole hotel.
Speed's important, boy,
Bring it on the run.
I'm hungry – what?

(Speaks)

Yes, just for one.
You heard me, damn it!
I said service for one!

(Hangs up phone – sings)

Why do they ask me every time I phone?
What's so bizarre about a man alone?
Sure I know it's not ideal.
I still have thoughts of her I can't forget.
But that's a thing they say that time will heal.
I wonder why it hasn't done it yet.

Now cut it out! Go out and have a whirl!
You know the spots! Go out and have a spree!
You've got a phone! Go get yourself a girl!
Go on you dope! Youre absolutely free!

*(About to pick up phone when suddenly
a thought stops him. He puts receiver
slowly back on hook)*

Free!
I wish I were free of that dream I keep dreaming!
The three of them swimming then starting to drown –
And I'm somewhere else and I don't hear them screaming –
And thousands of people just watch them go down.

(Shakes himself out of it)

No! I'm not sitting in again tonight!
I'm heading out where the lights are bright!

(He picks up the phone violently – speaks)

Room service!

(Sings)

I've got my freedom! The thing is done!
But what's the use if I don't have fun!

(Into phone)

This is Samu'l Cooper! The order's dead!
You've been too long! I'm going out instead!

(Slams down phone)

Yeah! I'm going out!
I need a change of view!
There must be something
Out there to do!
I got my freedom,
The perfect life!
Don't have a fam'ly,
A home, a wife!
This is the life, the life for me!
This is the way it ought to be!
I'm free! Free! Free!

Economics

Man and woman you got to admire.
They conquered cold and they conquered fire.
They stuck together through thick and thin;
Through lots of good and lots of sin.

But there's one thing that beats them;
That they just can't subdue;
One thing that defeats 'em,
And splits 'em up in two.
And that love-defyin' thing
About which we's gonna sing
Is Economics!

Now Cora had a husband makin' seven a day.
She left him for a guy who made eleven a day.
Now that's good economics,
That's good economics,
But awful bad for love!

Now Sarah and her husband they were doin' okay;
For Sarah had an ev'nin' job and he worked all day.
Now that's good economics,
That's good economics,
But awful bad for love!

Economics are rough on love!
Economics are tough on love!
You got a little money;
You got a little honey;
Money go!
Honey go!

Now Ruby was a woman who could needle your spine,
But when you went to kiss her it was cash on the line.
Now that's good economics,
That's good economics,
But awful bad for love!

Now Joe he had a job and worked with all of his might;
He worked so doggone hard that he was tired at night.
Now that's good economics,
That's good economics,
That's good economics,
But awful bad for love!

Now Henry and Mathilda got along very nice;
But when inflation came Mathilda boosted her price.
Now that's good economics,
That's good economics,
That's good economics,
But awful bad for love!

Economics are sad for love!
Economics are bad for love!
Now Flo she can't be trusted,
She'll leave you when you're busted.
Dough come back!
Flo come back!

Now Edna used to slip her husband's pay down her chest,
And just to keep it extra safe she never undressed.
Now that's good economics,
That's good economics,
That's good economics,
But awful bad for love!

'Susan's Dream', placed in the score after the ragtime quartet 'Economics', was, in the opinion of Weill's biographer, the best melody in the score. Heavily influenced by the traditional blues form, it was to be sung by a black woman who emerges from the group involved in 'Economics' and sings of her vision of a better life, one which is, in many regards, identical to her life at the present moment. When Lerner and Weill first played the score to Mary Martin, this was the only piece she liked. Unfortunately it was not a song she could very well perform in the role of the heroine. The song was eventually dropped from the score before opening night.

Susan's Dream

Susan,
She had a husband man to make a home for,
Made it shine because she loved him so.
Susan
Got lucky with the Lord and had some children,
Gave 'em all her heart to help 'em grow.

But now and then her man went drinkin';
The kids got sick and cried till morn!
And now and then Susan, oh Susan,
Plumb got tired of home and livin'
And began to wish she'd not been born.

Yes, she did.
She wished she'd not been born.

And then one night she was all wearied out,
The kids had worn her ragged and her man was not about,
And she flopped on her knees by the side of her bed
And she wiped her flaming eyes and looked up and said:
Oh God, let 'em sleep and when I sleep let me see
A heavenly dream of the way life could be.
That's all that I want,
So do that for me.
When I sleep let me dream of the way life should be.
Then she got into bed and her achin' slipped away.
And soon she was asleep and she heard a voice say:
Susan, oh Susan,
I heard you pray,
Susan, oh Susan,
You shall have your way.
There's good in your soul and so you shall see
The dream that you want of the way life should be.

And Susan then dreamed she had a man to make a home for;
Made it shine because she loved him so.
Susan she dreamed she had a pair of angel children;
Gave 'em all her heart to help 'em grow.
And now and then her man went drinkin';
The kids got sick or acted bad.
And suddenly Susan woke up and with a sob she started smilin'
And she felt no longer blue and sad.
Susan dreamed exactly what she had.

Love Song

New York, Tennessee, Oregon, Maine;
Wichita, Little Rock, Butte and Spokane.
I've seen 'em all, mister.
I've heard their noisy hum.

You know 'em all, mister,
When you're a bum.

Wherever I go I listen.
And I watch with open eyes.
And I've heard and seen a woman
Singin' freedom to the skies.
And I've heard the song of Wall Street
Singin', climb you market, climb!
And a drinkin' song that whispers
That it's prohibition time.
Yes, I've heard a song of harvest
From the green and copper hills;
As the copper turns to pennies
And the green to dollar bills.

Yes, I've heard 'em all, mister,
But you can't go sing 'em back,
I sing another song
Along the track.

I sing a song about the ocean,
Sing of how endless is the ocean,
Sing of however near the shore and sea,
And that's how true love should ever be.

I sing a song about the snowfall,
Sing of how gentle is the snowfall,
Sing of how pure the snow on every tree,
And that's how true love should ever be.

I've sung my song on the plain,
With the wind and the rain
Around me.

I've sung it high to a cloud
And to people who crowd
Along.

Oh, I sing a song about forever,
Only a song about forever,
Sing of how empty hearts forever long,
But nobody listens to my song.

Hear me, I only sing a love song,
Hear me, I only sing a love song,
Sing of how when it dies the world turns
  grey;
But nobody hears me what I say.

Madrigal

Oh, once upon the month of May
While strolling willy-nilly,
And wond'ring how I'd pass the day,
I met my good friend Billy.

Ho, Billy O!
The wind of spring is blowing.
Ho, Billy O!
So tell me where you're going.

He looked at me and sadly said:
The world is idiotic.
Oh, faith is gone and faith is dead;
And worse, I am neurotic.

Ho, Billy O!
The wind of spring is blowing.
Sing fa la la la la la la
And nowhere to be going.
Fa la la la la la la la
The world is idiotic.
Fa la la la la la la la
And Billy is neurotic.

I said: Oh, Billy, look at me
I'm overly aggressive,
And doctors ev'rywhere agree
I'm manic and depressive.

Ho, Billy O!
The wind of spring is blowing.
Ho, Billy O!
And nowhere to be going.

My father used to stay away,
With home he'd never bother.
And mother hid me twice a day
Because I looked like father.

Ho, Billy O!
The wind of spring is blowing.
Sing fa la la la la la la la
And nowhere to be be going.
Fa la la la la la
What folly lies in thinking.
Fa la la la la la la la
Come, Billy, let's go drinking.

So down we went
(Ay, down we went),
To a bar we knew
(A bar we knew),
And on the way
(Ay, on the way)
We met a lass named Mary Lou.
We met a lass named Mary Lou.

A lass that Billy and I both knew;
A lass that we knew through and through.
Fa la la la la la la la la
We knew her through and through.

Oh, sweet she was, I must admit,
Her dress all pink and frilly,
She curtseyed low and smiled a bit,
And coyly said to Billy:

Ho, Billy O!
The wind of spring is blowing.
Ho, Billy O!
So tell me where you're going.

Said Billy, with a hopeless grin,
The world is too chaotic.
The golden rule has turned to tin;
And worse, we're both neurotic.

Ho, Billy O!
The wind of spring is blowing.
Ho, Billy O!
So tell me where you're going.

Said she: Oh Billy, look at me,
I also am disgusted.
The doctors say that sexu'lly
I'm very maladjusted.

Ho, Billy O!
The wind of spring is blowing.
Sing fa la la la la la la
And nowhere to be going.
Fa la la la la la la la
The world cannot be mastered.
Fa la la la la la la la
Come, Billy, let's get plastered.

So went we three
(So went we three)
To the Club Nineteen
(The Club Nineteen),
And on the way
(Ay, on the way)
We met a lass named Geraldine.
We met a lass named Geraldine.
A lass who lived in a mansion big
A lass we thought an awful pig!
Fa la la la la la la la la
She was an awful pig!

    Oh, plump she was from head to toe,
    Her figure very hilly,
    But come she did and curtsey low,
    And shyly say to Billy:

Ho, Billy O!
The wind of spring is blowing.
Ho, Billy O!
So tell me where you're going.

    Said Billy: Boy, we're up the creek;
    The world is too despotic.
    We've disinherited the meek,
    And so we're all neurotic.

Ho, Billy O!
The wind of spring is blowing.
Ho, Billy O!
So tell me where you're going.

    Said she: Oh Billy, look at me,
    A piece of bad construction,
    And what is more sub-consciously
    I'm bent on self-destruction!

Oh, Billy O!
The wind of spring is blowing.
Sing fa la la la la la la
And nowhere to be going.
Fa la la la la la la
What folly lies in thinking.
Fa la la la la la la la
Come, Billy, let's get stinking.

So on we went
(Ay, on we went),
We neurotic four
(Neurotic four),
And drink we did
(Ay, drink we did)
'Till we fell flat on the floor.
'Till we fell flat on the floor.
Then off to bed went we one and all;
But whose we simply can't recall.
Fa la la la la la la la la
We simply can't recall.

Ho, Billy O!
The wind of spring is blowing.
Ho, Billy O!
Where in heaven are we going?
Fa la la la la la la
Fa la la la la la la.

Blues

Ladies, Ladies!
Ladies! – and new members – of the women's club, local branch,
Chapter seventeen – which was founded two years ago in
Eighteen ninety-two –

On a very cold night!
We're gathered here because the world is changing,
And our traditional position's out of fashion!
And the time has come to redirect our passion!

I toss and turn in bed alone at night,
My body aching for the right
To vote.

And when I'm gazing at the stars above
I tremble thinking how I'd love
To vote!

I've got a mouth as red as roses,
Crimson red as roses,
Hardly ever touched at all.
But from now on
I want to use it.
I'm gonna use it
To shout in ev'ry public meeting and hall.

I've got an urge, a powerful urge
For someone to squeeze me –
For someone to squeeze me in line at the polls.
I've got a desire, a mounting desire
For someone to seize me –
And make me free and equal as a male!
I'm sick of my domestic jail!

And when the moon is out at night
I start to dream about the right
To work!

And when the lamp begins to flicker low
My heart begins to pound to go
To work!

I've got a pair of satin shoulders,
Soft as satin shoulders,
I can move 'em like an eel.
But from now on
I want to use 'em,
I'm gonna use 'em,
I'm gonna put those shoulders right to the wheel!

I want to have the right to go and be a doctor.
A woman ought to have the right to be a doctor.
A doctor has to know about the facts of life.
And that you never learn about when you're a wife!

I want to have the right to be a country judge.
A woman should be free to be a country judge.
A judge, it is his job to sit and punish men.
It must be great to sit around and punish men.

I want to have the right to be a trav'lling salesman
A woman should be free to be a trav'lling salesman.
To travel through the country must be lots of fun.
I'll bet that now and then the farmer has a son!

I've got a figure white as iv'ry.
Smooth and white as iv'ry.
Once it used to hold a throb.
Well, from now on
I want to use it,
I'm gonna use it,
I'm gonna make that figure useful holding a job!

Green up Time

Yesterday morning I did see
Blossoms on the apple tree.
I took a breath and thought could it be
It's green up time.

Then I began to look around,
And in every field I found
Greens were a-pushing up through the ground
For green up time.

And sure enough the blue bells tinkled April in the glen.
And sure enough I fell in love with love again.
Then

I started feeling awful bright!
Had a thought that hit me right.
I'll have m'honey dance me tonight
And have a time
To welcome in the green up time.

Is It Him or Is It Me?

What happens now?
What do I do?
I never really thought
We ever would be through.

I never dreamed
I'd see the day,
But maybe he is right;
We're better off this way.

No! I'm not gonna cry!
I won't! What's done is done!
It's time that I was happy!
Oh, Sam, what have we done?

When I came home from work each evening
As tired and worn as I could be,
Why was he cold instead of tender?
Is it him or is it me?

Why, when I need his arms around me,
Did he pretend he didn't see?
Why was he numb to all my needing?
Is it him or is it me?

Why did we have all those senseless quarrels
Lasting 'till the early dawn?
Why would he go off sometimes and leave me
Not even knowing
Where he's going?

Why were there days of no one talking?
Why did we always disagree?
Oh, who's to blame he's gone and left me to be free?
Is it him or is it me?

Gone were all the idle dreams and fancies;
Silent were the future plans.
And I know when all the dreams
Are torn into tatters,
Nothing matters.

No, nothing matters when it's over,
The only thing is to be free.
But what's the use of all the endless wondering?
Is it him or is it me?

☆ ROYAL WEDDING ☆

In 1952, at the invitation of Arthur Freed, Lerner went to Hollywood for ten weeks, the idea being that he 'hang around', in the hope that an idea for a picture might develop, perhaps for Fred Astaire. Freed and Lerner chatted one day about the great stage career when Fred's partner had been his sister Adele. That alliance had come to an end when, after the success on Broadway of *The Bandwagon* in 1931, Adele had retired to marry Charles Cavendish, a son of the Duke of Devonshire. The two had met when the Astaires came to London in 1928 to repeat their New York success in the Gershwin show *Funny Face*. Lerner's screenplay for *Royal Wedding* kept in close touch with these facts. 1928 became 1947, Fred and Adele became Tom and Ellen Bowen, *Funny Face* became *Every Night at Seven*, and Cavendish became Lord John Brindale. In order to supply Fred with the obligatory love interest, a fourth character, eventually played improbably by Sarah Churchill, was added.

Astaire's partner-sister was to be played by June Allyson, but her pregnancy caused a change in the plans. It was then decided that Judy Garland be called in, but her failure to arrive at rehearsals, caused by her poor physical condition, caused further changes, which at last were resolved with the recruiting of Jane Powell. The production always embarrassed Lerner:

Although Burton Lane wrote some spiffy songs and Fred danced in a way that made all superlatives inadequate, my contribution left me in such a state of cringe that I could barely straighten up.

Every Night at Seven

LADIES

Your Majesty, what shall we wear to the dance?
Lame, or satin or silk?
Sequins or jersey or maybe perchance
That stuff they're making from milk?

TOM

My royal day can be a royal bore,
It leaves me colder than a basement floor,
The only moment I keep waiting for,
Is when the day will be through.
I never notice if it's dark or clear,
What people say to me I hardly hear,
The passing hours are an endless year,
Until at last I'm alone with you, for . . .

> *(Tom and Ellen rise up from throne, and start
> into dance routine, which continues after
> finish of following chorus.)*

TOM

Every night at seven, you walk in as fresh as clover,
And I begin to sigh all over again.

Every night at seven, you come by like May returning,
And me, oh my, I start in yearning again.

You seem to bring far away spring near me,
I'm always in full bloom, when you're in the room.

For – every night at seven, every time the same thing happens,
I fall once again in love, but only with you.

> *(At end of dance routine, which involves groups
> of guards who enter through both sides of stage,
> Tom chases Ellen who has stolen his crown,
> around and through the guards – to finale of
> number.)*

GUARDS

Every night at seven, every time the same thing happens,
I fall once again in love,

TOM

But only with you.

Sunday Jumps

Sunday is a thing you lie around on,
A day of peace and gathering new reserves.
Sunday's calm routine,
Tranquil and serene,
But brother, how it gets on my nerves.
I've got the Sunday jumps,
The fidgety kind of screaming jumps
I only seem to get on Sunday.
All week I'm happier than a daisy,
Then comes the day to relax and I go crazy.
They tell me get some rest,
But all that I get is depressed,
I count the ages till Monday.
I'm far away from the world and in the dumps.
No date with anyone,
No place I've gotta run,
And so I've got the Sunday jumps.

Open Your Eyes

Open your eyes
There's a saphire sky above us
High above us
Made for us
When you
Open your eyes.

Open your eyes
There's a carpet of jade
Around us
Made around us
All for you
When you
Open your eyes.

Let me show you the sights
Take you
On a tour of this
Great new
Fabulous world
We own
We alone
So open your eyes
And you'll see how this
Momentary
Ordinary
Night can seem
More unreal than a dream.

Let me show you the sights
Take you
On a tour of this
Great new
Fabulous world
We own
We alone
So open your eyes
And you'll see how this
Momentary
Ordinary
Night can seem
More unreal than a dream
More unreal than a dream.

How Could You Believe Me When I Said I Love You When You Know I've Been a Liar all my Life?

How could you believe me when I said I love you
When you know I've been a liar all my life?
I've had that reputation
Since I was a youth,
You must have been insane to think
I'd tell you the truth.
How could you believe me when I said we'd marry!
When you know I'd rather hang than have a wife.
I know I said
I'd make you mine,
But who would know that you would go
For that old line?

How could you believe me when I said I love you
When you know I've been a liar,
Nothing but a liar,
All my doggone
Cheatin' life?

GIRL

You said you would love me long,
And never would do me wrong.
And faithful you'd always be.

BOY

Oh, baby, you must be loony to trust a lower than low two-timer like me.

GIRL

You said I'd have ev'rything,
A beautiful diamond ring,
A bungalow by the sea.

BOY

You're really naive to ever believe a full of baloney phoney like me.

GIRL

Say! How about the time you went to Indiana?

BOY

I was lyin' I was down in Alabam!

GIRL

You said you had some business
You had to complete.

BOY

What I was doin' I would be
A cad to repeat.

GIRL

What about the evenings you were with your mother?

BOY

I was romping with another honey lamb.

GIRL

To think you swore
Our love was real.

BOY

But, baby, let us not forget,
That I'm a heel.

How could you believe me when I said I love you
When you know I've been a liar,
Nothing but a liar,
All my doggone
No good life?

GIRL

No good
Good for nothin' life.

Too Late Now

Too late now to forget your smile;
The way we cling when we've danced a-while;
Too late now to forget and go on to someone new.

Too late now to forget your voice;
The way one word makes my heart rejoice;
Too late now to imagine myself away from you.

All the things we've done together
I relive when we're apart.
All the tender fun together
Stays on in my heart.

How could I ever close the door
And be the same as I was before?
Darling, no, no, I can't any more;
It's too late now.

'You're All the World to Me' is one of those examples, rare but not quite unknown, of a song with a double life, dual parentage, contradictory functions. In *Royal Wedding* it served, as the reader can see at a glance, as a declaration of love comprising a travelogue. In the choreographic sense, it was one of the most stunning songs in the history of the cinema, being the one which Astaire sings in an ecstasy of gravity-defying euphoria while dancing up the walls and across the ceiling of his hotel bedroom. Just as remarkable is the fact that the melody, composed by Burton Lane, had already appeared on screen in another guise. The Astaire version is slowish and intensely romantic, but in 1934 when Lane had originally conceived it, while working with the lyricist Harold Adamson on a Samuel Goldwyn production called *Kid Millions*, starring Eddie Cantor, the piece had been designed as an up-tempo spectacular performed by the precocious Nicholas Brothers, Harold and Fayard, who sang and danced the song supported by a phalanx of top-hatted chorus girls. It is revealing to compare the urbanity of Lerner's version with the energetic celebration of a dead tradition which Lane and Adamson had written:

> We always love a minstrel man,
> He thrills us like nobody can,
> The way he dances sure is dandy,
> And sings the songs about his sugar candy.
> He's learned to love the minstrel ways,
> Oh, bring them back, the minstrel days,
> Give us a man like George M. Cohan,
> We want a minstrel man.

When I asked Alan about this extraordinary reincarnation of an ancient melody, he professed to be flabbergasted, but it seemed a little too far-fetched to me that he, an intense student of popular music, should not have known that the song had had a previous incarnation. This suspicion was confirmed when later I discussed it with Lane, who recalled the circumstances as follows: 'I wrote the melody as my expression of what I would like to do if I were to write a song for Astaire. Then someone suggested we make the tune fit Eddie Cantor. I said okay. So we wrote a song which I never felt realized everything the tune could have. I was never happy with "I Want To Be a Minstrel Man". But it worked in the picture. Many years later, when I got the assignment to do *Royal Wedding*, I remembered this tune and I said, "I'm gonna see if I can get the rights back from Sam Goldwyn, because this is the tune I always dreamed would be good for Astaire." And when I played it for Astaire, he loved it.' When I asked about Goldwyn, Lane surprised me by replying, 'He was very generous with me, very decent.'

You're All the World to Me

You're like Paris
In April and May.
You're New York
On a silvery day.
A Swiss Alp
As the sun grows fainter;
You're Loch Lomond
When autumn is the painter.
You're moonlight
On a night in Capri
And Cape Cod
Looking out at the sea.
You're all the places
That leave me breathless;
And no wonder,
You're all the world to me.

Ev'rywhere that beauty glows
You are.
Ev'rywhere an orch'd grows
You are.
Ev'rything that's young and gay,
Brighter than a holiday,
Ev'rywhere the angels play
You are.

You're Lake Como
When dawn is aglow.
You're Sun Valley
Right after a snow,
A museum,
A Persian palace,
You're my shining
Aurora Borealis.
You're like Christmas
At home by a tree
The blue calm of
A tropical sea.
You're all the places
That leave me breathless;
And no wonder,
You're all the world to me.

I Left my Hat in Haiti

I left my hat in Haiti,
In some forgotten flat in Haiti;
I couldn't tell you how I got there
I only know it was so hot there.
She took my hat politely
And wound her arms around me tightly,
But I remember nothing clearly
Except the flame when she came near me.
Her eyes had the fire of surrender
And her touch, it was tender;
And with someone as fi'ry as that*
You forget about your hat!

So if you go to Haiti,
There is a girl I know in Haiti.
If you can find her
You'll adore-a;
Just look around
Till you've found
Someone who has a blue grey fedora.

I think of that gorgeous creature when I'm all alone,
Whenever I do from down inside there comes a groan.
That son of a gun in Haiti
Has got the prettiest hat I own.
And when it is bleak and chilly
And life is flat,
I think of that Haitian dilly.
And think I'd better go get my hat.

*Astaire sings: 'And I guess in a moment as that'.

The Happiest Day of my Life

I wake up and sigh each morning, happy the night's gone by,
I wake up and pray each morning, pray that the day will fly,
And then I sit back and smile, and dream of that day when

I'll be standing by your side, my love, the happiest day of my life,
How my heart will swell with pride, my love,
The happiest day in a lifetime.
Then as the last words are spoken, the bells in the steeple will chime,
And I will love you so, and you will see,
It will be for a lifetime.

☆ PAINT YOUR WAGON ☆

The resumption of the partnership with Fritz Loewe was a happy event artistically, less happy for its investors. In this story of a town which owes its genesis to a gold rush, there were overtones of *Oklahoma!*, underlined by the choreography of Agnes de Mille, but Lerner's story was more adventurous than the Rodgers and Hammerstein operetta. The setting was California in 1853. The arrival of prospectors in search of gold brings about the birth of the town of Rumson, named after its first sheriff, and also its judge and mayor. When there is no more gold the town withers, but is saved by irrigation schemes and the birth of agriculture. A celebration of the old Far West, the show opened on 12 November 1951, ran for 289 performances and left the parodists with the promising material of its best-known ballad, 'I Talk to the Trees'.

I'm On My Way

Where'm I goin', I don't know.
Where'm I headin', I ain't certain.
All I know is I am on my way!

When will I be there, I don't know.
When will I get there, I ain't certain.
All I know is I am on my way!

Got a dream, boy?
Got a song?
Paint your wagon
And come along!

Where'm I goin', I don't know.
When will I be there, I ain't certain.
What will I get, I ain't equipped to say.
But who gives a damn...
I'm on my way!

Wand'rin' Star

I was born under a wand'rin' star.
I was born under a wand'rin' star.
Wheels are made for rollin',
Mules are made to pack.
I never seen a sight
That didn't look better lookin' back.
I was born under a wand'rin' star.

Mud can make you pris'ner and the plains can make you dry.
Snow can burn your eyes but only people make you cry.
Home is made for comin' from, for dreams of goin' to,
Which, with any luck, will never come true.

I was born under a wand'rin' star.
I was born under a wand'rin' star.
Do I know where hell is?
Hell is in hello.
Heaven is 'Goodbye forever,
It's time for me to go'.
I was born under a wand'rin' star,
A wand'rin', wand'rin' star.

I was born under a wand'rin' star.
I was born under a wand'rin' star.
When I get to heaven
Tie me to a tree,
Or I'll begin to roam,
And soon you know where I will be.
I was born under a wand'rin' star,
A wand'rin', wand'rin' star.

Gold Fever

I would give the world to see
How I used to be
When I had no axe to grind
Except for choppin' wood.
Day was day and night was night;
Wrong was never right;
Didn't matter where I went
As much as where I stood.
I had dreams,
Av'rage size.
There were stars
In the skies;
Not in my eyes.
Then I got

Gold fever!
No rompin', rollin' girl and fellow stuff
Can cure the
Gold fever!
Nothin' can help you but the yellow stuff.
What
Can stop that itchin',
Ain't
Around the kitchen.
Gold! Gold!
Hooked am I!
Susannah, go ahead and cry.

Once we all did honest work:
Farmer, lawyer, clerk;
Married men and single men
And some who ain't too sure.
Now I look at them and see
Duplicates of me;
Cured of what we suffered from
And suff'rin from the cure.
Who can say
Why we came?
Where's the hope?
Where's the flame?
We're the same.
Then you got

Gold fever!
No rompin', rollin' girl and fellow stuff
Can cure the
Gold fever!
Nothin' can help you but the yellow stuff.
What
Can stop that itchin',
Ain't
Around the kitchen.
Gold! Gold!
Hooked am I!
Susannah, go ahead and cry.

The First Thing You Know

God made the mountains,
God made the sky,
God made the people,
God knows why.
He fixed up the planet
As best as He could;
Then in come the people
And gum it up good.

The first thing you know
They civilize the foothills
And ev'rywhere He put hills
And mountains and valleys below
They came along and take 'em
And civilize and make 'em
A place where no civilized person would go.
The first thing you know.

The first thing you know
They civilize what's pretty
By puttin' up a city
Where nothin' that's pretty can grow.
They muddy up the winter
And civilize it into
A place too uncivilized even for snow.

The first thing you know
They civilize left and they civilize right
Till nothin' is left and nothin' is right.
They civilize freedom 'till no one is free;
No one except, by coincidence, me!

The first thing you know
The boozer's in prison,
The criminal, he isn',
And only the rascals have dough.
But soon as there's a parson
I want to put my arse on
A wagon that follows the tail of a crow.
I pick up and blow
The first thing you know.

A Million Miles Away Behind the Door

Send back the world,
There's too much night for me.
The sky is much too high
To shelter me when darkness falls.
Four cabin walls
Would be just right for me.
I need a threshold I can cross
Where I can sit and gather moss
For ever more,
A million miles away behind the door.

Roll up the plains.
There's too much view for me.
There's so much space
Between the waiting heart and whispered word,
It's never heard.
One room will do for me;
Where ev'ry evening I can stare
At someone smiling from his chair
Across the floor,
A million miles away behind the door.

No fears; no fools;
No lies; no rules.
Just doing with my life
What life is for.
A million miles away behind the door.

I Talk to the Trees

I talk to the trees
But they don't listen to me.
I talk to the stars
But they never hear me.

The breeze hasn't time
To stop and hear what I say.
I talk to them all in vain.

But suddenly my words
Reach someone else's ears;
Touch someone else's heartstrings, too.

I tell you my dreams,
And while you're list'ning to me,
I suddenly see them come true.

I can see us on an April night
Sipping brandy underneath the stars.
Reading poems in the candle light
To the strumming of guitars.

I will tell you how I passed the day,
Thinking only how the night would be.
And I'll try to find the words to say,
All the things you mean to me.

But suddenly my words
Reach someone else's ear;
Touch someone else's heartstrings, too.

I tell you my dreams,
And while you're list'ning to me,
I suddenly see them come true.

I Still See Elisa

I still see Elisa;
She keeps on returning
As breathless and young as ever.

I still hear Elisa,
And still feel a yearning
To hold her against me again.

Her heart was made of holidays;
Her smile was made of dawn.
Her laughter was an April song
That echoes on and on.

Since I saw Elisa
The shadows are falling,
The winter is calling above.
But I still see Elisa
Whenever I dream of love.

They Call the Wind Maria

Away out here they got a name
For wind and rain and fire;
The rain is Tess, the fire's Jo,
And they call the wind Maria.
Maria blows the stars around
And sends the clouds a-flyin',
Maria makes the mountains sound
Like folks were up there dyin'.

Maria! Maria! They call the wind Maria!

Before I knew Maria's name
And heard her wail and whinin'.
I had a girl and she had me
And the sun was always shinin',
But then one day I left my girl,
I left her far behind me.
And now I'm lost, so goldurn lost
Not even God can find me.

Maria! Maria! They call the wind Maria!

Out here they got a name for rain
For wind and fire only.
But when you're lost and all alone
There ain't no word but lonely.
And I'm a lost and lonely man
Without a star to guide me.
Maria, blow my love to me;
I need my girl beside me.

Maria! Maria! They call the wind Maria!
Maria! Maria! Blow my love to me!

How Can I Wait?

How can I wait, can I wait till tomorrow comes?
How can I live till tomorrow comes?
How can I make every minute fly
Till that breathless moment when
I'll be seein' him again?

I'm gonna die,
Gonna die or be old and grey!
Why is tomorrow so far away?
How can I talk, can I breathe, can I eat?
What can I do with my hands and my feet?
How can I wait, can I wait till tomorrow comes?

Starlight, go away, fade away, blow away!
Sunrise, come again, make a new sunny day!

Oh, what can I do, can I think about?
How can my heart keep from jumpin' out?
How can I sleep – couldn't sleep if I tried!
Where can I run till I run to his side?
How can I wait till tomorrow comes!

Coach Comin' In

There's a coach comin' in!
If you listen you can hear it – a
Clip-cloppin' over the hill,
And the sound that you hear is as good to your ear
As the call of a wild whipperwill.

There's a coach comin' in!
You can feel it gettin' near
All at once and it bursts into view,
And it looks to your eye like it fell from the sky,
Like a coach full of dreams come true.

For it's bringin' me eyes that are moonlight,
And it's carryin' lips that are wine,
And it's comin' with arms that are pillows,
And this evenin' it all will be mine.

There's a coach comin' in!
And you're smellin' like a steer,
Get the soap out, it ain't far away!
Cut the socks from your feet
Rake your hair 'til it's neat
There's a coach comin' in,
There's a coach comin' in today!

There's a coach comin' in!
Hurry, hurry, do you hear?
With a cargo of joy from Paree.
Drop the tables and chairs,
Get them beds up the stairs,
And be sure ev'ry lock has a key.

Fot it's coming mitt girls who buy perfume
Who wear powder and rouge from Paree.
Who will haff to go somewhere to get them
And that somewhere to go will be me.

There's a coach comin' in!
And it's flyin' like a deer.
Thank the Lord there's relief on the way.
Thank with all of your hearts
For them half dozen tarts
There's a coach comin' in,
There's a coach comin' in today!

There's a coach comin' in!
If you listen you can hear it – a
Clip-cloppin' over the hill,
And the sound that you hear is as good to your ear
As the call of a wild whipperwill.

For it's bringin' me eyes that are moonlight,
And it's carryin' lips that are wine,
And it's comin' with arms that are pillows,
And this evenin' it all will be mine.

There's a coach comin' in!
If you listen you can hear it – a
Clip-cloppin' over the hill,
And the sound that you hear is as good to your ear
As the call of a wild whipperwill.

There's a coach comin' in!
You can feel it gettin' near
All at once and it bursts into view,
And it looks to your eye like it fell from the sky
Like a coach full of dreams come true.

For it's bringin' me eyes that are moonlight,
And it's carryin' lips that are wine,
And it's comin' with arms that are pillows,
And this evenin' it all will be mine.

There's a coach comin' in!
Now it's ridin' in the clear,
And the sound of it grows to a din!
Now there ain't far to go,
No there ain't far to go,
Now they're hollerin' 'Whoa!'
Yes, they're hollerin' 'Whoa!'
There's a coach comin' in,
There's a coach comin' in,
And it's in.

Some years after its Broadway production *Paint Your Wagon* was adapted into a film. This entailed some re-writing, including the following amended version of this song.

There's a Coach Comin' In

There's a coach comin' in!
If you listen you can hear
It a clip-cloppin' over the hill,
And the sound that you hear
Is as good to your ear
As the call of a wild whipperwill.

There's a coach comin' in!
You can feel it gettin' near
All at once and it bursts into view,
And it looks to your eye
Like it fell from the sky,
Like a coach full o' dreams come true.

For it's bringin' me eyes that are moonlight,
And it's carryin' lips that are wine,
And it's comin' with arms that are pillows,
And this evenin' it all will be mine.

There's a coach comin' in!
Now it's ridin' in the clear,
And the sound of it grows to a din.
Now there ain't far to go!
Now they're hollerin', 'Whoa!'
There's a coach comin' in,
There's a coach comin' and it's in!

It's a clip-cloppin' over the hill,
And the sound that you hear
Is as good to your ear
As the call of a wild whipperwill.

There's a coach comin' in!
You can feel it gettin' near
All at once and it bursts into view,
And it looks to your eye
Like it fell from the sky,
Like a coach full o' dreams come true.

For it's bringin' me eyes that are moonligh
And it's carryin' lips that are wine,
And it's comin' with arms that are pillows,
And this evenin' it all will be mine.

There's a coach comin' in!
Now it's ridin' in the clear,
And the sound of it grows to a din!
Now there ain't far to go!
Now they're hollerin' 'Whoa!'
There's a coach comin' in, and
The coach comin' came today!

Another Autumn

Winter's comin' on
I feel it all around
The leaves are movin' faster along the ground.

Why have all the dreams
Been broken wide apart?
And where is all the hope that was in my heart?

Another autumn . . .
I've known the chill before
But every autumn
I feel it more and more,
For you can dream up spring
When every hope is high,
But when the fall comes in
They all begin
To fade and die.

Another autumn . . .
So sweet when all is well;
But how it haunts you when all is wrong.
For one thing time has shown:
If you're alone
When autumn comes
You'll be alone all winter long.

The Gospel of No Name City

You want to see sin of the wickedest kind?
Here it is!
Want to see virtue left behind?
Here it is!
Sodom was vice and vice versa.
Want to see where the vice is worser?
Here it is!
I mean,
Here it is!

No Name City,
No Name City,
The Lord don't like it here.
No Name City,!
No Name City,
Your reck'nin' day is near.
No Name City,
No Name City,
Here's what He's gonna do:
Gobble up this town
And swallow it down
And goodbye to you.

You want to live life in the rottenest way?
Here it is!
Women and whisky, night and day?
Here it is!
You want to embrace the golden calf,
Ankle and thigh and upper half?
Here it is!
I mean,
Here it is!

No Name City,
No Name City,
The Lord don't like it here.
No Name City,
No Name City,
Your reck'nin' day is near.
No Name City,
No Name City,
Here's what He's gonna do:
Gobble up this town
And swallow it down
And goodbye to you.

Will you go to heav'n, will you go to hell?
Go to hell!
Either repent or fare thee well.
Fare thee well!
God will take care of No Name City.
Comes the end, it won't be pretty.
Here it is!
I mean,
Here it is!

No Name City,
No Name City,
The Lord don't like it here.
No Name City,
No Name City,
Your reck'nin' day is near.
No Name City,
No Name City,
Here's what He's gonna do:
Gobble up this town
And swallow it down
And goodbye to you.
Here it is!
I mean, here it is!
Here it is!
I mean, here it is!
Amen!

Hand Me Down That Can o' Beans

JAKE

Hand me down that can o' beans,
Hand me down that can o' beans,
Hand me down that can o' beans,
I'm throwin' it away!

Out the winder go the beans,
Out the winder go the beans,
Out the winder go the beans,
I had a lucky day!

CHORUS

Mary!
Ma-ma-ma-Mary!
My sweet canary,
We're goin' out this evenin'!
Mary!
Ma-ma-ma-Mary!
I'm gonna take you out tonight!
So!
Hand me down that can o' beans,
Hand me down that can o' beans,
Hand me down that can o' beans,
I'm throwin' it away!

Out the winder go the beans,
Out the winder go the beans,
Out the winder go the beans, go the beans, go the beans,
Good times are here to stay!

So hand me down that can o' beans,
Hand me down that can o' beans,
Out the winder go the beans,
Good times are here to stay!

What's Goin' On Here?

I've been in lots of camps before
But this one is by far the most bewild'rin',
I never seen so many growed up people
Actin' like a bunch o' children.
What's goin' on? What's in the air?
The way this town's behavin' is enough
To make a person tear her hair.

I sit down to tie my shoe
And ev'ry single time I do,
I'm circled by a hundred men or more.
What's goin' on here? What's goin' on?
Ain't no one ever seen a shoe before?

Liftin' me across the mud,
A miner dropped me with a thud
And said he'd never pick me up again.
What's goin' on here? What's goin' on?
I only weigh a hundred nine or ten.
I never seen a camp so crazy.
They must've all had too much sun.

When the days are hot as steam
And ev'ry one goes in the stream,
When I jump in, they all jump out and run.
Oh, what's goin' on here? What's goin' on here?
What did I done?

No one will walk with me.
Ev'ryone leaves me high and dry.
No one will talk with me.
Tell me why, why, why?

Once I asked a miner if
He'd rub my neck 'cause it was stiff,
And feelin' like the handle of a mop.
What's goin' on here? What's goin' on?
I couldn't get the crazy fool to stop.

Of all the camps that I have been to,
I never had so little fun.

Yesterday I passed a man
Who asked me how to clean a pan,
When I bent over, Lordy, did he run!
Oh, what's goin' on here? What's goin' on here?
What did I done?

☆ MY FAIR LADY ☆

In the spring of 1952, while Lerner was in Hollywood writing the screenplay for *Brigadoon*, there arrived in town that most professional of all professional Hungarians, Gabriel Pascal, who had somehow persuaded Bernard Shaw to part with the screen rights of several of his plays. Pascal, currently involved in the transformation of *Androcles and the Lion* into a picture, took time out to lunch with Lerner, announcing his desire to make a musical of *Pygmalion* using Lerner's music. Lerner explained that he did not write music but that Frederick Loewe did. Pascal then instructed Lerner to fetch Loewe from New York, and left to demand a libretto from Aldous Huxley which never was forthcoming. At the first meeting between Lerner, Loewe and Pascal, the Hungarian told them that they alone could realize his dream of a musical *Pygmalion*, which struck the partners as curious in view of the fact that it was common knowledge inside the profession that he had already offered it to Rodgers and Hammerstein. Lerner and Loewe agreed to proceed, after explaining to Pascal that he must find a theatrical producer and that he must be prepared to wait two years, which was the standard period of time required by Lerner and Loewe to write a new show.

During 1952 Lerner became increasingly disillusioned with the whole idea. The problems seemed insuperable. The play was all talk, and Lerner could see no way of 'tearing down the walls of the drawing-room and allow the play to unfold in a setting and atmosphere that suggested music.' And where was the ensemble? Where was the sub-plot? Where was the love interest? One night at a rally for Adlai Stevenson, Lerner met Oscar Hammerstein who asked him how things were coming along. 'Slowly,' answered Lerner, to which Hammerstein shook his head and said, 'It can't be done. Dick and I worked on it for over a year and gave it up.' Soon after, Lerner and Loewe abandoned the project.

That summer something serious had happened to Gabriel Pascal. As Lerner puts it, 'He gave up the ghost and become one,' having in the intervening two years offered the *Pygmalion* deal to every composer and lyricist in the business, all of whom had turned it down. Meanwhile Lerner was going through crises both physical and spiritual. A loss of professional confidence, brought about by a fear that he was losing touch with his times, made it impossible for him to settle down to work. His anguish spawned a brain fever which developed into spinal meningitis. Delirium and a paralysed left leg followed, at which point it is interesting to reflect on the unawareness of those who assume that writing songs for a living is a carefree existence. Fritz Loewe tried to carry on by writing a show with Harold Rome, while Lerner, once he felt well enough, began collaborating with Burton Lane on a musical version of *Li'l Abner*, which he saw as 'a sort of *Good Soldier Schweik'*. But Lerner found he was still unable to write, and in desperation turned to the producer Herman Levin, asking him to promise to stage *Li'l Abner* should it ever be completed. Levin then went off for a Mediterranean cruise, and while he was away Lerner picked up his newspaper one morning and read an obituary of Pascal. This sent his thoughts racing back to *Pygmalion*. Within hours he had telephoned Loewe. They lunched together:

It was like going home. As we began to discuss it, I saw, for the first time in two years, the thin line of a distant dawn on the horizon. I felt like a long-distance runner slowly catching up with the herd.

What had caused this reawakening? Had Lerner solved the problems which had caused him to give up with such finality two years earlier? He had not, but had simply decided that they were not problems after all. Why not write a musical without a chorus, without a sub-plot, without a romantic ending? (Eventually the ultra-romantic Lerner could not bring himself to swallow the anti-romantic pill which Shaw insisted must be taken with every performance of the play.) But the absence of a chorus and a sub-plot proved no impediment. In his memoirs Lerner writes at some length and with great flair about the genesis of *My Fair Lady*. All that needs to be noted here is that he decided to follow the ground-plan of Shaw's screen version, linking Shaw's scenes with additional scenes of his own where they seemed to be called for:

Example: *Pygmalion* is in five acts. In the first act Higgins meets Eliza in her native habitat of Covent Garden, then meets Pickering, who is on his way home from the opera, explains to him how, by phonetics, he can turn this 'squashed cabbage leaf' into a duchess at an embassy ball, invites Pickering to stay with him at his house on Wimpole Street, and off they go. End of Act One.

Act Two. It is the following day, and Higgins is demonstrating to Pickering his phonetic equipment when Eliza appears asking for speech lessons. 'Now,' said Fritz and I to each other, 'what was Eliza doing between Higgins' departure from Covent Garden and her arrival at Higgins' house the following morning?' She probably went home to her parents. But she had no parents – that is, at home. Later in the play we are told that she lives alone, has no mother and that her father is a dustman living with another woman. So that is precisely what we wrote. Eliza goes home, meets her father and two of his cronies. Brief scene between them. Song by father to establish his character, 'With a Little Bit of Luck', and on into the next scene when Eliza comes to Wimpole Street.

How easy Lerner makes it all seem, how obvious, how inevitable. Among the details he omits to mention are his uncanny mastery of the old English music hall genre, which he echoes later in the play when Doolittle sings 'Get Me to the Church on Time', and his instinctive feeling that Eliza would have gone looking for her father. As to the hardest decisions of all, the placing of the songs, once again Lerner over-simplifies to the point where the reader begins to feel that anyone might have written *My Fair Lady*, instead of the truth, which is the nobody else could:

We finally arrived at those moments where music and lyrics could reveal what was implied and not repeat what was already in the text, and could catch the drama at the hill-tops where it could ascend no farther without the wings of music and lyrics, at the same time remaining faithful to the spirit of the Irish Pope.

Levin, having returned from his sea trip, was duly informed that he was producing, not *Li'l Abner* (which was eventually written, quite brilliantly, by Johnny Mercer and Gene de Paul), but *Pygmalion*, after which he met the partners regularly to discuss production and financial details. Meanwhile Lerner reached the conclusion that the key to the show would be the casting of Higgins:

Empathy for him came easily to me. There was no doubt in my mind that Higgins was Shaw, and Shaw, as far as women were concerned, was a man of overwhelming shyness. His love affairs existed on paper only, and his ardour, though magnificently articulate, romantic, exalted and bewitching, was all by post. What always moved me so deeply about Higgins was that he, a master in the language of the poets, was incapable of putting together a few words to relieve his own loneliness, a loneliness which he (Shaw and/or Higgins) so gallantly and wittily concealed. So the first person we began to look for was not an Eliza Doolittle, but a Henry Higgins. And the first person I thought of was Rex Harrison.

There then followed an extraordinary passage with Mary Martin, who had heard of the project and had decided to offer herself as Eliza, which calls to mind the regiments of mature ladies who had once suggested themselves as believable Scarlett O'Haras. The Martin phase having ended, Lerner and Loewe happened to see a Broadway production about the Twenties, 'as seen through the eyes of someone who was not there'. This was *The Boy Friend*, whose eighteen-year-old leading lady, one Julie Andrews, instantly commended herself to the partners. But soon Harrison had announced he hated the first two songs written for him. Lerner and Loewe, realizing his judgement was better than theirs, instantly discarded the songs and started again. The next step was to discover if Harrison could sing. He was led up to Fritz's room and asked to sing. He chose 'Molly Malone'; after one chorus Fritz stopped him and said, 'Fine. That's all you need.'

Claridge's was also the scene of Doolittle's recruitment. Stanley Holloway, asked if his singing voice was still intact, petrified the dining-room, even down to the string quartet, by bursting into an irresistible baritone performance.

The rest of the story concerns the protracted battle for rights, the recruitment of Moss Hart as director, the investment of $400,000 by CBS, the New Haven and Philadelphia try-outs, and the final triumphant Broadway opening, followed by the rather less perfect screen version by Warner Brothers. On 15 March 1956, New York audiences first saw what is generally agreed to be the closest thing to a faultless musical ever written, comprised of a libretto so lovingly constructed by a dedicated Shavian that almost no damage has been done to the original, lyrics unsurpassed in their elegance and wit, and a score bursting with memorable tunes. In retrospect it can also be seen that in Harrison, Andrews and Holloway, casting had been achieved of so consummate a nature that it seems highly unlikely that any comparable group will ever interepret the work with as much flair. What Lerner had achieved was the masterwork of his life, something so magnificent that it is hard to imagine even Shaw, the dedicated Wagnerian, having much objection to the transformation of his work.

It has often gone unnoticed that *My Fair Lady* is rare in not having a title song. This had not always been the intention. The first choice of title had been 'Liza', rejected because 'Rex Harrison in "Liza"' would have seemed peculiar. 'Lady Liza' was discarded for the same reason. The next selection was 'My Fair Lady' – soon discarded because it sounded too much like an operetta. Then Loewe became an advocate of 'Fanfaroon', an arcane English term for someone who blows his own fanfare. There was also a lobby for the song 'Come to the Ball' to be adopted as the title song. The company were rehearsing for the New Haven opening, still without a title. At this stage, Levin, who had taken out newspaper ads announcing 'Rex Harrison and Julie Andrews in "?"', made a speech:

Now listen. We've got to have a title. People have to know the name of what they have seen so they can tell their friends to go and see it. Call it anything. You can always change it on the road. After all, when *Oklahoma!* opened it was called 'Away We Go'.

Lerner then suggested, 'Why don't we just take the title that we all dislike the least?' There followed a brief discussion, and 'My Fair Lady' it was. 'A few months later,' says Lerner, 'we all thought it was brilliant – except Fritz, who still liked "Fanfaroon".'

There was a postscript. Lerner happened to mention to his good friend Ira Gershwin the projected title of the new show. Ira told him that it had already been used. In 1925 the Gershwin brothers had written a Broadway show called *My Fair Lady* which was changed to *Tell Me More*. Lerner was astonished to hear this, and went to check the details. He found that there had been not one but several shows called *My Fair Lady*. One more could do no harm.

When Harrison first began learning this lyric he complained that it made him feel 'like an inferior Noël Coward'. At first Lerner was baffled by the complaint, but then came to the conclusion that perhaps he ought to change the rhyme-scheme. In its original form he had written:

> Why can't the English teach their children how to speak?
> In Norway there are legions
> Of literate Norwegians.

He rewrote this as:

> Why can't the English teach their children how to speak?
> This verbal class distinction by now should be antique.

The rewriting had the double effect of rendering the lyric less 'lyricky' and of pleasing Harrison. Lerner later testified that finding a style for Harrison was like finding a style for himself. 'To this day, time after time I find myself instinctively writing for Rex and constantly reminding myself that I am not writing for Rex. Nevertheless, he was then and always will be my natural extension.'

Why Can't the English?

Why can't the English teach their children how to speak?
This verbal class distinction by now should be antique.
If you spoke as she does, sir,
Instead of the way you do,
Why, you might be selling flowers, too.

An Englishman's way of speaking absolutely classifies him;
The moment he talks he makes some other Englishman despise him,
One common language I'm afraid we'll never get.
Oh, why can't the English learn to set
A good example to people whose English is painful to your ears?
The Scotch and the Irish leave you close to tears.

There even are places where English completely disappears.
In America, they haven't used it for years!
Why can't the English teach their children how to speak?
Norwegians learn Norwegian; the Greeks are taught their Greek.
In France every Frenchman knows his language from 'A' to 'Zed'.
The French never care what they do, actually, as long as they pronounce it properly.
Arabians learn Arabian with the speed of summer lightning.
The Hebrews learn it backwards, which is absolutely frightening.
But use proper English, you're regarded as a freak.
Why can't the English,
Why can't the English learn to speak?

This was the first lyric which Lerner completed when commencing to adapt *Pygmalion*. Armed with Loewe's melody, he describes the excitement of being able to begin. But he was horrified to find himself faced with writer's block. After three weeks in which he had achieved not a single line, had lost eight pounds and had, in his own words, 'become a basket case', he went to see a psychiatrist, who listened to the story and then remarked, 'You know, you write as if your life depends on every line,' to which Lerner answered, 'It does.' Lerner then told the unfortunate tale of his brush with Mary Martin and her husband, who, having been the first outsiders to hear the early attempts of the partners to write some numbers for the show, had reacted so rudely as to have shattered Lerner's confidence completely. Once the correlation of the rebuff and the block had been suggested to him, Lerner went home and wrote the words to this song in thirty-six hours. Although he allowed the following version to stand, he was never convinced it was right. His intent had been to compose a lyric comprised entirely of references to creature comforts like warmth, chocolates and so on. But he confessed he had never been able to find a suitable climax to the song and had finally allowed into the lyric the intrusion of some second party, 'someone's head resting on my knee'.

Wouldn't it be Luverly?

All I want is a room somewhere,
Far away from the cold night air;
With one enormous chair . . .
Oh, wouldn't it be luverly?

Lots of choc'late for me to eat;
Lots of coal makin' lots of heat;
Warm face, warm hands, warm feet . . .!
Oh, wouldn't it be luverly?

Oh, so luverly sittin' absobloominlutely still,
I would never budge till spring
Crept over me winder sill.

Someone's head restin' on my knee,
Warm and tender as he can be,
Who takes good care of me . . .
Oh, wouldn't it be luverly?
Luverly! Luverly!
Luverly! Luverly!

I'm an Ordinary Man

I'm an ordinary man;
Who desires nothing more
Than just the ordinary chance
To live exactly as he likes
And do precisely what he wants.
An average man am I
Of no eccentric whim;
Who likes to live his life
Free of strife,
Doing whatever he thinks is best for him.
Just an ordinary man.

But let a woman in your life
And your serenity is through!
She'll redecorate your home
From the cellar to the dome;
Then get on to the enthralling
Fun of overhauling
You.

Oh, let a woman in your life
And you are up against the wall!
Make a plan and you will find
She has something else in mind;
And so rather than do either
You do something else that neither
Likes at all.

You want to talk of Keats or Milton;
She only wants to talk of love.
You go to see a play or ballet,
And spend it searching for her glove.

Oh, let a woman in your life
And you invite eternal strife!
Let them buy their wedding bands
For those anxious little hands;
I'd be equally as willing
For a dentist to be drilling
Than to ever let a woman in my life!

I'm a very gentle man;
Even-tempered and good-natured,
Whom you never hear complain;
Who has the milk of human kindness
By the quart of ev'ry vein.
A patient man am I
Down to my fingertips;
The sort who never could,
Ever would,
Let an insulting remark escape his lips.
Just a very gentle man.

But let a woman in your life
And patience hasn't got a chance.
She will beg you for advice;
Your reply will be concise.
And she'll listen very nicely
Then go out and do precisely
What she wants!

You were a man of grace and polish
Who never spoke above a hush.
Now all at once you're using language
That would make a sailor blush.

Oh, let a woman in your life
And you are plunging in a knife!
Let the others of my sex
Tie the knot around their necks;
I'd prefer a new edition
Of the Spanish Inquisition
Than to ever let a woman in my life!

I'm a quiet living man
Who prefers to spend his evenings
In the silence of his room;
Who likes an atmosphere as restful
As an undiscovered tomb.
A pensive man am I
Of philosophic joys;
Who likes to meditate,
Contemplate,
Free from humanity's mad, inhuman noise.
Just a quiet living man.

But let a woman in your life
And your sabbatical is through!
In a line that never ends
Come an army of her friends;
Come to jabber and to chatter
And to tell her what the matter
Is with you.

She'll have a booming, boist'rous fam'ly
Who will descend on you en masse.
She'll have a large Wagnerian mother
With a voice that shatters glass!

Oh, let a woman in your life . . .
Let a woman in your life . . .
Let a woman in your life . . .
I shall never let a woman in my life!

On the last day of rehearsal before the company departed for the New Haven opening, there was a complete run-through of the show, which revealed that this song would not work. As the libretto stood, it was done twice in the first act, and the very best that could now be hoped for it was to be performed once only. Even with one performance, it seemed unlikely to Lerner and Loewe that it was a strong enough item to stand as the third song of the evening. The show was scheduled to open on a Saturday night, but on that afternoon a dispute between Harrison and the writers caused the cancellation of the opening. Lerner and Loewe decided to spend their spare time cutting 'With a Little Bit of Luck'. At the last moment Harrison was prevailed upon to change his mind and make an appearance. There was now no time to cut the song. The show started on time and a few minutes later it had stopped cold again, arrested in its progress by the tumultuous reception for Holloway as the singing dustman. There was no further talk of cutting the item.

With a Little Bit of Luck

The Lord above gave man an arm of iron,
So he could do his job and never shirk.
The Lord above gave man an arm of iron – but
With a little bit of luck,
With a little bit of luck
Someone else'll do the blinkin' work!

With a little bit . . . with a little bit . . .
With a little bit of luck
You'll never work!

The Lord above made liquor for temptation,
To see if man could turn away from sin.
The Lord above made liquor for temptation – but
With a little bit of luck,
With a little bit of luck,
When temptation comes you'll give right in!

With a little bit . . . with a little bit . . .
With a little bit of luck
You'll give right in.

Oh, you can walk the straight and narrow;
But with a little bit of luck
You'll run amuck!

The gentle sex was made for man to marry,
To share his nest and see his food is cooked.
The gentle sex was made for man to marry – but
With a little bit of luck,
With a little bit of luck
You can have it all and not get hooked.

With a little bit . . . with a little bit . . .
With a little bit of luck
You won't get hooked.
With a little bit . . . with a little bit . . .
With a little bit of bloomin' luck!

The Lord above made man to help his neighbour,
No matter where, on land, or sea, or foam.
The Lord above made man to help his neighbour – but
With a little bit of luck,
With a little bit of luck,
When he comes around you won't be home!

With a little bit . . . with a little bit . . .
With a little bit of luck
You won't be home.

They're always throwin' goodness at you;
But with a little bit of luck
A man can duck!

Oh, it's a crime for man to go philanderin'
And fill his wife's poor heart with grief and doubt.
Oh, it's a crime for man to go philanderin' – but
With a little bit of luck,
With a little bit of luck,
You can see the bloodhound don't find out!

With a little bit . . . with a little bit . . .
With a little bit of luck
She won't find out!
With a little bit . . . with a little bit . . .
With a little bit of bloomin' luck!

Just You Wait

Just you wait, 'enry 'iggins, just you wait!
You'll be sorry but your tears'll be too late!
You'll be broke and I'll have money;
Will I help you? Don't be funny!
Just you wait, 'enry 'iggins, just you wait!

Just you wait, 'enry 'iggins, till you're sick,
And you scream to fetch a doctor double-quick.
I'll be off a second later
And go straight to the the-ater!
Oh ho ho, 'enry 'iggins, just you wait!

Ooooooooh 'enry 'iggins!
Just you wait until we're swimmin' in the sea!
Ooooooooh 'enry 'iggins!
And you get a cramp a little ways from me!

When you yell you're going to drown
I'll get dressed and go to town!
Oh ho ho, 'enry 'iggins!
Oh ho ho, 'enry 'iggins!
Just you wait!

One day I'll be famous! I'll be proper and prim;
Go to St James so often I will call it St Jim!
One evening the King will say: 'Oh, Liza, old thing,
I want all of England your praises to sing.
Next week on the twentieth of May
I proclaim Liza Doolittle Day!
All the people will celebrate the glory of you,
And whatever you wish and want I gladly will do.'

'Thanks a lot, King,' says I, in a manner well-bred;
'But all I want is 'enry 'iggins' 'ead!'
'Done,' says the King, with a stroke.
'Guard, run and bring in the bloke!'

Then they'll march you, 'enry 'iggins, to the wall;
And the King will tell me: 'Liza, sound the call.'
As they raise their rifles higher,
I'll shout: 'Ready! Aim! Fire!'
Oh ho ho! 'enry 'iggins!
Down you'll go! 'enry 'iggins!
Just you wait!!!

As a general rule Lerner was a slow and painstaking worker, and *My Fair Lady* in particular proved to be a protracted and exhausting campaign. But there was one song in the score which came at lightning speed and with great ease. Lerner recalls it as 'an unexpected visitation from the muses'. The entire song, words and music, was completed in ten minutes. 'In fact,' recalls Lerner, 'it had happened so spontaneously and easily that we were suspicious of it. Moss dispelled our suspicions.'

The Rain in Spain

SERVANTS
Poor Professor Higgins!
Poor Professor Higgins!
Night and day
He slaves away!
Oh, poor Professor Higgins!
All day long
On his feet;
Up and down until he's numb;
Doesn't rest;
Doesn't eat;
Doesn't touch a crumb!

Poor Professor Higgins!
Poor Professor Higgins!
On he plods
Against all odds;
Oh, poor Professor Higgins!
Nine P.M.
Ten P.M.
On through midnight ev'ry night.
One A.M.
Two A.M.
Three . . . !

Quit, Professor Higgins!
Quit, Professor Higgins!
Hear our plea
Or payday we
Will quit, Professor Higgins!
Ay not I,
O not Ow,
Pounding, pounding in our brain.
Ay not I,
O, not Ow,
Don't say 'Rine', say 'Rain'. . .

continued . . .

ELIZA

The rain in Spain stays mainly in the plain.

HIGGINS

What was that?

ELIZA

The rain in Spain stays mainly in the plain.

HIGGINS

Again.

ELIZA

The rain in Spain stays mainly in the plain.

HIGGINS

I think she's got it! I think she's got it!

ELIZA

The rain in Spain stays mainly in the plain!

HIGGINS

(Triumphantly)

By George, she's got it!
By George, she's got it!
Now once again, where does it rain?

ELIZA

On the plain! On the plain!

HIGGINS

And where's that soggy plain?

ELIZA

In Spain! In Spain!

ALL

The rain in Spain stays mainly in the plain!
The rain in Spain stays mainly in the plain!

HIGGINS

In Hertford, Hereford and Hampshire . . . ?

ELIZA

Hurricanes hardly happen.

*(Higgins taps out 'How kind of you to
let me come.')*

ELIZA

How kind of you to let me come!

HIGGINS

Now once again, where does it rain?

ELIZA

On the plain! On the plain!

HIGGINS

And where's that blasted plain?

ELIZA

In Spain! In Spain!

ALL

The rain in Spain stays mainly in the
plain!
The rain in Spain stays mainly in the
plain!

I Could Have Danced All Night

Bed! Bed! I couldn't go to bed!
My head's too light to try to set it down!
Sleep! Sleep! I couldn't sleep tonight!
Not for all the jewels in the crown!

I could have danced all night!
I could have danced all night!
And still have begged for more.
I could have spread my wings
And done a thousand things
I've never done before.

I'll never know
What made it so exciting;
Why all at once
My heart took flight.
I only know when he
Began to dance with me,
I could have danced, danced, danced all night!

When in New Haven the inquests revealed that the first act was running twenty-five minutes too long, there was a unanimous feeling – except for Lerner – that this song had to go. On the previous night it had been greeted 'with mute disinterest', and Loewe, who had always hated the melody, was eager to dump it. Lerner begged to differ:

I liked the melody and thought the flagrantly romantic lyric that kept edging on the absurd exactly right for the character. But obviously one cannot leave in a number that dies. I could not for the life of me understand why it failed so dismally.

Before proceeding with Lerner's recollection, it may be as well to acquaint ourselves with the form the song took during the discussions as to its suitability. Instead of the song subsequently popularized, the original version had a different verse, and an interlude to be sung just before the middle section.

On the Street Where You Live

Darling, there's the tree you run to
When it starts to rain.
See the way it's filled with bloom.
And isn't there a garland round the window pane?
That could only be your room.
This street is like a garden and your door a garden gate,
What a lovely place to wait.

I have often walked down this street before,
But the pavement always stayed beneath my feet before.
All at once am I
Several storeys high,
Knowing I'm on the street where you live.

Are there lilac trees in the heart of town?
Can you hear a lark in any other part of town?
Does enchantment pour
Out of ev'ry door?
No, it's just on the street where you live.

Some men hate to wait and wait,
If by chance the girl is late.
I don't mind the waiting part at all.
Some get bored and wander on,
Curse their fate and soon are gone.
I would wait through winter, spring and fall.

And oh, the towering feeling,
Just to know somehow you are near.
The overpowering feeling
That any second you may suddenly appear.

People stop and stare. They don't bother me.
For there's nowhere else on earth that I would rather be,
Let the time go by,
I won't care if I
Can be here on the street where you live.

At last it occurred to Lerner that the reason why audiences were failing to react to the song was that they were not sure of the identity of the character singing it. His previous appearance, as one of several men dressed in Ascot greys, might well have had the effect of rendering him anonymous. And yet the original purpose of the song had been to establish Freddie as a major secondary character and a possible threat to Higgins for the hand of Eliza. So Lerner now decided to write a new verse in which Freddie, by echoing the events of the previous scene, would be reminding the audience of his place in the plot. 'And to fortify that,' thought Lerner, 'I'll have somebody open the door and say who he is.' With these changes the song stopped the show.

> FREDDIE
>
> When she mentioned how her aunt bit off the spoon,
> She completely done me in.
> And my heart went on a journey to the moon
> When she told about her father and the gin.
> And I never saw a more enchanting farce
> Than the moment when she shouted 'Move yer bloomin –'
>
> MAID
> Yes, sir?
>
> FREDDIE
> Is Miss Doolittle at home?
>
> MAID
> Whom shall I say is calling?
>
> FREDDIE
> Freddie Eynsford-Hill.
>
> MAID
> Oh, yes sir.
>
> FREDDIE
> And if she doesn't remember me, tell her I'm the fellow who was sniggering at her.
>
> MAID
> Yes sir.
>
> FREDDIE
> And you needn't rush. I want to drink in this street where she lives.
>
> MAID
> Yes sir.
>
> FREDDIE
> SINGS THE VERSION OF THE SONG KNOWN TO ALL.

In describing the details of his difficulties with that song, Lerner makes the revealing comment that he constructed the wrong rhyme-scheme deliberately. In theory, the versifier knows that, given the structure of 'On the Street Where You Live', he must provide triple rhymes, e.g.: *heart of town, part of town* and *start of town*. Lerner found this boring, and so wrote two sets of double rhymes: *heart* and *start, enchantment pour* and *ev'ry door*, hoping as he put it, 'that it would slide by'. What pleased him much more was the pattern of the middle section, with its intricate scheme of interlocking rhymes, *And oh, the towering, Just to know,* and *The overpowering; near* and *appear*. He had clearly been content to settle for the faint blemish of *bother me* and *rather be*. But what is most surprising of all is the one American blemish on an otherwise near-perfect simulation of British vocabulary and diction. No Briton, whether from the classes like Freddie, or the masses like Eliza, would ever have talked of being *on* a street. The British live in streets, Americans on them. The slip is all the more astonishing in that none of the three British stars of the production pointed out the error, especially as it could have been corrected without spoiling either the rhyme-scheme or the rhythmic stress.

Ascot Gavotte

Ev'ry duke and earl and peer is here.
Ev'ry one who should be here is here.
What a smashing, positively dashing
Spectacle: the Ascot op'ning day.

At the gate are all the horses
Waiting for the cue to fly away.
What a gripping, absolutely ripping
Moment at the Ascot op'ning day.

Pulses rushing!
Faces flushing!
Heartbeats speed up!
I have never been so keyed up!

Any second now
They'll begin to run.
Hark! A bell is ringing,
They are springing
Forward
Look! It has begun . . . !

What a frenzied moment that was!
Didn't they maintain an exhausting pace?
'Twas a thrilling, absolutely chilling
Running of the Ascot op'ning race.

Although this song always received an enthusiastic reaction, there was a feeling that perhaps at the climax of the story, where Karpathy announces that Eliza is a Hungarian princess, there ought to be a more impressive climax. So Lerner added the following couplet, which incorporates one of the most endearing rhymes in the entire show:

> I know each language on the map, said he,
> And she's as Hungarian as the first Hungarian rhapsody.

The new couplet was given to Harrison one night in Philadelphia. When the moment came to sing the song, he forgot them and the rest of the words. The new couplet went out.

You Did It

PICKERING

Tonight, old man, you did it!
You did it! You did it!
You said that you would do it,
And indeed you did.
I thought that you would rue it.
I doubted you'd do it.
But now I must admit it
That succeed you did.
You should get a medal
Or be even made a knight.

HIGGINS

It was nothing. Really nothing.

PICKERING

All alone you hurdled
Ev'ry obstacle in sight.

HIGGINS

Now, wait! Now, wait!
Give credit where it's due.
A lot of the glory goes to you.

PICKERING

But you're the one who did it,
Who did it, who did it!
As sturdy as Gibraltar,
Not a second did you falter.
There's no doubt about it,
You did it!
I must have aged a year tonight.
At times I thought I'd die of fright.
Never was there a momentary lull.

HIGGINS

Shortly after we came in
I saw at once we'd easily win;
And after that I found it deadly dull.

PICKERING

You should have heard the ooh's and ah's;
Ev'ry one wond'ring who she was.

HIGGINS

You'd think they'd never seen a lady before.

PICKERING

And when the Prince of Transylvania
Asked to meet her,
And gave his arm to lead her to the floor . . .!
I said to him: You did it!
You did it! You did it!
They thought she was ecstatic
And so damned aristocratic,
And they never knew
That you
Did it!

HIGGINS
(Speaking)

Thank Heavens for Zoltan Karpathy. If it weren't for him I would have died of boredom. He was there, all right. And up to his old tricks.

MRS PEARCE

Karpathy? That dreadful Hungarian? Was he there?

HIGGINS
Yes.
That blackguard who uses the science of speech
More to blackmail and swindle than teach;
He made it the devilish business of his
'To find out who this Miss Doolittle is.'

continued . . .

Ev'ry time we looked around
There he was, that hairy hound
From Budapest.
Never leaving us alone.
Never have I ever known
A ruder pest.
Fin'lly I decided it was foolish
Not to let him have his chance with her.
So I stepped aside and let him dance with her.

Oozing charm from ev'ry pore,
He oiled his way around the floor.
Ev'ry trick that he could play,
He used to strip her mask away.
And when at last the dance was done
He glowed as if he knew he'd won!
And with a voice too eager,
And a smile too broad,
He announced to the hostess
That she was a fraud!

MRS PEARCE

No!

HIGGINS

Yavol!
Her English is too good, he said,
Which clearly indicates that she is foreign.
Whereas others are instructed in their native language
English people aren.
And although she may have studied with an expert
Di'lectician and grammarian,
I can tell that she was born Hungarian!
Not only Hungarian, but of royal blood, she is a princess!

SERVANT

Congratulations, Professor Higgins,
For your glorious victory!
Congratulations, Professor Higgins!
You'll be mentioned in history!

FOOTMAN	THE REST OF THE SERVANTS
This evening, sir, you did it!	Congratulations,
You did it! You did it!	Professor Higgins!
You said that you would do it!	For your glorious
And indeed you did.	Victory!
This evening, sir, you did it!	Congratulations,
You did it! You did it!	Professor Higgins!
We know that we have said it,	Sing hail and halleluia,
But you did it and the credit	Ev'ry bit of credit
For it all belongs to you!	For it all belongs to you!

Show Me

Words!
Words! Words! I'm so sick of words!
I get words all day through;
First from him, now from you!
Is that all you blighters can do?

Never do I ever want to hear another word.
There isn't one I haven't heard.
Here we are together in what ought to be a dream;
Say one more word and I'll scream!

Don't talk of stars
Burning above;
If you're in love,
Show me!

Haven't your arms
Hungered for mine?
Please don't 'expl'ine',
Show me! Show me!

Tell me no dreams
Filled with desire.
If you're on fire,
Show me!

Don't wait until wrinkles and lines
Pop out all over my brow,
Show me now!

Here we are together in the middle of the night!
Don't talk of spring! Just hold me tight!
Anyone who's ever been in love'll tell you that
This is no time for a chat!

Haven't your lips
Longed for my touch?
Don't say how much,
Show me! Show me!

Don't talk of love lasting through time.
Make me no undying vow.
Show me now!

Sing me no song!
Read me no rhyme!
Don't waste my time,
Show me!

Don't talk of June!
Don't talk of fall!
Don't talk at all!
Show me!

Get Me to the Church on Time

FRIENDS

There's just a few more hours,
That's all the time you've got.
A few more hours
Before they tie the knot.

DOOLITTLE
(Speaking)

There are drinks and girls all over
  London,
and I have to track 'em down
in just a few more hours.

I'm getting married in the morning!
Ding dong! the bells are gonna chime.
Pull out the stopper!
Let's have a whopper!
But get me to the church on time!

I gotta be there in the morning
Spruced up and lookin' in me prime.
Girls, come and kiss me,
Show how you'll miss me,
But get me to the church on time!

If I am dancin'
Roll up the floor.
If I am whistlin'
Whewt me out the door!

For I'm getting married in the morning!
Ding dong! the bells are gonna chime.
Kick up a rumpus,
But don't lose the compass,
And get me to the church,
Get me to the church,
For Gawd's sake, get me to the church on time!

I'm getting married in the morning!
Ding dong! the bells are gonna chime.
Drug me or jail me,
Stamp me and mail me,
But get me to the church on time!

I gotta be there in the morning
Spruced up and lookin' in me prime.
Some bloke who's able,
Lift up the table,
And get me to the church on time!

If I am flying
Then shoot me down.
If I am wooin'
Get her out of town!

For I'm getting married in the morning!
Ding dong! the bells are gonna chime.
Feather and tar me,
Call out the Army,
But get me to the church,
Get me to the church,
For Gawd's sake, get me to the church
  on time!

A Hymn to Him

What in all of heaven could have prompted her to go?
After such a triumph at the ball?
What could have depressed her?
What could have possessed her?
I cannot understand the wretch at all!

Women are irrational, that's all there is to that!
Their heads are full of cotton, hay and rags!
They're nothing but exasperating, irritating,
Vacillating, calculating, agitating,
Maddening and infuriating hags!

Pickering, why can't a woman be more like a man?

Yes, why can't a woman be more like a man?
Men are so honest, so thoroughly square;
Eternally noble, historically fair;
Who when you win will always give your back a pat.
Why can't a woman be like that?
Why does ev'ryone do what the others do?
Can't a woman learn to use her head?
Why do they do everything their mothers do?
Why can't they grow up like their father instead?
Why can't a woman take after a man?
Men are so pleasant, so easy to please;
Whenever you're with them, you're always at ease.
Would you be slighted if I didn't speak for hours?
        Of course not.

Would you be livid if I had a drink or two?
        Nonsense.

Would you be wounded if I never sent you flowers?
        Never.

Why can't a woman be like you?

One man in a million may shout a bit.
Now and then there's one with slight defects.
One perhaps whose truthfulness you doubt a bit.
But by and large we are a marvellous sex!

Why can't a woman behave like a man?
Men are so friendly, good-natured and kind;
A better companion you never will find.
If I were hours late for dinner, would you bellow?
        Of course not.

continued . . .

If I forgot your silly birthday, would you fuss?
>Nonsense.

Would you complain if I took out another fellow?
>Never.

Why can't a woman be like us?

Why can't a woman be more like a man?
Men are so decent, such regular chaps.
Ready to help you through any mishaps.
Ready to buck you up whenever you are glum.
Why can't a woman be a chum?

Why is thinking something women never do?
Why is logic never even tried?
Straightening up their hair is all they ever do.
Why don't they straighten up the mess that's inside?

Why can't a woman be more like a man?
If I were a woman who'd been to a ball,
Been hailed as a princess by one and by all;
Would I start weeping like a bathtub overflowing?
And carry on as if my home were in a tree?
Would I run off and never tell me where I'm going?
Why can't a woman be like me?

It comes as much as a surprise to the modern researcher as it did to Lerner and Loewe at the time that this proved to be the most contentious item in the score. The difficulty was with Harrison, who was obliged to stand on the stage with nothing to do while Julie Andrews sang the song. Lerner decorously quotes Harrison on the subject: 'I am not going to stand up there and make a cunt of myself.' It was eventually decided that the best way of mollifying Harrison would be to write for him an interpolated interruption at the climax of the song, but this idea was rejected out of hand. Moss Hart then said to Harrison: 'Rex, Julie is going to sing "Without You" whether you are on the stage or not. In my personal opinion you will look like a horse's ass if you leave the stage when she begins it and return when she has finished. However, if you will give me the opportunity, I will show you how it can be staged.' And so it proved.

Without You

ELIZA

What a fool I was! What a dominated fool!
To think you were the earth and sky.
What a fool I was! What an addle-pated fool!
What a mutton-headed dolt was I!
No, my reverberating friend,
You are not the beginning and the end!

There'll be spring ev'ry year without you.
England still will be here without you.
There'll be fruit on the tree,
And a shore by the sea;
There'll be crumpets and tea
Without you.

Art and music will thrive without you.
Somehow Keats will survive without you.
And there still will be rain
On that plain down in Spain,
Even that will remain
Without you.
I can do
Without you.

You, dear friend, who talk so well,
You can go to Hertford, Hereford and Hampshire!

They can still rule the land without you.
Windsor Castle will stand without you.
And without much ado
We can all muddle through
Without you!

Without your pulling it, the tide comes in.
Without your twirling it, the earth can spin.
Without your pushing them, the clouds roll by
If they can do without you, ducky, so can I!

I shall not feel alone without you.
I can stand on my own without you.
So go back in your shell,
I can do bloody well
Without . . .

HIGGINS

By George, I really did it!
I did it! I did it!
I said I'd make a woman
And indeed I did!

I knew that I could do it!
I knew it! I knew it!
I said I'd make a woman
And succeed I did!

I've Grown Accustomed to her Face

I've grown accustomed to her face!
She almost makes the day begin.
I've grown accustomed to the tune
She whistles night and noon.
Her smiles. Her frowns.
Her ups, her downs,
Are second nature to me now;
Like breathing out and breathing in.
I was serenely independent and content before we met;
Surely I could always
Be that way again – and yet
I've grown accustomed to her looks;
Accustomed to her voice;
Accustomed to her face.

Marry Freddie! What an infantile idea! What
A heartless, wicked, brainless thing to do!
But she'll regret it! She'll regret it. It's
Doomed before they even take the vow!

I can see her now:
Mrs Freddie Eynsford-Hill,
In a wretched little flat above a store.
I can see her now:
Not a penny in the till,
And a bill collector beating at the door.

She'll try to teach the things I taught her,
And end up selling flow'rs instead;
Begging for her bread and water,
While her husband has his breakfast in bed!

In a year or so
When she's prematurely grey,
And the blossoms in her cheek have turned to chalk,
She'll come home and lo!
He'll have upped and run away
With a social climbing heiress from New York!

(Tragically)

Poor Eliza!
How simply frightful!
How humiliating!

(Irresistibly)

How delightful!

I've grown accustomed to her face!
She almost makes the day begin.
I've grown accustomed to the tune
She whistles night and noon.
Her smiles. Her frowns.
Her ups, her downs,
Are second nature to me now;
Like breathing out and breathing in.
I was serenely independent and content before we met;
Surely I could always
Be that way again – and yet
I've grown accustomed to her looks;
Accustomed to her voice;
Accustomed to her face.

But I'm so used to hear her say:
'Good morning' every day.
Her joys, her woes,
Her highs, her lows
Are second nature to me now;
Like breathing out and breathing in.
I'm very grateful she's a woman
And so easy to forget;
Rather like a habit
One can always break – and yet
I've grown accustomed to the trace
Of something in the air;
Accustomed to her face.

Every one of the foregoing songs eventually achieved an intimacy with audiences all over the world. Some, like 'On the Street Where You Live' and 'I Could Have Danced All Night', became symbolic of the show, while others, like 'Just You Wait', remained tethered to the libretto for obvious reasons. 'I've Grown Accustomed to her Face' at last sailed away from its moorings up into the rarefied air of the standard song, where to this day it is enjoyed by artists and audiences who know or care little about the romantic obduracy of Henry Higgins and even less about the social philosophies of Bernard Shaw. *My Fair Lady* ran for 2,717 performances in New York, and for 2,281 in London, which means that night after night, for year after year, the songs were insinuating themselves into the consciousness of the general public. But there was one song in *My Fair Lady* whose life spanned not 2,717 performances but only one. When the show began its pre-Broadway try-out in New Haven, it included the piece which follows, a fast, swooping waltz placed at a juncture, after the Ascot Gavotte, where Eliza, having lost all confidence in herself, decides to discontinue the experiment. From the very earliest days of his work on the project, Lerner had been convinced that there would have to be a song in which Eliza's flagging confidence would be boosted by encouragement from Higgins, and had written a song called 'Lady Liza' to serve this function. He had also written a song in which Eliza confides to her fellow-conspirators her deep misgivings about what might happen to her at the Palace. This was called 'Say a Prayer for Me Tonight'. 'Lady Liza' subsequently disappeared from the records; 'Say a Prayer for Me Tonight' was more fortunate, eventually finding a home in *Gigi*. But the song which replaced 'Lady Liza', a piece called 'Oh, Come to the Ball', in which Higgins attempts to persuade Eliza to go through with the imposture, was not so fortunate, having been so tightly integrated into the texture of one play that it was inapplicable to any other. Lerner had done his work too well.

The song is the perfect expression of the exasperation which so dominates Higgins' temperament. Aghast at the prospect of losing his bet with Pickering and seeing all his painstaking labours go for nothing, he remonstrates with Eliza, cajoles her, honeys her with every blandishment he can muster, painting a resplendent picture of the stunning magnitude of her conquest at the ball if only she can muster the courage to attend it. The brilliance of the lyric speaks for itself, and it comes as no surprise to learn that it always held a special place in the affections of the man who wrote it. Lerner often took the chance to evangelize on its behalf. At our musicless recital, staged appropriately enough at a London venue called The Bernard Shaw Theatre, he recited it. At his one-man concert in New York in December 1971 he sang it. In the television show at which he was flanked by Andre Previn and myself, he sang it again. To the very end he was never quite sure why the song had failed on that fatal first night in New Haven. He told his New York audience: 'There was a song we wrote for *My Fair Lady* that Fritz and I and Moss Hart were absolutely positive would be Rex's *pièce de résistance*, that it was going to be his big number. He thought so. It was rehearsed and we opened with it in New Haven. And it lasted one performance.'

Oh, Come to the Ball

Oh, Come to the Ball, Oh, Come to the Ball,
It wouldn't be fair
To the men who'll be there
To deny them
All the dreams you'll supply them.
There even may be
A dashing marquis
Who, feature by feature,
Will swear you're the creature
He always prayed for,
Single stayed for.
If you aren't there
His complete despair
Will be painful to see,
So Come to the Ball, Come to the Ball, Come to the Ball, Come to the Ball
With me.

Consider the lord
So frantically bored
He's leaving his kin
And becoming an In-
Dian lancer,
Hoping danger's the answer.
Your innocent glow
Will dazzle him so
That glancing at you
Will restore his illu-
Sions and as he glances,
Farewell, Lancers.
Should he die, alas,
At the Khyber Pass,
What a loss it would be,
So come the Ball, Come to the Ball, Come to the Ball, Come to the Ball
With me.

I can see you now in a gown by Madame Worth,
When you enter ev'ry monocle will crash.
I can see you now, like a goddess come to earth,
I can hear the ladies' teeth begin to gnash.
Little chaps will wish they were Atlas,
A Queen will want you for her son.
Portly men will wish they were fatless,
And the married men will wish they were Un.

What a triumph, through and through,
What a moment, what a coup.

continued . . .

And off by a wall,
Unnoticed by all,
A man with a smile
You could see for a mile
Will be standing,
His dimensions expanding,
The pride in his eyes
Will double their size,
As sweetly and neatly
You somehow completely
Electrify them,
Lorelei them.
Search the world around
There could not be found
Someone prouder than he,
So Come to the Ball, Come to the Ball, Come to the Ball, Come to the Ball
With me.

☆ GIGI ☆

When Lerner went to Hollywood to work on the screenplay of *Brigadoon* for MGM, he had signed a three-picture contract with the company. After *Brigadoon* he began working out the contract by collaborating with Burton Lane on a musical version of *Huckleberry Finn*, to star Danny Kaye and Gene Kelly. Two weeks after shooting began, Kelly, encouraged by changes in the American tax laws, decamped to Europe and the project was abandoned. There remained one film for Lerner to write, and when *My Fair Lady* was playing in Philadelphia, he was visited by Arthur Freed, the ex-

songwriter in charge of musical production at MGM. He suggested to Lerner a musical version of Collette's novella *Gigi*, the story of an ugly duckling who is trained to become the most desirable courtesan in Paris.

In August 1956, by which time *My Fair Lady* had been settled into its New York run for six months, Lerner was beginning to find that the strain of relaxing was inducing insomnia, so he flew to California, began circling round *Gigi*, and soon saw that if he built up the off-stage character of Gaston's uncle, he would have something to offer his great hero Maurice Chevalier. There was, however, one grave problem. Fritz Loewe had always sworn never to defile himself by contact with the movie industry, and each time the partners were offered deals, Fritz would react with telegrams of abrupt and sarcastic rejection. Reluctantly Lerner resigned himself to writing the songs with a different partner, consoling himself with the thought that there would be only four songs. He then completed the screenplay and persuaded Loewe to read it. Fritz liked what he saw and surprisingly agreed to write the music. The partners then left for Paris and a meeting with Chevalier.

The meeting went well, and was soon followed by discussions about casting, with Audrey Hepburn mooted as a possible Gigi, and Dirk Bogarde as the perfect Gaston. But Hepburn had already portrayed Gigi on stage and did not wish to repeat the experience. The Rank Organization refused to release Bogarde, but Lerner and Loewe were delighted to discover that Louis Jourdan had a pleasant singing voice. Leslie Caron was then recruited and found, in the opinion of the partners, to have an unpleasant singing voice, which meant, after much diplomatic confusion and displays of tempera-ment, some adept dubbing by the singer Marni Nixon. By this time the score had swollen to six songs.

When shooting was complete, everybody involved acknowledged that one or two of the songs would have to be re-shot and that cost of these repairs would be $300,00. The studio baulked at the extra expense, and it seemed that either the picture would be released in its imperfect form, or not at all. Lerner and Loewe then performed the most reckless act of gallantry of their careers. They offered MGM $3,000,000 for the print of the picture, a bid so sensational that Freed and the two executives involved asked to be excused for a few minutes to confer. Lerner and Loewe then retired to the Men's Room, where the following exchange took place:

FRITZ: (At the washstand following nervous relief): Dear boy, where the fuck are we going to get three million dollars?
ALAN: We don't know. Don't you remember?
FRITZ: Don't remind me.
ALAN: What about Bill Paley?
FRITZ: Bill Paley? Put three million dollars into a picture which isn't very good? My boy, he's not an idiot. Who would make such an offer?
ALAN: We just did.
FRITZ: That's because we don't have three million dollars. Bill Paley has, that's the big difference.

The eventual effect of the offer was that MGM, impressed by the apparent faith of the two writers in the picture, agreed to spend the extra $300,000. The show was on the road.

Thank Heaven for Little Girls was the first completed song in the score. Before leaving for Paris, Lerner had given Loewe this working title for a song to be sung by Chevalier which would establish the style of the production. On arrival in Paris, the pair of them began working on the song, of which Lerner later wrote:

In order to establish the musical style, Chevalier plays the role of narrator or *raisonneur,* and in the first scene addresses the audience and introduces Paris, the period, the atmosphere and Gigi. The style of a film must be established within the first few minutes, as it is in the opening sequences that the audience adjusts its emotional body temperature to the climate of the film.

The song was speedily completed except for the release, or the bridge, or, as it is called in Britain, the middle eight:

I had written pages and pages, but none of the versions seemed right. One evening Fritz was going out, as was his wont, and said that when he returned he would call and if I was still awake come up to see how I was doing. If I had gone to sleep I was to turn off the phone. He returned about six in the morning, as was his wont, and I was still up. I read him everything I had, which he liked enormously. I then told him what I had been going through with those damn middle lines. Said Fritz: 'What are you trying to say, dear boy?' Said I, picking up a piece of paper I had written some twenty-four hours earlier: 'I am trying to say something like this:

> Those little eyes so helpless and appealing,
> One day will flash
> and send you crash-
> ing through the ceiling.'

Said Fritz: 'What's wrong with that?' I replied: 'You can't crash through the ceiling. You crash through the floor.' Said Fritz: 'Who says so? It's your lyric and if you want to crash through the ceiling, crash through the ceiling.' At six in the morning I was easily persuaded. And so I crashed through the ceiling.

Thank Heaven for Little Girls

Each time I see a little girl
Of five or six or seven,
I can't resist the joyous urge
To smile and say

    Thank heaven
For little girls!
For little girls get bigger every day.
Thank heaven for little girls!
They grow up in the most delightful way.

Those little eyes so helpless and appealing
One day will flash
And send you crashing through the ceiling!

Thank heaven for little girls!
Thank heaven for them all,
No matter where, no matter who.
Without them what would little boys do?

Thank heaven . . .
Thank heaven . . .
Thank heaven for little girls!

It's a Bore

HONORE
Look at all the captivating
Fascinating things there are to do!

GASTON
Name two!

HONORE
Look at all the pleasures,
All the myriad of treasures we have got!

GASTON
Like what?

HONORE
Look at Paris in the spring,
When each solitary thing
Is more beautiful than ever before.
You can hear ev'ry tree
Almost saying: Look at me. . . !

GASTON
What colour are the trees?

HONORE
Green.

GASTON
What colour were they last year?

HONORE
Green.

GASTON
And next year?

HONORE
Green.

GASTON
It's a bore.

HONORE
Don't you marvel at the pow'r
Of the mighty Eiffel tow'r,
Knowing there it will remain evermore?
Climbing up to the sky,
Over ninety storeys high . . .

GASTON
How many storeys?

HONORE
Ninety.

GASTON
How many yesterday?

HONORE
Ninety.

GASTON
And tomorrow?

HONORE
Ninety.

GASTON
It's a bore.

HONORE
The river Seine . . .

GASTON
All it can do is flow.

HONORE
But think of wine!

GASTON
It's red or white.

HONORE
But think of girls!

GASTON
It's either yes or no.
And if it's no or if it's yes
It simply couldn't matter less.

HONORE
But think of a race
With your horse in seventh place,
Then he suddenly begins
And he catches up and wins
With a roar!

GASTON
It's a bore!

HONORE
Life is thrilling as can be!

GASTON
Simply not my cup of tea.

HONORE
It's a gay romantic fling!

GASTON
If you like that sort of thing!

HONORE
It's intriguing!

GASTON
It's fatiguing!

HONORE
It's a game!

GASTON
It's the same
Dull world wherever you go,
Whatever place you are at.
The earth is round
But ev'rything on it is flat!

HONORE
Don't tell me Venice has no lure.

GASTON
Just a town without a sewer.

HONORE
The leaning tower I adore!

GASTON
Indecision is a bore.

HONORE
But think of the thrill
Of a bull fight in Seville,
When the bull is uncontrolled
And he charges at a bold
Matador!

GASTON
It's a bore.

HONORE
Think of lunch beneath the trees!

GASTON
Stop the carriage, if you please.

HONORE
You mean you don't want to come?

GASTON
The thought of lunch leaves me numb.

HONORE
But I implore. . . !

GASTON
Oh no, uncle. It's a bore!

I Don't Understand the Parisians

A necklace is love.
A ring is love.
A rock from some obnoxious
Little king is love.
A sapphire with a star is love.
An ugly black cigar is love.
Ev'rything you are is love.
You would think it would embarrass
All the people here in Paris
To be thinking ev'ry minute of love!

I don't understand the Parisians.
Making love ev'ry time they get a chance.

I don't understand the Parisians
Wasting ev'ry lovely night on romance.

Any time
And under ev'ry tree in town
They're in session two by two.
What a crime
With all there is to see in town
They can't find something else to do!

I don't understand how Parisians
Never tire of walking hand in hand.
But they seem to love it,
And speak highly of it!
I don't understand the Parisians.

I don't understand the Parisians
Making all this to-do about *l'amour.*

I don't understand the Parisians.
All this la-di-da is so immature.

When it's warm
They take a carriage ride at night,
Close their eyes and hug and kiss.
When it's cold
They simply move inside at night.
There must be more to life than this!

I don't understand the Parisians
Thinking love so miraculous and grand.
But they rave about it,
And won't live without it!
I don't understand the Parisians!

This was the song which caused the $300,000 crisis. When the footage arrived in Hollywood, it was found that the absence of close-ups made nonsense of the sequence. At this juncture of the plot, Jourdan was supposed to be incensed by the spectacle of Gigi having a good time without his presence. The entire lyric is delivered unseen, as it were, with Jourdan watching Gigi swirling around while the words of the song are supposed to be what he is thinking. But, as Lerner asks, 'How can an audience know a song is being sung in someone's head if one cannot see the head? Facial expressions definitely demand a face. Without a close-up of Louis, all one heard was a disembodied voice which, for all anyone knew, could have been coming from the bandstand, and the whole scene made no sense at all.' It eventually made sense, at a cost of $300,000.

She's Not Thinking of Me
(Waltz at Maxim's)

She's so gay tonight!
She's like spring tonight!
She's a rollicking, frolicking thing tonight,
So disarming,
Soft and charming,
She is not thinking of me,
No, she's not thinking of me!

In her eyes tonight
There's a glow tonight,
They're so bright
They could light
Fontainebleau tonight.
She's so gracious,
So vivacious,
She is not thinking of me!

Bless her little heart,
Crooked to the core.
Acting out a part . . .
What a rollicking, frolicking bore!

She's such fun tonight!
She's a treat tonight!
You could spread
Her on bread
She's so sweet tonight.

So devoted,
Sugar-coated,
That it's heart-warming to see.
She's simmering with love,
She's shimmering with love,
Oh, she's not thinking of me!

Someone has set her on fire,
It is Jacques, is it Paul, or Léon?
Who's turning her furnace up higher?
Oh, she's hot but it's not for Gaston.

Oh, she's gay tonight!
Oh, so gay tonight!
A gigantic, romantic cliché tonight.
How she blushes!
How she gushes!
How she fills me with ennui!
She's so ooh la-la-la-la!
So untrue la-la-la-la!
Oh, she's not thinking of me!

There appear to be two versions of this lyric. In the screenplay Jourdan sings the accepted version, but in Lerner's manuscript version the lyric reads as follows:

She Is Not Thinking of Me

She's so gay tonight!
She's like spring tonight!
She's a rollicking, frolicking thing tonight,
So disarming,
Soft and charming,
She is not thinking of me!

In her eyes tonight
There's glow tonight,
They're so bright they could light Fontainebleau tonight.
She's so gracious,
So vivacious,
She is not thinking of me!

Bless her little heart,
Crooked to the core.
Acting out her part . . .
What a rollicking, frolicking bore!

She's such fun tonight!
She's a treat tonight!
You could spread her on bread she's so sweet tonight.
So devoted,
Sugar-coated,
That it's heart-warming to see.
Oh, she's simmering with love!
Oh, she's shimmering with love!
Oh, she's not thinking of me!

She is not thinking of me.
She is not thinking of me.
Is it that painter from Brussels?
Is it that count with the muscles?
Is it that ice skating lout?
That long English lord with the gout?
Is it Jacques?
Or Léon?
Oh, she's hot
But it's not for Gaston!

Oh, she's gay tonight!
Oh, so gay tonight!
A gigantic, romantic cliché tonight.
How she blushes!
How she gushes!
How she fills me with ennui!
She's so ooh la-la-la-la!
So untrue la-la-la-la!
Oh, she's not thinking of me!

The Night They Invented Champagne

GIGI

What time tomorrow will we get there?
Can I watch you play roulette there?
May I stay up late for supper?
Is it awf'lly, awf'lly upper?

MAMITA

Gigi! You'll drive us wild.
Stop, you silly child.

GIGI

Is ev'rybody celebrated,
Full of sin and dissipated?
Is it hot enough to blister?
Will I be your little sister?

MAMITA

Gigi, you are absurd.
Not another word.

GASTON

Let her gush and jabber,
Let her be enthused.
I cannot remember
When I have been more amused.

GIGI

The night they invented champagne
It's plain as it can be
They thought of you and me,
The night they invented champagne
They absolutely knew
That all we'd want to do
Is fly to the sky on champagne
And shout to ev'ryone in sight
That since the world began
No woman or a man
Has ever been as happy as we are tonight!

I Remember It Well

HONORE
We met at nine.

GRANDMAMA
We met at eight.

HONORE
I was on time.

GRANDMAMA
No, you were late.

HONORE
Ah yes! I remember it well.
We dined with friends.

GRANDMAMA
We dined alone.

HONORE
A tenor sang.

GRANDMAMA
A baritone.

HONORE
Ah yes! I remember it well.
That dazzling April moon!

GRANDMAMA
There was none that night.
And the month was June.

HONORE
That's right! That's right!

GRANDMAMA
It warms my heart
To know that you
Remember still
The way you do.

HONORE
Ah yes! I remember it well.
How often I've thought of that Friday –

GRANDMAMA
– Monday

HONORE

     . . . night,
When we had our last rendez-vous.
And somehow I've foolishly wondered if you might
By some chance be thinking of it too.
That carriage ride . . .

GRANDMAMA

You walked me home.

HONORE

You lost a glove.

GRANDMAMA

I lost a comb.

HONORE

Ah yes! I remember it well.
That brilliant sky.

GRANDMAMA

We had some rain.

HONORE

Those Russian songs.

GRANDMAMA

From sunny Spain.

HONORE

Ah yes! I remember it well.
You wore a gown of gold.

GRANDMAMA

I was all in blue.

HONORE

Am I getting old?

GRANDMAMA

Oh no! Not you!
How strong you were,
How young and gay;
A prince of love
In ev'ry way.

HONORE

Ah yes! I remember it well.

Lerner's confession that once having worked with Rex Harrison, he found that everything he wrote seemed to be for Harrison, is borne out by the shape and mood of this song, which, if it were switched from Paris to St Marylebone, anglicized and filtered through the temperament of Henry Higgins, would have expressed more or less accurately the transformation of Eliza from baggage to princess. Harrison's style as an actor had left Lerner with an obvious weakness for depicting angry men whose irascibility is no more than a mask to conceal their romantic vulnerability. Gaston's insistence to himself that Gigi is a mere child smacks of Higgins in his 'Hymn to Him' mood, and once the song flowers into the elegaic confessional of the main theme, 'I've Grown Accustomed to her Face' comes instantly to mind. But the charges that *Gigi* was nothing much more than warmed-over Shaw were unfounded. The similarities were between Eliza and Gigi, and the resemblance of the adventures of both of them to those experienced by that most ancient of all musical comedy heroines, Cinderella.

Gigi

She's a babe! Just a babe!
Still cavorting in her crib;
Eating breakfast with a bib;
With her baby teeth and all her baby curls.
She's a tot! Just a tot!
Good for bouncing on your knee.
I am positive that she
Doesn't even know that boys aren't girls.

She's a snip! Just a snip!
Making dreadful baby noise;
Having fun with all her toys;
Just a chickadee who needs her mother hen.
She's a cub! A papoose!
You could never turn her loose.
She's too infantile to take her from her pen.

Of course that week-end in Trouville
In spite of all her youthful zeal,
She was exceedingly polite,
And on the whole a sheer delight.
And if it wasn't joy galore,
At least not once was she a bore
That I recall.
No, not at all.

Hah!

She's a child! A silly child!
Adolescent to her toes,
And good heaven how it shows!
Sticky thumbs are all the fingers she has got.
She's a child! A clumsy child!
She's as swollen as a grape,
And she doesn't have a shape.
Where the figure ought to be it is not.

Just a child! A growing child!
But so backward for her years:
If a boy her age appears
I am certain he will never call again.
She's a scamp and a brat!
Doesn't know where she is at.
Unequipped and undesirable to men.

Of course I must in truth confess
That in that brand new little dress
She looked surprisingly mature
And had a definite allure.
It was a shock, in fact, to me,
A most amazing shock to see
The way it clung
On one so young.

Ah!

She's a girl! A little girl!
Getting older, it is true,
Which is what they always do;
Till that unexpected hour
When they blossom like a flower. . . !

Oh, no. . . !
Oh, no. . . !
But. . . !
But. . . !

There's a sweeter music when she speaks,
Isn't there?
A diff'rent bloom about her cheeks,
Isn't there?
Could I be wrong? Could it be so?
Oh where, oh where did Gigi go?

continued . . .

Gigi, am I a fool without a mind
Or have I merely been too blind
To realize?
Oh, Gigi, why you've been growing up
    before my eyes.
Gigi, you're not at all that funny,
    awkward little girl I knew!
Oh no! Over night there's been a
    breathless change in you.
Oh, Gigi, while you were trembling on
    the brink
Was I out yonder somewhere blinking
At a star?
Oh, Gigi, have I been standing up too
    close
Or back too far?
When did your sparkle turn to fire?
And your warmth become desire?
Oh, what miracle has made you the
    way you are?

Gigi..!
Gigi....!!
Gigi......!!!
Oh no! I was mad not to have seen the
    change in you!

Oh, Gigi, while you were trembling on
    the brink
Was I out yonder somewhere blinking
At a star?
Oh, Gigi, have I been standing up too
    close
Or back too far?
When did your sparkle turn to fire?
And your warmth become desire?
Oh, what miracle has made you the way you are?

This was the song originally written for Eliza Doolittle to sing on the eve of her daring attempt to pass herself off as an aristocrat at the ball. The fact that it applied just as well to Gigi on her emergence as a social butterfly underlines the striking parallels between the two plays, and especially between the two heroines, both of whom begin as ugly ducklings, both of whom are taken in hand by a sophisticated man, and both of whom fall in love with their mentor. At the time *Gigi* was first seen, several critics complained that the songs sounded like remnants left over from *My Fair Lady*. There was some truth in the observation, but it had nothing to do with any failure on the part of Lerner and Loewe to change gear from Shaw to Colette. It was simply that the basic situation of each play was identical.

Just as the two partners had had a difference of opinion over the merits of 'On the Street Where You Live', so they did over 'Say a Prayer for Me', except that this time the positions were reversed. Lerner disliked the song, saying of its disappearance from the score of *My Fair Lady*, 'I was not sad to see it go. I never liked it. Fritz did. I told him I thought it sounded like a cello solo. He said it did sound like a cello solo, but a very nice cello solo. It would never have found its way into *Gigi* except Fritz, that dirty dog, played it one night for Arthur Freed and Vincente Minnelli when I was not around, and the following morning I was outvoted three to one.'

Lerner later retracted, saying that the sequence in the picture, in which Leslie Caron sings the song to her cat, 'was one of the most touching moments in the film'.

Say a Prayer for Me Tonight

Say a prayer for me tonight.
I'll need ev'ry prayer
That you can spare
To get me by.

Say a prayer and while you're praying
Keep on saying:
She's much too young to die.

On to your Waterloo, whispers my heart.
Pray I'll be Wellington, not Bonaparte.

Say a prayer for me this evening.
Bow your head and please
Stay on your knees
Tonight.

When Lerner and Loewe paid their first visit to Chevalier, before the score of the picture had been written, they found him enthusiastic for the project and full of energy. He discussed his age frankly –

... remarking that being seventy-two was not all that bad considering the alternative. He also said something else that stuck in my mind. 'At seventy-two,' he said, 'I am too old for women, too old for that extra glass of wine, too old for sports. (He had started his life as a boxer and was always very athletic.) All I have left is the audience but I have found it is quite enough.' Months later his words returned to me, and undoubtedly led me to the idea for 'I'm Glad I'm Not Young Any More'.

When the song was pre-recorded with orchestra in Hollywood, Chevalier asked Lerner if the accent had been acceptable, to which Lerner replied that he had understood every word. Chevalier said, 'That's not what I mean. Was there enough?'

I'm Glad I'm Not Young Any More

I

Poor boy. Poor boy.
Down-hearted and depressed and in a spin.
Poor boy. Poor boy.
Oh, youth can really do a fellow in.

How lovely to sit here in the shade
With none of the woes of man and maid.
I'm glad I'm not young any more.

The rivals that don't exist at all;
The feeling you're only two feet tall;
I'm glad that I'm not young any more.

No more confusion.
No morning-after surprise.
No self-delusion,
That when you're telling those lies,
She isn't wise.

And even if love comes through the door;
The kind that goes on for evermore,
For evermore is shorter than before.
Oh, I'm so glad that I'm not young any more.

II

The tiny remark that tortures you;
The fear that your friends won't like her too;
I'm glad I'm not young any more.

The longing to end a stale affair
Until you find out she doesn't care.
I'm glad that I'm not young any more.

No more frustration.
No star-crossed lover am I.
No aggravation.
Just one reluctant reply;
Lady, goodbye.

The fountain of youth is dull as paint.
Methuselah is my patron saint.
I've never been so comfortable before.
Oh, I'm so glad that I'm not young any more.

In This Wide, Wide World

GIGI
(Into the phone; the music begins under)
Gaston?

(Sings)

I've been hoping you'd call.
Yes I called you.
I've been thinking, that's all I've been doing today.
Am I sorry?
I'm sorry you wounded me so.
No, please not again.
Don't try to explain.
What matters to me
Is you forced me to see
Something buried inside
I can no longer hide . . .
In this wide, wide world
Must be oh so many girls better for you than I.
In this wide, wide world
There is someone who
Is more ideal for you.
Someone who's more your world:
Wiser arms, a far more knowing smile.
Charm galore, she'll have,
Much more she'll have
Than I possess;
With so much more finesse and style;
Someone used to this wide, wide world
Who can love and still not hope too high:
Who can live your life
And give your life
The things I can't supply. . . !
And if you find her . . .
I'll die!
So I called you today,
Called you to say
After reflecting and pond'ring and thinking about you
I would rather be mis'erable with you than without you.

Paris Is Paris Again

Night in the sky . . .
From the street comes the cry
Of the rooster in search of the hen.
And Paris is Paris again.

Stars on their beat
Looking down on the sweet
Intertwining of women and men.
And Paris is Paris again.

Lovers in closets and shoes in the drawer:
Screams on the Rue Madeleine.
Swords in the park:
A shot in the dark:
And Paris is spicely,
Vicely Paris again.

Moon burning bright
And like bats in the night
Come the well-feathered demimondaine.
And Paris is Paris again.

Ladies you know
Arm in arm with their low
Classanovas meander the Seine.
And Paris is Paris again.

Meetings at nine that tomorrow will be
Meetings with lawyers at ten.
Handfuls of hair:
A tooth on the chair:
And Paris is gallicly, phallicly
Paris again.

The song of the cuckold is heard in the land
Hailing La Vie Parisienne.
Joy and remorse:
Delight and divorce:
And Paris is gaudily, bawdily,
Physically,
Aph-er-o-disically
Paris again.

I Never Want to Go Home Again

If I had a wish
I would be a fish,
Even just a clam.

Leave me here, I beg,
Here for ever eg-
Zactly where I am . . .

I never want to go home again.
I never want to go home again.
Where I want to hide is
Anywhere the tide is;
Staring at the ocean for ever,
And never go home again.

I never want to see Paris again.
No, never want to see Paris again.
All I want to do is
Be where not a shoe is;
Strolling by the ocean for ever,
And never go home again.

I have daydreams, I have feelings
Much too large to have any more dealings
With apartments and with ceilings;
Or anywhere a door is;
Anywhere a floor is;
Anywhere the waves cannot go.
Oh no! No!

I never want to go home again.
I never want to go home again.
Where I want to be is
Anywhere that free is;
Anywhere the sea is for ever,
And never go home again.

The Earth and Other Minor Things

The postman or Mama or Aunt Alicia –
That's all it seems to be a question of;
A pauper or a slave or Aunt Alicia –
And not a mention anywhere of love.
What is there that anyone can teach
If everything I want is out of reach?

I know about the earth and other minor things;
Why caterpillars smile
And summertime has wings.
How if somewhere there's always a dawn,
The Earth must be worth being on.
But there's one thing that makes
A continual riddle of it:
Why oh why I'm here in the middle of it all?

I don't belong where the crowds are.
Why don't I go where the clouds are?

I know about the leaves
That fall and then are gone;
How small a kite becomes
With no one holding on.
And I can't be a cloud in a storm
With nowhere to go to be warm.
And as long as I can't find
A clue to the riddle of it,
What am I to do in the middle of it all?

I don't belong where the crowds are.
I don't belong where the clouds are.
Then where do I belong?

☆ CAMELOT ☆

In 1470 the English poet, soldier, politician and jailbird Sir Thomas Malory beguiled the long days of a prison sentence by translating into English the *Morte d'Arthure*, a fourteenth-century French poem which took several forms. By the time the French had treated it, the myth of an English king who had conceived an order of chivalric knights was already widely known. Malory's version was first published in 1485 by Caxton, and was to become the great source-book for a succession of writers, none of whom earned greater renown than Alfred Tennyson, who in 1842 published his *Morte d'Arthur*, the overture to his *Idylls of the King*, on which he worked for the next forty years. Other writers attracted by the legend included Mark Twain, whose introduction to Malory in 1885 caused him a year later to write the anglophobe story *A Connecticut Yankee*; also, surprisingly, John Steinbeck, whose lifelong passion for Malory finally expressed itself in his last published work, *The Acts of King Arthur and his Noble Knights* (1976). By then, there had already been two considerable versions of the Arthurian legend written by contemporary English writers, T. H. White's *The Once and Future King* (1958), and Rosemary Sutcliff's *Sword at Sunset* (1963). Miss Sutcliff's masterly evocation of the myth has tended to be eclipsed somewhat by White's massive, idiosyncratic, cranky and brilliantly executed series of books, of which *The Sword in the Stone*, the first of four parts, was purchased by the Disney Studios and was therefore unavailable to Lerner when he first began work on his libretto.

White was a schoolteacher at an English public school, something of a recluse and an eccentric, a man at home in the fields but not particularly enamoured of modern urban life, about which he knew little and cared less. In view of the popularization of his masterwork as a musical, it is revealing to learn why he wrote it and what he intended it to say:

I have had the Matter of Britain on my hands for twenty years. That is what it has been called since before the days of Malory, and it is a serious subject. I have tried to deal with every side of it – with the clash between Might and Right, man's place in nature, the problem of war, the racial background which is an important part of the story, and with King Arthur's personal doom – the Aristotelean tragedy which made Malory call his long book the *Morte* d'Arthur. I have tried to look at it through the innocent eyes of young people, because I don't very much believe in the modern theory that the whole object of life is gratified desire. Malory didn't either. I have tried to make the seriousness acceptable by getting as much fun as possible out of the comic characters. I have invented a love affair for King Pellinore – the only addition to Mallory, except that he did not say that Lancelot was ugly. Almost all the people in this book are in his wonderful one, and have the same characters in both. I hope the moral is not too heavy, but the story was always a deep one. After all, it is the major British epic – more so than Milton's Italian excursion. English writers, including great ones like Tennyson, have been mulling it over for a thousand years, and for that matter Milton himself thought of doing it before he decided to deal with Adam.

Not quite the most promising theme for a musical comedy. Indeed, there is a sense in which *Camelot* is nothing of the sort, but its converse, a musical tragedy, in which the fortunes of all the principals, to say nothing of their principles, decline in the course of the action, which slides from light-hearted contentment to doom and death. Lerner acknowledged the problem:

In *Camelet* the first half was joyous and romantic. But the second act told the story of the disintegration of the Round Table and it became pure drama. Unfortunately, there is no way of making a downhill story go uphill.

What has generally been overlooked is the *Camelot* was not the first attempt by Broadway to go looking for Camelot. In 1927 Twain's novel had been adapted by Rodgers and Hart and had enjoyed a highly profitable run. More significantly, it had been revived in 1943, the year of Lerner's Broadway début with *What's Up?* and had featured the last scintillating lyrics of Lerner's friend and mentor, Lorenz Hart. Yet it should be said that Lerner's *Camelot* was a far more serious and demanding affair than anything conceived by Rodgers and Hart. It hedged no bets, spurned the joke of anachronism which had fuelled so much of the laughter of its predecessor, and omitted none of the tragic overtones, although not even the sombre shades of the plot were very much more deadly that the real-life circumstances behind the making of the musical.

On the eve of the opening in London of *My Fair Lady* in 1958, Fritz Loewe had almost died after suffering a massive coronary, and was for the rest of his career hardly able to undertake the rigorous chores which a musical demands. While *Camelot* was still running wildly over length and the great problem was to know how to cut it down to shape without letting too much blood, Moss Hart, very much the navigator of the ship and Lerner's great hero, was stricken with a heart attack at the very moment Lerner was in hospital recovering from a burst ulcer. What followed was too macabre for contrivance:

On Saturday afternoon I dressed and packed, said my thank-you's to the members of the staff who had been so kind to me and walked down the corridor to the elevator. My nurse was with me. While waiting for it to arrive, I happened to look back and I saw a hospital bed, obviously occupied, being wheeled into the room I had just vacated. As we rode down in the elevator the nurse told me who it was. It was Moss.

To this day *Camelot* carries the structural impurities which were a direct result of the confusion following the disappearance of Hart. The disputes which ensued regarding the possibility of hiring a new director caused a rift between Lerner and Loewe which was never quite healed during their working partnership. The production staggered down from Toronto to Boston, where T.H. White appeared for the first time:

I had forewarned him by mail that the task of converting his beautiful six-hundred-page book to a form whose dimensions had to be limited to two and a half hours, was less a matter of dramatizing incidents than capturing the spirit. After recovering from the first shock of seeing it on the stage in a shape that must have seemed light years away from what his imagination had envisioned, he was enthusiastic and encouraging, and magnanimously gave me free rein to do whatever I thought was best for the play.

By now Lerner had taken on the duties of director, and later testified that only the dedication, expertise and good faith of his two stars saved the day. Of Burton he writes: 'In simple language he kept the boat from rocking, and *Camelot* might never have reached its final destination on 44th Street had it not been for him.' And of Julie Andrews: 'A professional in the proudest sense of the word. She meets any challenge with a smile and an unbatted eyelid that makes you wonder how Britain ever lost the Empire.'

By the time the caravan reached New York the advance booking had reached two million dollars and the show was still not ready. Its opening received mixed notices, but after a slow start it established itself, ran over two years, two further years in London, longer in Australia, became a best-selling album and was sold to the movies for one million dollars. It changed the lives of all its principals, bringing about the retirement from Broadway of Loewe and thereby altering utterly the circumstances of Lerner's life. It also saw the last of Julie Andrews as a musical comedy star. Moss Hart died shortly after. The one contributor to *Camelot* whose life was in a sense enhanced by the experience was the man whose creative work had inspired everyone to make the attempt:

For Tim White, the stage version of *The Once and Future King* proved to be more lucrative than all his previous works. After the play opened in New York he returned to Alderney and I never saw him again. However, he sent me his last book of poetry in which he wrote: 'Dear Alan, How extraordinary it is that you, a stranger from a far-off land, should have been responsible for making me my fortune. Affectionately, Tim.'

The only slight irritant to the reclusive White was that from now on he was a celebrity. Easily recognized by his messianic white beard, he became a mark for gossip columnists and self-seekers of all kinds. But he had his ways of repulsing their attacks. One day there came knocking at his door some proselytizers who announced themselves as Jehovah's Witnesses. 'Well I'm Jehovah,' snapped White and slammed the door on them.

I Wonder What the King is Doing Tonight

I know what my people are thinking tonight,
As home through the shadows they wander.
Ev'ryone smiling in secret delight,
They stare at the castle and ponder.
Whenever the wind blows this way,
You can almost hear ev'ryone say:

I wonder what the King is doing tonight.
What merriment is the King pursuing tonight?
The candles at the Court, they never burn'd as bright.
I wonder what the King is up to tonight.
How goes the final hour
As he sees the bridal bower
Being legally and regally prepared?
Well, I'll tell you what the King is doing tonight:
He's scared! He's scared!

You mean that a king who fought a dragon,
Whack'd him in two and fix'd his wagon,
Goes to be wed in terror and distress?
Yes!
A warrior who's so calm in battle
Even his armour doesn't rattle,
Faces a woman petrified with fright?
Right!
You mean that appalling clamouring
That sounds like a blacksmith hammering
Is merely the banging of his royal knees?
Please!
You wonder what the King is wishing tonight . . .
He's wishing he were in Scotland fishing tonight.
What occupies his time while waiting for the bride?
He's searching high and low for some place to hide.
And oh, the expectation,
The sublime anticipation
He must feel about the wedding night to come!
Well, I'll tell you what the King is feeling tonight:
He's numb! He shakes!
He quails! He quakes!
Oh, that's what the King is doing tonight.

The Simple Joys of Maidenhood

St Genevieve! St Genevieve!
It's Guinevere. Remember me?
St Genevieve! St Genevieve!
I'm over here beneath this tree.
You know how faithful and devout I am.
You must admit I've always been a lamb.
But, Genevieve, St Genevieve,
I won't obey you any more!
You've gone a bit too far.
I won't be bid and bargain'd for
Like beads at a bazaar.

St Genevieve, I've run away,
Eluded them and fled;
And from now on I intend to pray
To someone else instead.
Oh, Genevieve, St Genevieve,
Where were you when my youth was sold?
Dear Genevieve, sweet Genevieve,
Shan't I be young before I'm old?

Where are the simple joys of maidenhood?
Where are all those adoring, daring boys?
Where's the knight pining so for me
He leaps to death in woe for me?
Oh, where are a maiden's simple joys?

Shan't I have the normal life a maiden should?
Shall I never be rescued in the wood?
Shall two knights never tilt for me
And let their blood be spilt for me?
Oh, where are the simple joys of maidenhood?

Shall I not be on a pedestal,
Worshipped and competed for?
Not to be carried off, or betterst'll,
Cause a little war?
Where are the simple joys of maidenhood?
Are those sweet, gentle pleasures gone for good?
Shall a feud not begin for me?
Shall kith not kill their kin for me?
Oh, where are the trivial joys. . . !
Harmless, convivial joys. . . ?
Where are the simple joys of maidenhood?

Fie on Goodness

ALL
Fie!
Fie on goodness, fie.
Fie on goodness, fie.
Eight years of kindness to your neighbour . . .

MORDRED
Making sure that the meek are treated well.

ALL
Eight years of philanthropic labour.

MORDRED
Derry down dell.

ALL SINGERS
Gad but it's hell.

ALL
Fie on goodness, fie.
Fie, fie, fie . . .

SAGRAMORE
There's not a folly to deplore.

ALL DANCERS
Derry down.

ALL SINGERS
Derry down.

DINADAN
Virgins may wander . . .

MORDRED
Unmolested?

DINADAN, SAGRAMORE AND LIONEL
Unmolested!

MORDRED
Lolly to let.

ALL
Gad it's a sweat.
Oh fie on goodness, fie.
Fie, fie, fie . . . ah fie!

ALL DANCERS
(Nasally)
Naaaaa . . . Naaaaa . . . Naaaaa . . . Naaaaa . . .

CASTOR
How we roared and brawled in Scotland
Not a law was e'er obeyed
And when wooing called in Scotland . . .

A KNIGHT, LIONEL, DINADAN, DAP
AND CASTOR
We'd grab any passing maid.

CASTOR
Ah, my heart is still in Scotland
Where the lassies woo'd the best . . .
On some bonnie hill in Scotland
Stroking someone's bonnie . . .

MORDRED
Fie on Scotland!

ALL
Fie!
Fie on Scotland, fie.

THREE KNIGHTS (DAP, LIONEL AND
A KNIGHT)
No one repents for any sin now.

CASTOR AND DINADAN
Ev'ry soul is immaculate and trim.

SAGRAMORE AND DANCERS
No one is covered with chagrin now.

MORDRED
Nonny no nin.

DINADAN
Confession Sunday is a bore.

ALL DANCERS
Derry Down.

ALL SINGERS
Derry Down.

MORDRED
Ah, but to spend a tortured evening
Staring at the floor . . .
Guilty and alive once more.

continued . . .

ALL

Fie on goodness, fie.
Fie, fie, fie, fie, fie.

DAP

When I think of the rollicking pleasures
That earlier filled my life . . .

ALL SINGERS

Lolly lo, lolly lo.

DAP

Like the night I beheaded a man
who was beating his naked wife.

ALL KNIGHTS

Lolly lo, lolly lo.

DAP

I can still hear his widow say,
Never moving from where she lay . . .
'Tell me, what can I do, I beg, sir, of you . . .
Your kindness to repay . . .'

ALL
(With a groan)

Oh fie on goodness, fie.
Fie on goodness, fie.

LIONEL

Lechery and vice have been arrested . . .

MORDRED

Well.

SAGRAMORE

Not a maiden is evermore in threat.

MORDRED

Well.

ALL

Gad but it's grim
Oh fie on goodness, fie.
Fie, fie, fie . . .

ALL

It's been depressing all the way,
Derry down, Derry down.
And getting glummer every day,
Derry down, Derry down.

MORDRED

Ah, but to burn a little town,
Or slay a dozen men . . .
Anything to laugh again . . .

ALL
(Sing)

Eight years of kindness to your neighbour
Making sure that the meek are treated well
Eight years of philanthropic labour
Derry down dell!
Gad but it's hell!

Oh, fie on virtue, fie!
Fie on mercy, fie!
Fie on justice, fie on goodness
Fie, fie, fie, fie, fie!

MORDRED

Fie!!

Camelot

It's true! It's true! The crown has made
  it clear:
The climate must be perfect all the year.

A law was made a distant moon ago here,
July and August cannot be too hot;
And there's a legal limit to the snow here
In Camelot.

The winter is forbidden till December,
And exits March the second on the dot.
By order summer lingers through September
In Camelot.

Camelot! Camelot!
I know it sounds a bit bizarre;
But in Camelot, Camelot
That's how conditions are.

The rain may never fall till after sundown,
By eight the morning fog must disappear.
In short, there's simply not
A more congenial spot
For happ'ly-ever-aftering than here
In Camelot.

Camelot! Camelot!
I know it gives a person pause
But in Camelot, Camelot
Those are the legal laws.

The snow may never slush upon the hillside.
By nine p.m. the moonlight must appear.
In short, there's simply not
A more congenial spot
For happ'ly-ever-aftering than here
In Camelot.

Each evening from December to December
Before you drift to sleep upon your cot,
Think back on all the tales that you remember
Of Camelot.

Ask ev'ry person if he's heard the story;
And tell it strong and clear if he has not:
That once there was a fleeting wisp of glory
Called Camelot.

Camelot! Camelot!
Now say it out with love and joy!

Camelot! Camelot!

Yes, Camelot, my boy . . .

Where once it never rained till after sundown;
By eight a.m. the morning fog had flown . . .
Don't let it be forgot
That once there was a spot
For one brief shining moment that was known
As Camelot . . .

The Jousts

A KNIGHT

Sir Dinadan's in form and feeling in his prime.

OTHERS

Yah! Yah! YAH! Oh, we'll all have a glorious time!

GUILLIAM

Sir Sagramore is fit, and Sir Li'nel feels sublime.

ALL

Yah! Yah! Yah! Oh, we'll all have a glorious time!
Now look you there! Sir Dinadan's astride.

GIRLS

He's astride!

ALL

It's obvious he will be the first to ride.

GIRLS

Oh, look!

ALL

Good fortune, Dinadan! We hail you, Dinadan!
Yah! Yah! Yah! Yah! Yah! Yah!
Sir Dinadan! Sir Dinadan!
Oh, there he goes with all his might and main.

A KNIGHT

There he goes!

ALL

He's got a steady grip upon the rein.

LADY 1

Steady, steady, steady!

ALL

Steady!
Sir Dinadan! Sir Dinadan!
Oh, try to gallop by him on the right.

LADY 1

On the right, on the right.

ALL

For that's the arm where you have all the might.

A KNIGHT

On the right.

ALL

On the right, on the right!
By jove, they're coming near . . .

OTHERS

They're close!

ALL

Sir Dinadan is raising up his spear . . .
Oh, charge him, Dinadan!

A MAN

Charge him!

ALL

You have him now, so charge him, Dinadan!
Here comes the blow! Here comes the blow!
OH, NO!

A KNIGHT

'Twas luck, that's all it was; pure luck and nothing more.

LADY 2

Sagramore will even up the score.

MAN 2

The Frenchman struck him first, but the blow was not that great.

LADY 3

Sagramore will open up his pate.

A GROUP

Sir Sagramore! He's riding on the field!

MAN 2

Oh, there's the black and crimson of his shield.

ALL

There he goes! There he goes!
He's bending low and spurring on his steed.

LADY 3

There he goes!

ALL

He's charging him at record breaking speed.

LADY 1

Charge! Charge!

ALL

Sagramore!
Oh, make his armour crack and split in two. . . .

LADY 3

Crack him!

ALL

A mighty whack as only you can do.

LADY 3

Whack him!

continued . . .

ALL

Now, look you through the dust . . . Look!
Sir Sagramore is ready for the thrust . . .
And now they're circling 'round . . .

LADY 3

Split him!

ALL

Sir Sagramore will drive him to the ground!
Here comes . . . the blow! Here comes . . . the blow!
OH, NO!

ARTHUR

He did that rather well, don't you think, dear?

GUINEVERE

That horse of Sagramore's is too old.

ARTHUR

But felling Dinadan with one blow, dear . . .

GUINEVERE

Sir Dinadan, I am told, has a nasty cold.

ALL

Sir Lionel! Sir Lionel!
On, charge at him and throw him off his horse! . . . Go!
Oh, show him what we mean by English force.

LADY 3

Throw him down!

ALL

Throw him down!
Sir Lionel! Sir Lionel!
I've never seen him ever ride as fast . . . Yah!
That Frenchman will be hopelessly outclass'd . . . Yah! Yah! Yah! Yah!
His spear is in the air!
I tell you Lancelot hasn't got a pray'r,
His shield is much too low.

LADY 3

Charge!

ALL

A good hard thrust and downward he will go!
And here's the blow! Here comes . . . the blow!
OH, NO! OH, NO!
Sir Lionel is down!
Dear God it isn't true!
Sir Lionel is dead!
The spear has run him through!

Follow Me

Through the clouds, grey with years,
Over hills, wet with tears;
To a world
Young and free
We shall fly.
Follow me.
April green ev'rywhere,
April's song always there.

Come and hear,
Come and see.
Follow me.

To the tree where our hopes hang high,
To the dream that should never die,
Where our long-lost tomorrows still are in
The sweet by and by.

Time goes by, or do we?
Close your eyes and you'll see,
As we were we can be.
Weep no more,
Follow me,
Follow me,
Follow me,
Follow me.

Far from day, far from night . . .
Out of time, out of sight . . .
Follow me . . .
Dry the rain, warm the snow . . .
Where the winds never go . . .

In a cave by a sapphire shore
We shall walk through an em'rald door.
And for thousands of evermores
To come, my life you shall be.

Only you, only I,
World farewell, world goodbye,
To our home 'neath the sea,
We shall fly,
Follow me . . .

C'est Moi

Camelot! Camelot!
In far off France I heard your call.
Camelot! Camelot!
And here am I to give my all.
I know in my soul what you expect of me;
And all that and more I shall be!

A knight of the table round should be invincible;
Succeed where a less fantastic man would fail;
Climb a wall no one else can climb;
Cleave a dragon in record time;
Swim a moat in a coat of heavy iron mail.
No matter the pain he ought to be unwinceable,
Impossible deeds should be his daily fare.
But where in the world
Is there in the world
A man so extraordinaire?

C'est moi! C'est moi,
I'm forced to admit!
'Tis I, I humbly reply.
That mortal who
These marvels can do,
C'est moi, c'est moi, 'tis I!
I've never lost
In battle or game.
I'm simply the best by far.
When swords are cross'd
'Tis always the same:
One blow and au revoir!
C'est moi! C'est moi,
So admir'bly fit;
A French Prometheus unbound.
And here I stand with valour untold,
Exception'lly brave, amazingly bold,
To serve at the Table Round!

The soul of a knight should be a thing remarkable:
His heart and his mind as pure as morning dew.
With a will and a self-restraint,
He could easily work a miracle or two!
To love and desire he ought to be unsparkable.
The way of the flesh should offer no allure.
But where in the world
Is there in the world
A man so untouch'd and pure?

C'est moi!

C'est moi! C'est moi,
I blush to disclose,
I'm far too noble to lie.
The man in whom
These qualities bloom,
C'est moi, c'est moi, 'tis I!

I've never stray'd
From all I believe.
I'm bless'd with an iron will.
Had I been made
The partner of Eve,
We'd be in Eden still.
C'est moi! C'est moi,
The angels have chose
To fight their battles below.
And here I stand as pure as a pray'r
Incredibly clean, with virtue to spare,
The godliest man I know. . . !
C'est moi!

The Lusty Month of May

Tra la! It's May!
The lusty month of May!
That lovely month when ev'ryone goes
Blissfully astray.

Tra la! It's here!
That shocking time of year!
When tons of wicked little thoughts
Merrily appear.

It's May! It's May!
That gorgeous holiday;
When ev'ry maiden prays that her lad
Will be a cad!

It's mad! It's gay!
A libellous display.
Those dreary vows that ev'ryone takes,
Ev'ryone breaks.
Ev'ryone makes divine mistakes
The lusty month of May!

Whence this fragrance wafting through the air?
What sweet feelings does its scent transmute?
Whence this perfume floating ev'rywhere?
Don't you know it's that dear forbidden fruit!
Tra la tra la. That dear forbidden fruit!
Tra la la la la.

Tra la la la la la la la la la la la
La la! It's May!
The lusty month of May!
That darling month when ev'ryone throws
Self-control away.

It's time to do
A wretched thing or two.
And try to make each precious day
One you'll always rue.

It's May! It's May!
The month of 'yes you may',
The time for ev'ry frivolous whim,
Proper or 'im'.

It's wild! It's gay!
A blot in ev'ry way.
The birds and bees with all of their vast
Amorous past
Gaze at the human race aghast
The lusty month of May!

Tra la! It's May!
The lusty month of May!
That lovely month when ev'ryone goes
Blissfully astray.

Tra la! It's here!
That shocking time of year!
When tons of wicked little thoughts
Merrily appear.

It's May! It's May!
The month of great dismay;
When all the world is brimming with fun,
Wholesome or 'un'.

It's mad! It's gay!
A libellous display.
Those dreary vows that ev'ryone takes,
Ev'ryone breaks.
Ev'ryone makes divine mistakes
The lusty month of May!

Then You May Take Me to the Fair

Sir Lionel,
Do you recall the other night
That I distinctly said you might
Serve as my escort
At the next Town Fair?

Well, I'm afraid there's someone who
I must invite in place of you.
Someone who plainly is
Beyond compare.

That Frenchman's power is more tremendous
Than I have e'er seen anywhere,
And when a man is that stupendous
He by right should take me to the Fair.

    LIONEL

Your Majesty, let me tilt with him and smite him.
Don't refuse me so abruptly, I implore.
Oh give me the opportunity to fight him
And Gaul will be divided once more.

    GUINEVERE

You will bash and thrash him?

    LIONEL

I'll smash and mash him.

    GUINEVERE

You'll give him trouble?

    LIONEL

He will be rubble.

    GUINEVERE

A mighty whack?

    LIONEL

His skull will crack.

    GUINEVERE

Well,
Then you may take me to the Fair
If you do all the things you promise.
In fact my heart will break
Should you not take me to the Fair.

Sir Sagramore,
I have some rather painful news
Relative to the subject who's
To be beside me at the
Next Court Ball.

You were the chosen one
I know,
But it's tradition
It should go
To the unquestion'd
Champion in the hall.

And I'm convinced that splendid French
Can eas'ly conquer one and all;
And besting all our local henchmen
He should sit beside me at the Ball.

    SAGRAMORE

I beg of you Ma'am
Withhold your invitation.
I swear to you
This challenge will be met.
And when I have finished
Up the operation
I'll serve him to your Highness,
En brochette!

    GUINEVERE

You'll pierce right through him?

    SAGRAMORE

I'll barbecue him.

    GUINEVERE

A wicked thrust?

    SAGRAMORE

Will be dust to dust.

    GUINEVERE

From fore to aft?

    SAGRAMORE

He'll feel a draft!

    GUINEVERE

Well then,
You may sit
By me at the Ball
If you demolish him in battle.
In fact I know I'd cry
Were you not beside
Me at the Ball.

Sir Dinadan,
Didn't I promise that you may
Guide me to London on the day
That I go up to
Judge the Cattle Show?

As it is quite a nasty ride,
There must be someone
At my side
Who'll be defending me
From beast and foe.

So when I choose
Whom I prefer go
I take the strongest
Knight I know.
And young DuLac seems
Strongest ergo,
He should take me to the
Cattle Show.

DINADAN
Your Majesty can't believe
This blust'ring prattle!
Let him prove it
With a sword or lance instead.
I promise you
When I'm done this gory battle
His shoulders will be
Lonesome for his head!

GUINEVERE
You'll disconnect him?

DINADAN
I'll vivisect him.

GUINEVERE
You'll open wide him?

DINADAN
I'll subdivide him.

GUINEVERE
Oh dear, dear dear, dear,
Then you may guide me to the Show
If you can carry out your programme.
In fact I'd grieve inside
Should you not
Guide me to the Show.

KNIGHTS
Milady we shall put an end to
That Gallic bag of noise and nerve.
When we do all that we intend to
He'll be a plate of French hors d'oeuvres.

GUINEVERE
I do applaud your noble goals;
Now let us see if you achieve them.
And if you do then you will be
The three
Who will go
To the Ball
To the Show
And take me to the Fair!

How to Handle a Woman

You swore that you had taught me ev'rything from A to Zed,
With nary an omission in between.
Well, I shall tell you what
You obviously forgot:
That's how a ruler rules a Queen!

And what of teaching me by turning me to animal and bird,
From beaver to the smallest bobolink!
I should have had a whirl
At changing to a girl,
To learn the way the creatures think!

But wasn't there a night, on a summer long gone by,
We pass'd a couple wrangling away;
And did I not say, Merlyn: What if that chap were I?
And did he not give counsel and say . . .
What was it now? . . . My mind's a wall.
Oh, yes! . . . by jove, now I recall.

How to handle a woman?
There's a way, said the wise old man;
A way known by ev'ry woman
Since the whole rigmarole began.

Do I flatter her? I begged him answer . . .
Do I threaten or cajole or plead?
Do I brood or play the gay romancer?
Said he, smiling: No indeed.

How to handle a woman?
Mark me well, I will tell you, Sir:
The way to handle a woman
Is to love her . . . simply love her . . .
Merely love her . . . love her . . . love her.

Before I Gaze at You Again

Before I gaze at you again
I'll need a time for tears.
Before I gaze at you again
Let hours turn to years.
I have so much
Forgetting to do
Before I try to gaze again at you.

Stay away until you cross my mind
Barely once a day.
Till the moment I awake and find
I can smile and say

That I can gaze at you again
Without a blush or qualm,
My eyes a-shine like new again,
My manner poised and calm.
Stay far away!
My love, far away!
Till I forget I gazed at you today . . . today.

If Ever I Would Leave You

If ever I would leave you,
It wouldn't be in summer.
Seeing you in summer, I never would go.
Your hair streaked with sunlight . . .
Your lips red as flame . . .
Your face with a lustre
That puts gold to shame.

But if I'd ever leave you,
It couldn't be in autumn.
How I'd leave in autumn, I never would know.
I've seen how you sparkle
When fall nips the air.
I know you in autumn
And I must be there.

And could I leave you running merrily through the snow?
Or on a wintry evening when you catch the fire's glow?

If ever I would leave you,
How could it be in springtime,
Knowing how in spring I'm bewitch'd by you so?
Oh, no, not in springtime!
Summer, winter or fall!
No, never could I leave you at all.

If ever I would leave you,
How could it be in springtime,
Knowing how in spring I'm bewitch'd by you so?
Oh, no, not in springtime!
Summer, winter or fall!
No, never could I leave you at all.

The Seven Deadly Virtues

Virtue and proper deeds, Your Majesty?
Like what?
Courage, Milord?
Purity and Humility, my liege?
Diligence? Charity? Honesty? Fidelity?
The seven deadly virtues?
No, thank you, Your Majesty.

The seven deadly virtues,
Those ghastly little traps,
Oh, no, Milord, they weren't meant for me.
Those seven deadly virtues,
They're made for other chaps,
Who love a life of failure and ennui.

Take Courage! Now there's a sport –
An invitation to the state of rigor mort!

And Purity! A noble yen!
And very restful ev'ry now and then.

I find Humility means to be hurt;
It's not the earth the meek inherit, it's the dirt.

Honesty is fatal and should be taboo.
Diligence? A fate I would hate.
If Charity means giving, I give it to you,
And Fidelity is only for your mate.

You'll never find a virtue
Unstatusing my quo,
Or making my Be-elzebubble burst.
Let others take the high road,
I will take the low;
I cannot wait to rush in
Where angels fear to go.
With all those seven deadly virtues,
Free and happy little me has not been cursed.

What Do the Simple Folk Do?

GUINEVERE

What do the simple folk do
To help them escape when they're blue?
The shepherd who is ailing,
The milkmaid who is glum,
The cobbler who is wailing
From nailing
      His thumb?

When they're beset and besieged,
The folk not noblessely obliged . . .
However do they manage
To shed their weary lot?
Oh, what do simple folk do
We do not?

ARTHUR

I have been informed
By those who know them well,
They find relief in quite a clever way.
When they're sorely pressed,
They whistle for a spell;
And whistling seems to brighten up their day.
And that's what simple folk do;
So they say.

GUINEVERE

They whistle?

ARTHUR

So they say.

GUINEVERE

What else do the simple folk do
To perk up the heart and get through?
The wee folk and the grown folk
Who wander to and fro
Have ways known to their own folk
We throne folk
      Don't know.

When all the doldrums begin,
What keeps each of them in his skin?
What ancient native custom
Provides the needed glow?
Oh, what do simple folk do?
Do you know?

ARTHUR

Once along the road
I came upon a lad
Singing in a voice three times his size.
When I asked him why,
He told me he was sad,
And singing always made his spirits rise.
So that's what simple folk do,
I surmise.

GUINEVERE

They sing?

ARTHUR

I surmise.

GUINEVERE AND ARTHUR

Arise, my love! Arise, my love!
Apollo's lighting the skies, my love.
The meadows shine
With columbine
And daffodils blossom away.

Hear Venus call
To one and all:
Come taste delight while you may.
The world is bright,
And all is right,
And life is merry and gay. . . !

GUINEVERE

What else do the simple folk do?
They must have a system or two.
They obviously outshine us
At turning tears to mirth;
Have tricks a royal highness
Is minus
      From birth.

What then I wonder do they
To chase all the goblins away?
They have some tribal sorc'ry
You haven't mentioned yet;
Oh, what do simple folk do
To forget?

ARTHUR

Often I am told
They dance a fiery dance,
And whirl till they're completely uncontrolled.
Soon the mind is blank,
And all are in a trance,
A vi'lent trance astounding to behold.
And that's what simple folk do,
So I'm told.

GUINEVERE

What else do the simple folk do
To help them escape when they're blue?

ARTHUR

They sit around and wonder
What royal folk would do,
And that's what simple folk do.

I Loved You Once in Silence

I loved you once in silence,
And mis'ry was all I knew.
Trying so to keep my love from showing,
All the while not knowing
You loved me too.

Yes, loved me in lonesome silence;
Your heart filled with dark despair . . .
Thinking love would flame in you for ever,
And I'd never, never
Know the flame was there.

Then one day we cast away our secret longing;
The raging tide we held inside would hold no more.
The silence at last was broken!
We flung wide our prison door.
Ev'ry joyous word of love was spoken . . . !

And now there's twice as much grief,
Twice the strain for us;
Twice the despair,
Twice the pain for us
As we had known before.

Guinevere

MAN 1
(In tower)

So they caught Guinevere
With her bold cavalier;
Tried and found her guilty of
One too many men to love.

MAN 2
(In tower)

Let them damn! Let them jeer!
But why burn Guinevere?
It's too heartless, too severe;
And I weep for Guinevere.

If they burn'd ev'ry wife
Who had stray'd in her life,
You know well, man, I am right,
Half of England would ignite.

MAN I
(In tower)

Calm your nerves; have no fear.
They shan't burn Guinevere.
Lance escaped them. He is free.
And he'll save her, you shall see.

MAN 3
(On stage to group)

I'll wager the King himself is hoping he will return.
Why would he have chosen five a.m. for the Queen to burn?
When all the world is black and grey
What time could be more ideal
For Lancelot to come and steal
Guinevere?

MAN 2
(In tower)

Five a.m.! Gad, it's near!
Soon they'll take Guinevere,
Why does Lancelot not appear?
Won't he rescue Guinevere?

WOMAN
(On steps)

Don't worry, if I know Lancelot he will be here on time.
Don't worry, he'll come before the bells in the tower chime.
For in the field of saving damsels
He is without a peer;
And ne'er would he fail his dear
Guinevere!

SMALL GROUP
(On steps)

Guinevere! Guinevere!
He will save Guinevere!
Any moment he'll appear
And he'll rescue Guinevere!

Guinevere! Guinevere!

He will save Guinevere!

Any moment he'll appear

And he'll rescue Guinevere!

MAN 2
(In tower)

Not a sign of him near.
Not a sound do I hear.
And the bells will soon ring clear.
Who will rescue Guinevere?

MAN 5

Oh hurry! Oh, Lancelot, hurry, there isn't too much time!
Oh hurry, or soon these evil bells in the tow'r will chime!
O hurry, Lance, the guard will soon be gath'ring around the stake;
And soon they will come to take
Guinevere!

GROUP

Oh my poor Guinevere,
There's no sign of him near,
And the bells will soon ring clear
For the end of Guinevere.

GROUP
(On steps)

Oh my poor Guinevere.
There's no sign of him near!
And the bells will soon ring clear
For the end of Guinevere!

ALL

Hurry, Lance! Five is near!
You must save Guinevere!
Oh, the bells will soon ring clear!
You must rescue Guinevere!

Guinevere! Guinevere!
You must save Guinevere!
Time is flying! Five is near!
You must rescue Guinevere!

GROUP
(On steps)

Don't worry, if I know Lancelot he will be here on time.
Don't worry, he'll come before the bells in the tower chime.
For in the field of saving damsels
He is without a peer;
And ne'er would he fail his dear
Guinevere!

GROUP
(On steps)

Oh hurry, Oh, Lancelot, hurry there isn't too much time.
Oh hurry, or soon those evil bells in the tow'r will chime!
Oh hurry, Lance, the guard will soon be
    gath'ring around the stake;
And soon they will come to take
Guinevere!

Guinevere! Guinevere!
You must save Guinevere!
Time is flying! Five is near!
You must rescue Guinevere!

You must save Guinevere!
You must save Guinevere!

BELLS

continued . . .

Out the room, down the hall;
Through the yard, to the wall;
Slashing fiercely, left and right,
Lance escaped them and took flight.

On a day, dark and drear,
Came to trial Guinevere.
Ruled the jury for her shame
She be sentenced to the flame.

As the dawn filled the sky,
On the day she would die,
There was wonder far and near:
Would the King burn Guinevere?

Would the King let her die?
Would the King let her die?
There was wonder far and near:
Would the King burn Guinevere?

She must burn. She must burn.
Spoke the King: She must burn.
And the moment now was here
For the end of Guinevere.

Slow her head, bowed her head,
To the stake she was led.
In his grief, so alone
From the King came a moan.

Then suddenly earth and sky were dazed by a pounding roar.
And suddenly through the dawn an army began to pour.
And lo! Ahead the army, holding aloft his spear,
Came Lancelot to save his dear
Guinevere!

By the score fell the dead,
As the yard turned to red.
Countless numbers felt his spear
As he rescued Guinevere.

In that dawn, in that gloom,
More than love met its doom.
In the dying candles' gleam
Came the sundown of a dream.

Guinevere! Guinevere!
In that dim, mournful year,
Saw the men she held most dear
Go to war for Guinevere.

Guinevere! Guinevere!
Guinevere! Guinevere!
Saw the men she held most dear
Go to war for Guinevere!
Guinevere! Guinevere! Guinevere!

☆ ON A CLEAR DAY YOU CAN SEE FOREVER ☆

Although in the conventional sense a confirmed atheist, Lerner adhered from adolescence to certain philosophies which deeply infused his work. The plot of *Brigadoon* showed an aspect of the paranormal, but it was not until *On a Clear Day You Can See Forever* that he explored in any depth his unshakeable belief in reincarnation. His heroine, Daisy Gamble, regards her own psychic gift as a toy which she cheerfully deploys in such harmless pursuits as inducing flowers to grow by talking to them. Unhappy about her habit of chain-smoking, she visits a psychiatrist who quickly perceives her alarming powers of extra-sensory perception. She knows instinctly where things are hidden and seems able to anticipate telephone calls before they happen. Under hypnosis her voice changes and she beomes metamorphosed into a nineteenth-century English orphan who has married a peer and cuckolded him for the love of an aristocratic gambler.

The doctor falls in love, not with Daisy but her Victorian alter ego, which reduces Daisy to despair. She is being upstaged by her own former self. The tangle is eventually resolved when the doctor uses telepathic communication to implore Daisy to come back to him, which she eventually does. For this daring adventure into the paranormal, Lerner turned to his Hollywood partner of a few years earlier, Burton Lane, who was something of an enigma. Since his brilliant worldwide success in 1947 with *Finian's Rainbow*, written in collaboration with E. Y. Harburg, Lane had embarked on no further projects. Nineteen years elapsed before Lerner excited his interest with his plot about the many lives of Daisy Gamble:

Every day I looked for a new project. It's a search that never ends, and it's the most frustrating thing when you don't find it. But Alan came to me with *On a Clear Day,* and I thought the premise was simply wonderful. I had reservations and I told him the first day there were aspects of it that didn't please me. I thought the story in the past became too heavy-handed and not joyful, not fun. I think that's what held the show back. But it did have such wit and imagination and fun. I got excited about it.

Lerner's confession that the show was 'modestly received' would seem to justify Lane's slight misgivings about the unorthodox nature of the theme, but the contrast in attitude between the two partners underlines once again Lerner's instinctive understanding that if the stage musical is to flourish it must extend the area of its operations and embrace ideas and subjects which in the 1940s would have been regarded as quite mad. *On a Clear Day You Can See Forever* remains one of the most original musicals ever written.

A revealing postscript concerns Lerner's first attempts to interest a composer in the story. In 1961 he had had discussions with Richard Rodgers, and soon after they made a formal arrangement to collaborate on the paranormal story, which at this stage had a working title of 'I Picked a Daisy'. The collaboration was a disaster. Lerner recalls Rodgers telling him one day that Oscar Hammerstein had been known to disappear for three weeks before coming up with a lyric. And Lerner, who sometimes took longer than that, adds, 'I should have realized at once our collaboration was doomed.' The Rodgers account is unintentionally comic. He complains that Lerner would make an appointment and then not keep it, or, if he did show up, usually with only half a lyric. Rodgers concedes, 'It wasn't all Alan's fault. Perhaps he felt uncomfortable working with someone he found too rigid.' Perhaps also he felt uncomfortable working with someone whose tunes he found unappealing. Whatever the truth, Rodgers seemed to have the idea that lyrics could be written to office hours, and indeed thought so little of the craft that at one stage he appointed himself, with predictable results, in *No Strings*. The episode can be seen in retrospect as a narrow escape for both men.

Hurry! It's Lovely up Here!

Hey, buds below, up is where to grow,
Up with which below can't compare with.
Hurry! It's lovely up here!
Life down a hole, takes an awful toll,
What with not a soul there to share with.
Hurry! It's lovely up here!

Wake up! Bestir yourself,
It's time that you disinter yourself;
You've got a spot to fill, a pot to fill,
And what a gift package of shower, sun and love
You'll be met above ev'rywhere with,
Fondled and sniff'd by millions who drift by;
Life here is rosy, if you're a posy.
Hurry! It's lovely here!

Hey, Buttercup, buds are better up
Where in case of nuptials you're handy.
Hurry! It's lovely up here!
Hey, Rhododend, courage little friend,
Ev'rything'll end Rhododandy.
Hurry! It's lovely up here!

Climb up, Geranium,
It can't be fun subterraneum.
On the exterior it's cheerier.
R.S.V.P., Peonies, pollinate the breeze;
Make the queen of bees hot as brandy;
Come give at least a preview of Easta;
Come up and see the hoot we're giving;
Come up and see the grounds for living;
Come poke your head out,
Open up and spread out,
Hurry! It's lovely here!

Wait 'til We're Sixty-five

Guaranteed income.
House with a view.
Doctors and nurses, surgery too.
Everything paid for.
And it comes true
When we're sixty-five.

I

Ten, twenty, thirty, then we're forty
Wait 'til we're sixty-five.
No need to hurry, not a worry
Left but to keep alive.
Not another premium to pay
All we got to do now, is play and play.

Six years to seven, then to heaven
Me first the record shows.
You get the pension, not to mention
'Blue Cross' until you go.
If you ever thought you had fun
At twenty-one,
Wait 'til we're sixty.

II

Hop skip to forty.
Jump to fifty
Wait 'til we're sixty-five.
Paid up and grinning,
Just beginning now to become alive.
If the children never mature,
What the hell, the bonds will,
So we're secure.

Safe from disaster, no one 'haster'
Take care of ma and pa.
All brown and rosy, livin' cozy
Down there in Tampa, Fla.
If you feel like Catherine the Great
At twenty-eight,
Wait 'til we're sixty-five.

III

False teeth at forty.
Wig at fifty.
Hew heart at sixty-five.
They'll see you get a
Perfect setta new parts to keep alive.

They provide an eighteen hole course;
And they even pay for your first divorce.
Life will be gala,
Ev'ry malady all completely paid
And we've a plot-a
Terra cotta in which
We'll both be laid.
If you were a little forlorn
When you were born,
Wait 'til we're sixty-five.

Lane's misgivings about the premise of the show extended to the title, which he took to be a development of a cliché current at the time, 'On a clear day you can see Catalina Island'. He conceded later that he didn't know what the title was supposed to mean, but felt that if he wrote a melody and then Lerner wrote a lyric that made sense, then the show itself would make sense:

One night I sat down and I wrote a melody. I wrote half a melody really, I didn't have the middle section or the ending but I had half a melody, and what was going through my mind was that at no point should he give away the title until the very end of the song. I didn't have any words, but I tried to illustrate it by saying 'On a blue day diddle da-de-dah-dah, On a grey day . . . On a happy day . . . whatever, but on a clear day, on that clear day you can see forever' – saving the title for the very end.

Lerner found that the writing of the lyric was one of his toughest chores. He spent two weeks in the attempt before realizing that if he waited till he completed it the rest of the show would never be completed. So he moved on, allowing three hours a morning, seven days a week for working on the lyric. And that was the schedule to which he adhered. It took him eight months, and he remembered writing ninety-one complete sets of words and discarding them all. Of the ninety-one all but eight were thrown away and never even seen by Lane, who remembers going through eight versions of the song, each one worse than all the others. 'Alan, who is a genius, took eight stabs at the lyric and they were awful. I mean, you cannot conceive that someone with his kind of ability could come so far off. You'd say to yourself, whoever wrote this lyric never wrote a lyric before. It's hard to conceive, but one day he came in with the lyric that we now have, which is absolutely stunning. It's magic.'

Some years later Lerner was told by a friend that the lyric was to be used as the text for a sermon at a local church. Lerner reacted wryly, 'Tell the minister not to wait for the second chorus.'

On a Clear Day
You Can See Forever

Could anyone among us
Have an inkling or a clue
What magic feats of wizardry
And voodoo you can do?

And who would ever guess
What powers you possess?
And who would have the sense
To change his views
And start to mind
His ESP's and Q's?

For who would ever dream
Of hearing phones before they ring
Or ordering the earth
To send you up a little spring?

Or finding you've been crown'd
The Queen of Lost and Found?
And who would not be stunned
To see you prove
There's more to us
Than surgeons can remove?

So much more than we ever knew,
So much more we were born to do;
Should you draw back the curtain,
This, I am certain,
You'll be impressed with you.

On a clear day
Rise and look around you
And you'll see who you are.
On a clear day
How it will astound you
That the glow of your being
Outshines ev'ry star.
You feel part of
Ev'ry mountain, sea and shore;
You can hear, from far and near
A world you've never heard before;
And on a clear day
On that clear day
You can see forever
And ever, and ever, and evermore!

On the S.S. *Bernard Cohn*

Come and see the sights, said he.
New York in lights, said he.
Said I: It might be amusing.
Next thing I knew we were cruising
On the S.S. *Bernard Cohn.*

Chilly and shivery
Out on the river, we
Found us a corner to chat in;
As we were circling Manhattan
On the S.S. *Bernard Cohn.*

Dear Mr Cohn, if by chance you exist,
Tell Mrs Cohn you deserve to be kissed.
After tonight you're the number one Mist-
Er Cohn I've known.

Time went tick-tocking on;
Me, I kept yakking on;
Him, he just listened and listened!
He never looked
Once at a sight,
And if his kindness
Was being polite,
Somehow his eyes never left me alone
Aboard the S.S. *Bernard Cohn.*

Melinda

This is a dream, Melinda,
Just a mirage, so they say.
This whole affair, they all declare,
Was dream'd each step of the way.
You're a mere dream, Melinda,
Out for a gay little spin,
Dealing me lies, before my eyes,
Of days that never have been.

There's no Melinda!
They say for sure.
But don't go, Melinda!
I know and you know
That you're no mere dream, Melinda,
Gone when the dawn glimmers through.
You and I know that long ago
Before the dream there was you,
There once was you.

Go to Sleep

When you know there's someone loving you;
And you know there's someone you love, too;
And they're not the same, what do you do?
Got to sleep, girl. Go to sleep, go to sleep.

Close your eyes and hide from every care;
When you wake up, they may not be there.
   But tell me how can I sleep?
   Tell me who could,
   When you see your whole life
   Tangled up good?
   I could drink; I could weep;
   Oh, but how can I sleep?

   Go to sleep.
   Go to sleep.

And when you and someone have a date;
   (Which you made when you were thinking straight)
And when you and someone stay out late;
   (It was bad to,
   But I had to)
When they're not the same, who gets the gate?
   (This is not the way to find a mate)
Go to sleep, girl. Go to sleep, go to sleep.
   (Go to sleep, girl. Go to sleep, go to sleep)

There is nothing you can solve tonight.
   (One in love with two could not be right)
In the morning you will see the light.
   But tell me how can I sleep?
   Look what I've done.
   Mess around with two men,
   Soon you have none.
   As you sow, so you reap;
   Which is why I can't sleep.

   Go to sleep . . .
   Go to sleep . . .
   Go to sleep . . .

Love with All the Trimmings

My dearest love who existed in a dream
'Til this evening,
When a wave came and swept me out to sea,
None of the loves that you have known
Could prepare you for the love
Raging ev'rywhere in me;
For all the arms that have covered you,
The hands that have touched you,
And the lips you have lingered on before,
Added together would be less than an olive
In the banquet of love I have in store.

Love seasoned to entice,
Love with all the trimmings filled with spice,
Love flavoured to your whim,
Served piping hot with all the trimmings;
For I'll decode ev'ry breath and ev'ry sigh
'Til your ev'ry lover's wish
Is fulfilled before it's made.
Toss in some jealousy and doubt,
Should it be required;
Not rest 'til there's nothing more desired;
Thus loving as I do,
Never, never will you ever be untrue,
Having love with all the trimmings
Waiting home for you.

Come Back to Me

I

Hear my voice where you are;
Take a train, steal a car;
Hop a freight, grab a star,
Come back to me.
Catch a plane, catch a breeze;
On your hands, on your knees;
Swim or fly, only please
Come back to me!

On a mule; in a jet;
With your hair in a net,
In a towel wringing wet –
I don't care, this is where
You should be.
From the hills, from the shore,
Ride the wind to my door.
Turn the highway to dust.
Break the law if you must.
Move the world, only just
Come back to me.

II

Blast your hide, hear me call;
Must I fight City Hall?
Here and now, damn it all!
Come back to me.
What on earth must I do,
Scream and yell, 'til I'm blue?
Curse your soul, when will you
Come back to me?

Have you gone to the moon?
Or the corner saloon
And to rack an' to 'roon'?
Madem'selle, where in hell can you be?
Leave a sign on your door
Out to lunch evermore.
In a Rolls or a van;
Wrapped in mink or saran;
Anyway that you can;
Come back to me.

III

Hear my voice thru the din;
Feel the waves on your skin;
Like a call from within;
Come back to me.
Leave behind all you own;
Tell your flowers
You will phone;
Let your dog walk alone;
Come back to me.
Let your tub overflow.
If a date waits below
Let him wait for Godot.
Ride a rail, come by mail C.O.D.,
Come in pain or in joy,
As a girl, as a boy,
In a bag or a trunk,
On a horse or a drunk,
In a ford or a funk,
Come back to me.
Come back to me.
Come back to me.

He Isn't You — She Isn't You

DAISY

How could I be this at ease with him?
Pour out my heart as I please with him?
He isn't you.
He isn't you.

When will I feel so in bloom again?
When will a voice warm the room again?
He isn't you.
He isn't you.

Mem'ries may fade in the shadows behind me,
But there'll be the dream that will always remind me;

A dream that I'll be forever comparing him to,
For love me, he may; even die for me,
Sweep every cloud from the sky for me;
He may be king – but he'll never be you.

MARC

Why doesn't love touch the skies for me?
Why are there no lows and highs for me?
She isn't you.
She isn't you.

Why has the rhyme turned to prose for me?
Love never danced on its toes for me?
She isn't you.
She isn't you.

Soon you'll be gone in the shadows behind me,
But there'll be the dream that will always remind me;

A dream that I'll be forever comparing her to,
For love will be tied to the ground again,
Hope and surprise never found again;
Angel or queen, she will never be you.

When I'm Being Born Again

Who is that boy
Beaming out loud?
So many nurses
That it looks like a crowd.
Who could it be?
That boy is me!
When I'm being born again.

Look at that room
Filled up with toys;
Must be the property of two hundred boys.
Don't cross the line!
Those toy are mine!
When I'm being born again.

When I will be being on earth again
I will be the gladdest of little men.

My, what a heart!
My, what a soul!
He's putting back
The box of candy I stole.

And there's a lot of pride there,
That's because it's me inside there,
Feeling happy when
I am born again.
This will be my heaven
When I'm being born again!

Don't Tamper with my Sister

EDWARD

Don't tamper with my sister.
Don't tamper with my sister.
Don't tamper with my sister
On a publick walke.
Her name would not survive it.
Go yonder where it's private.
And don't arouse my sister
On a publick walke.

Nibble on her ear.
Tickle her about the waist.
Tantalize the dear.
Titillate with all due haste.
Doing it out here
I must say is bad taste.

Carry on, old man,
Do your best to do your worst.
Any sort of plan:
Good or bad or 'vice-a-versed'
Frolic all you can;
But do go elsewhere first!

CHORUS

Do go elsewhere first . . .

EDWARD

Don't tamper with my sister.
Don't tamper with my sister.
Don't tamper with my sister
On a publick walke.
'Tis safer to assault her
In China or Gibraltar,
But don't have at my sister on a publick walke.

CHORUS

But don't have at his sis . . .

EDWARD AND CHORUS

. . . ter on a publick walke.

EDWARD

As Cleopatra said
While leaping from her bed:
Great jumping Julius, can't you close the door?

Don Juan had once a royal marriage lined up
Until he left a blonde Venetian's blind up.

CHORUS

Don't stab at her . . .
Don't grab at her . . .

EDWARD AND CHORUS

Don't tamper with my sister.
Don't tamper with my sister.
Don't tamper with my sister
On a publick walke . . .!

When Daisy Gamble realizes that the man she loves is in love with her alter ego, and finds her uninteresting by comparison, she sings an extraordinarily complex and brilliantly written lyric describing the hopelessness of her dilemma. It was this song which instantly sprang into my mind during that nocturnal conversation in the Chichester Festival Theatre car park when Lerner glanced at me and told us that it was not the long words but the short ones that gave the problems. He called this song 'a puzzler', and went on to explain to a New York theatre audience why this was so:

No matter how many times I wrote it, it never sounded right. Finally I realized that the melody had a peculiar strength that demanded words of one syllable. Not only words of one syllable but strong words like 'knack of', 'lack of', harsh-sounding words.

Those who are familiar with the song will know what Lerner is trying to say, but he sells himself short by not nominating as an example of simple words delighting the ear with the unexpected felicity of their assonance as well as their intelligence the coupling of 'sequel' with 'equal'. It sounds quite obvious once heard, but it took three hours a day, seven days a week, for eight months, to arrive at it.

What Did I Have That I Don't Have Now?

(Barbra's Recorded Version)
I don't know why they redesigned me;
He likes the way he used to find me;
He likes the girl I left behind me;
I mean he, I mean me.

1st CHORUS
What did I have that I don't have?
What did he like that I lost track of?
What did I do that I don't do the way I did before?
What isn't there that once was there?
What have I got a great big lack of?
Something in me then, he could see then
Beckons to him no more.
I'm just a victim of time,
Obsolete in my prime!
Out of date and outclassed by my past.
What did he love that there's none of?
What did I lose the sweet warm knack of?
Wouldn't I be the late great me if I knew how?
Oh! what did I have I don't have now?

continued . . .

2nd CHORUS

What did I have that I don't have?
What do I need a big supply of?
What was the trick I did particularly well before?
What did he see that's gone in me?
What did I use that now I'm shy of?
Why is the sequel never equal?
Why is there no encore?
Where can I go to repair
All the wear and the tear
Till I'm once again the previous me?
What did he like that I'm not like?
What was the charm that I've run dry of?
What would I give if my old know-how still knew how?
Oh, oh, what did I know, tell me where did it go?
What, oh what did I have I don't have now?

☆ COCO ☆

In 1970, changing partners once again, Lerner collaborated with Andre Previn to write an original musical based on the life of the Parisian queen of fashion, Coco Chanel. Obviously a bravura role for an actress, it tempted Katharine Hepburn, at the age of sixty-two, to portray Coco, with great flair and surprising musical awareness.

That's the Way You Are

You wake up every day
Hoping love will come,
Fearing that it may,
But that's the way you are.

Wanting nothing deep,
Nothing that will last,
Guaranteed to keep
You the way you are.

Always sighing
For love undying,
You go on goodbyeing,
A dream unpossessable,
But so undressable.

Time silences the phone,
Empties every vase,
Leaving you alone,
With your mem'ries
Of au revoir.

Loving could save you,
It could have, that is, if you had learned how,
But that's the way you are.
That's the way you are.
That's the way you are.

The World Belongs to the Young

My mind's made up!
I've got to work!
For memories lose calories
And now I'm undernourished;
So, youth, en garde.
I'll serve you right,
You want the world?
You'll have to fight!

The world belongs to the young.
That's an order, so I hear.
Salute and praise them or hold your tongue.
Even better, disappear.

They say that I have had my day.
It's time for someone else to dance.
They say I ought to crawl away.
Mes enfants, not a chance.

I want it all again and more.
I want the world the young deplore.
So peck away, sweet birds of youth.
It's eye for eye and tooth for tooth.

I'll keep the good taste here at home;
And send the bad taste back to Rome.
I will let the British Isles
Keep all the gaudy styles.
I want Paree to wake and see
Without me there's a vacancy . . .

The world belongs to the young.
To the young – or to me?
We shall see. We shall see.
We shall see.

Let's Go Home

The Paris moon appears above.
It's time to bargain hunt for dreams again.
But all those dreams I'm weary of.
I want love,
Let's go home, let's go home, let's go home.

A fleeting escapade won't do.
A waste of love it always seems again.
I want a lifetime rendezvous.
I want you!
Let's go home, let's go home, let's go home.

I want you so, my love,
I cannot play with you
Or stroll the quai with you
Where lovers should roam.

No, my love!
No dancing floor tonight!
I want much more tonight.
Let's go home, let's go home,
Let's go home . . .

Where in my arms you'll come and stay . . .
And leave the world a world away . . .
And once you're there I'll never say
Goodnight.

Mademoiselle Cliché de Paris

More than regal,
Less than legal;
Siren singing,
Caution flinging –,
Mademoiselle Cliché de Paris.

Weak but able,
Ergo sable;
Laughing, winking,
Di'monds clinking –
Mademoiselle Cliché de Paris.

But this Mademoiselle
A sadder moiselle
I very soon became,
Try as I may
I just couldn't play
That wayward game,
Or do the same
As ev'ry standard
Courtesan did;
Cloying, giddy,
Grinning, idi-
Otically
Was too much for me.
Than do all that for bed and board
I'd rather be in bed and bored,
And never be
A worn-out cliché de Paris.

The Money Rings Out Like Freedom

Oh, the money rings out like freedom!
Clink-clink-a-jingle.
That primitive sound is freedom to me.
Free to parade up
The Rue de la Paid-up,
As equal as I can be.

Ev'ry franc in the bank is freedom!
Clink-clink they jingle.
We live in a world where cabbage is king.
So dime, mark and kroner,
Come make me your owner
And let freedom ring!

One day
In May
The duke and I
Let the tempers fly,
And I told him whither to go and stay;
So he invited to the next soirée
A buxon bore for whom he'd bought
A diamond bigger than a diamond ought
To be;
Did he.
And I knew why.
To make me cry.
But I came wearing imitation junk,
So large and gaudy that her diamond shrunk;

The crowd went wild for the glass display;
And costume jewelry was here to stay!
What a coup!
What luck!
Tell the bank to send a truck!

Oh, the money rings out like freedom!
Clink-clink-a-jingle.
That capital tune is chiming I'm free.
My heart rejoices,
When I hear invoices
That sing out so solvently.

One spring
The King
Of I forgot
Exactly what,
Picked the Grand Canal to have a fete
Which no one there ever will forget.
All the rich and famous in a great chorale
Saw me tumble in the Grand Canal.

It's true.
My shoe
Ensnared my gown
And I went down;
And 'down' in Venice means really under;
Which made me wet and made me wonder:
Would this have happened if by some chance
Instead of a gown I wore men's pants?

Then soon all the sisters and the cousins and the aunts
Were calling me the pirate of men's pants.

What a stroke!
How divine!
Call me up in Liechtenstein.
Oh, the money rings out like freedom!
Clink-clink they jingle.
A queen with a lot of jack is a king.
So kopeck and lire,
Come nearer and nearer
And let freedom ring.

Alex died
Without a word of warning.
To friends I cried:
I'll put the world in mourning!
And out of the depths of my distress
Came the basic little black dress.

Alex gone!
What a shame!
What a hit that dress became!
Oh, the money rings out like freedom.
Clink-clink they jingle.
Translated it means I kow-tow no more.
Up goes the income
And out go
The nincom-
Poops I had to please before.

All the pelf on the shelf is freedom.
Clink-clink they jingle.
With money to pay, oh, debt, where's thy sting?
So come, legal tender,
Be tender, surrender,
And let freedom ring.

So come, sweet peseta,
Come sooner, not later
And let freedom ring.

A Brand New Dress

I need a bright and holidaytime gown,
Today my life is starting over.
The me I used to be has fled the town,
My tears I've sent back to the sea.

I need a brand new dress,
A really grand new dress,
To find a brand new love for me.
To make him stop and stare,
And give my life then and there
A brand new reason to be.

There must be somewhere under all this sky,
A place where loving means forever.
Where no one knows about the word Goodbye,
And teardrops never leave the sea.

I need a brand new dress,
A fairyland new dress,
To find a brand new love for me.
To make a brand new life,
And be the lover and wife,
I know I'm eager to be.

But oh, if he who broke my heart today
Should pass me by not even staring,
Or caring
What I am wearing,
I know I'll throw my lovely brand new dress away.

A Woman Is How She Loves

A woman is not her dress,
Or if you see more or less;
It isn't her coat and gloves . . .

A woman is how she loves.
Don't tell me how high her fashion;
Tell me how deep her passion goes.

A woman is how she loves.
That magic that leaves you weaker
Isn't from wearing chiquer clothes.

Clothes make the man.
Make more money as fast as he can –
But I'm not a fan.
What a man goes to hell for
Don't go to Chanel for . . . !

A woman is how she loves.
What makes her an Aphrodite
Isn't the way her nightie flows.

Why should I care
If it's Cardin or Gucci
Or Lanvin or Pucci
Who makes what is left on the chair?

None of it's even part of
All that is in the heart of
Woman! What's a woman?
A woman, a woman,
A woman is how she loves!

A woman is how she loves.
Don't count on Balenciaga
Helping you sell monogamy.

Dior isn't shy;
He would like all the skirts raised up high.
How grand! So would I!
But who cares where the hems are
If dismal the stems are.

A woman is how she loves.
But women who get too slender
Make it confusing genderly.

'Twill be ever thus:
From some feminine reason
From season to season
You dress for each other not us.

We're more than satisfied with
Someone who's lined inside with
Woman, lots of woman.
A woman, a woman,
A woman is how she loves!

Gabrielle

Gabrielle...

There's a new and happy you
Not far away,
Gabrielle;
What became of what's-her-name
The world will say?
Gabrielle
Will be never seen again;
Amen
Gabrielle
Will be known as merry
Mimi...?
Momo...?
Kiki...?
Coco...!

Fare thee well,
Little drab unhappy
Gabrielle, farewell
Fare thee well
From that wild, delicious child,
Coco, farewell.
Gabrielle...
Dream away a little,
Play a little,
Pray a little,
Make the hours fly...
Till we tell
Gabrielle
Goodbye.

Coco

Coco, Coco...
Hoping too high,
Fell down from the sky,
And started to cry:

It's the end of Coco.
Coco...
Where is a friend
To trust and depend upon?

Scan the hills;
Rake the sky;
But your searching
Won't end till you try
To
Learn to turn to
Someone who's called
Coco, Coco, Coco.

Fiasco

Fiasco!
How I have waited and waited for you!
Fiasco!
Thank God, at last a disaster came true.

What Waterloo did;
And what Spain to Peru did;
Should be included,
Plus American wine.

A real fiasco!
The crowd was vicious, pernicious, divine!
And now she's battered
And splattered and shattered
And mine, all mine!

I dream of Chanel
In a Hilton Hotel, a new one,
Or stuck on a boat
With no guests on the Côte d'Azur;
Or losing her voice –
What an urge to rejoice runs through one –
But the wolf at her door
Somehow has even more allure.

What a fiasco!
The tweeds were hated and rated the worst.
Fiasco!
Put on the lamé, it damn well may burst.

To all Paree she's
From a primeval species.
To Givenchy she's
At the end of the line.

It's a unanimous, unqualified, unmatchable, incomparable,
incredible, fantastic and fabulous

Fiasco!
Oh, what a thrilling, fulfilling decline!
And while she's slipping and slipping . . .
I'm skipping and skipping.
For now this faded,
Degraded and jaded
Old maid is mine!

When Your Lover Says Goodbye

When you're young
It's like losing a watch in Switzerland.
When you're my age,
It's like two extra weeks in Baden-Baden.

When your lover says goodbye,
Wise are they who know . . .
When your lover says goodbye,
Let her go.

When your lover flies away
Sad are they who learn
There can be a darker day . . .
Her return.

She was kind to leave, my friend;
You're a fool to grieve, my friend;
This is your Bastille Day.

When your lover says goodbye
Wise men all agree
There can be but one reply . . .
Leave the key.

When your lover says goodbye
You are spared the worst
Lasting love that doesn't die – kills you first.

When your lover says goodbye,
Says: Chéri, we're through;
Hold her in your arms and sigh:
Toodle-oo
Au Revoir . . .
May you stay
Well and far.
For no sweeter words can love supply
Than hello
And Goodbye.

Ohrbach's, Bloomingdale's, Best and Saks

Paris hates the dresses;
Gave them all the ax.
But everything's fine
Right down the line
For Ohrbach's, Bloomingdale's and Best and Saks.

Horrible, says Paris;
Speaking of the slacks.
But wait till they see
The hit they'll be
At Ohrbach's, Bloomingdale's and Best and Saks.

Cheer up and smile, m'lady's
Face is too long.
One hundred eighty million
Growing Americans couldn't be wrong.

Clothes that have a simple line
Seem never old and sloppy.
Plus the fact the other kind
Is goddam hard to copy.

Out of date, says Paris.
Youth is what she lacks.
We guarantee this:
You just can't miss
At Ohrbach's, Bloomingdale's and Best and Saks.

Do all your copies wear as well
And last as long as a real Chanel?
And are all the copies you make and sell
Exactly the same as a real Chanel?

They're totally identical;
In every way authentical;
And made to a perfection
No collection could surpass.
Except the colours run a bit.
The seams may come undone a bit.
The wool is made of plastic
And the plastic's made of glass.
And occasionally they go up in flame.
But they're practically, yes, practically the same.

Tedious, says Paris;
Flatter than her chest.
But what'll they say
On opening day
At Ohrbach's, Bloomingdale's and Saks and Best?

Here they may not want you.
We want all you have.
For what do they know?
We know they'll go
At Ohrbach's, Bloomingdale's and Best
And Saks Fifth Ave.

Always Mademoiselle

Is this a sample of the joyous state of motherhood?
A taste of what maternal happiness is?
If this is the reward,
Then I'm grateful to the Lord
That all I have been pregnant with is dresses.

I'm glad I live alone without humanity;
Safe from all the dangers of devotion.
I've a selfish interest in
How they cover up their skin.
Beyond that they can all jump in the ocean.

Thank God there's no one always supervising me . . .
No one with a way of tenderizing me . . .
No one after whom I'm always cleaning . . .
Without whom life will barely have a meaning.

No one . . .
No one . . .

Clever Mademoiselle;
Brilliant Mademoiselle.
Everything that mattered
She scattered away.
Dazzling Mademoiselle
In her golden shell.
Life is just a merry,
Solitary holiday.

Gone is all the love
She had so much of;
Never more to be.
Never more will she
Cast another spell.
Through the winter night,
Now she dims the light
From the lonely bed she made;
Wondering why in hell she stayed
Always Mademoiselle.

Who the devil cares
What a woman wears?
Is it worth a stitch
Ending up a witch
In a golden shell?

One is as one does;
And, by God, it was!
Life was as it had to be.
It was not too bad to be
Always Mademoiselle.
Right or wrong, I'm glad to be
Gabrielle Chanel.

☆ LOLITA, MY LOVE ☆

Yet another new partner for Lerner was the British musician John Barry, with whom he collaborated on an ill-fated musical version of Vladimir Nabokov's scandalously popular novel *Lolita*, which tells the story of Humbert Humbert, a middle-aged man with the unfortunate ability to fall in love with schoolgirls. Lerner first offered the role of Humbert to Richard Burton, but the eventual choice was Burton's old Shakespearean partner, John Neville. A world première in Philadelphia was followed by a shortened run in that town and a closing-down for a month. There was then a second opening in the Shubert Theatre, Philadelphia, where after five days the show closed once again, this time for good. The general consensus of opinion was that the libretto, by being formed as a flash-back, surrendered the element of surprise, but at a deeper level it may well have been that the American public was not attracted by the subject. It is interesting that though all this took place in 1971, long after the Higgins-Camelot period, there were those who considered the lyrics for *Lolita, My Love* to rank among Lerner's finest.

Dante, Petrarch and Poe

HUMBERT
(Sings)
My series of lectures exclusively features
Poets enraptured and captured by creatures
Barely pubescent.

ALL
Pubescent?!

HUMBERT
Pubescent.
Who charm them, enthrall them;
What else is there to call them
But a nymphet?

ALL
A nymphet?!

HUMBERT
A demi-Delilah.
Artless –

A FEW
A nymphet?!

HUMBERT
A guileless beguiler.
And you discover
The moment you love her
That women lose colour
And every day get duller.

(Consternation abroad)

Look how Dante –

CHARLOTTE
Not Browning?

HUMBERT
Exploded like thunder,
When Beatrice –

CHARLOTTE
Not Barrett?

HUMBERT
Was ten years or under:
Dante exploded
As Petrarch and Poe did.
And this is the story
In all its nymphic glory
I shall dwell on.

ALL
A nymphet?

HUMBERT
A nymphet!

ALL
How awful!

HUMBERT
(Enjoying it)
Awful? Not awful; but highly unlawful.
Call it erotic.

MAN
It's unpatriotic.

HUMBERT
(Carried away)
It maddens. It shatters.
It's all that ever matters.

To a nymphic-driven man
Like Poe or Dante Alighieri,
Ordinary love is, all in all,
Too ordinary.
How can you compare
A woman's Chase-Manhattan charm
With dusty little toes,
A sticky hand, a scrawny arm?

*(The Friends back away, revealing
Quilty who has entered. He comes
toward Humbert)*

QUILTY
Dusty little toes?!

HUMBERT
A dimpled flank, a bony shoulder
Sink into the flab
And disappear when she is older.

QUILTY
Does that man imply
There may be thrills
I do not know?

HUMBERT
But Dante did,
And Petrarch did,
And Edgar Allan Poe.

*(Everybody turns away and begins
chatting as if the whole ghastly
thing never happened)*

GROUP ONE
And how are the children?

GROUP TWO
I could use a sweater.

GROUP THREE
Cook it outside and it always tastes better.

QUILTY
(Confidently, to Humbert)
WWhere can I buy one?
I'm dying to try one.

HUMBERT
(Contemptuously)
I hardly would know, sir.
Perhaps the corner grocer.

*(He walks away in search of alcoholic
relief. Charlotte enters carrying a
platter of very high hamburgers and
very long frankfurters)*

CHARLOTTE
Who is ready for seconds?

(Sees Quilty)

My God, it's Clare Quilty!

(Commotion)

ALL
Quilty? Clare Quilty?! It is! It's Clare Quilty!

QUILTY
(To Charlotte, indicating Humbert)
Who is that viper
Who likes them post-diaper?

(Before she can answer)

ALL
What play are you writing?
You lead the most exciting
Life.

QUILTY
(To Vivian)
A nymphet. A nymphet.
My knee-caps are water.

ALL
How's Arizona?

QUILTY
(To Charlotte)
Say, how is your daughter?

CHARLOTTE
You mean Lolita?

QUILTY
One day I must meet-a.

ALL
You've gotten much thinner.
Why don't you come for dinner
Sunday evening . . . Or Monday
    or Tuesday or Wednesday;
Or Thursday or Friday or Saturday
    or Sunday . . . etc.

Conversation

HUMBERT

And now for that topical dull conversation;
Hear it, you're ready for self-immolation.
If they must do it,
Let's hurry them through it.
The quicker we hear them,
The quicker we can clear them
From the yard.

EVERYONE

Abortion, Agnew, Bella Abzug;
Banking, babies, black and burger;
Cancer, Cairo, C.I.A., Cambodia;
Dien and Daley;
Egypt and ecology;
The F.B.I. and what's-her-name?

And grass, Hanoi and Ho Chi Minh;
Inflation, Israel, interest rates;
And Johnson, Junky, Jackson, Jew;
And Kennedy and Kent and Ky;
Lysurgic acid, Lindsay, Laird and Liberal
And Martha Mitchell;
Nixon, negro and pollution;
Peace, police and pornographic;
Supersonic, sex and Saigon;
Teddy, Trudeau, Vietnamese
And Women's Lib and War –
Youth –
War and Youth.

Sur les Quais de Ramsdale

CHARLOTTE

Wine français straight from Burgundy;
Onion soup du jour; and voilà, chéri!
We're monsieur, madame,
Sur les quais de Ramsdale, Vermont.

Here in our own bistro, if, by chance, you feel
As I do tonight, then for breakfast we'll
Have croissants and jam
Sur les quais de Ramsdale, Vermont.

Tonight my peonies seem like fleur-de-lis;
And across the yard staring down at me
I see Nôtre Dame,
Sur les quais de Ramsdale, Vermont.

And who would ever dream you could reach Paree
On the Interstate Highway 93?
Oh, but here I am
Sur les quais de Ramsdale, Vermont.

In the Broken Promise Land

One day when I was twelve and three . . .
I fell in love beside the sea.
We strolled, we kissed, we clung, we swore
We'd love for evermore.

In the broken promise land of fifteen
Tears that fell upon the sand still are seen.
And the memory of love is all that stays
Forever evergreen
In the broken promise land of fifteen.

A child was she, a child in years.
But who is not till love appears?
And love had placed beside the sea
An apple from the tree.

In the broken promise land of fifteen,
Nothing love has ever planned ends serene.
And in spite of all the signs along the road,
The end is unforeseen
In the broken promise land of fifteen.

Not far were we from heaven's door
When steps were heard along the shore.
We turned, we gasped, she rose in fright
And vanished in the night.

And the tide that drifted in, circling me,
Tried to sweep what-might-have-been out to sea;
But the memory of love lives on and on
Forever evergreen
In the broken promise land of fifteen . . .
In the broken promise land of fifteen . . .

The Same Old Song

CHARLOTTE
The same old song!
The same old song!
The same old:
'Oh-mother-Oh-mother'
All day long.

You couldn't say
Just once a day
'Yes-mother-dear'
In the familiar
Human way.

You keep your clothes
Under the chair.
Heaven knows what
Lives in your hair.
As for your feet,
What do you care?
You're nature's child!

You're never sweet;
Never polite;
Never a smile;
Never contrite;
All part of youth's
Uncivil right
To drive me wild!

(She looks through the open windows)

Put on some clothes.
Your what's-it shows . . .

LOLITA
(Offstage)
Oh, mother!

CHARLOTTE
Oh, mother!
There goes the same old
Oh, mother!
Without a let-up!

LOLITA
(Offstage)
Oh, mother!

CHARLOTTE
Why don't you get up?

LOLITA
(Offstage)
Oh, mother!

CHARLOTTE
Oh, mother!

LOLITA
(Offstage)
Oh, mother!

CHARLOTTE
Oh . . . !

CHARLOTTE
(Sings)
The same old song!

The same old song!

The same old:

Oh-mother-Oh-mother

All day long.

LOLITA
(Sings, as she trudges toward the door)
What is so wrong
In improving my mind,
Hearing beautiful po'ems
Edgar what's-his-name wrote?
Would you rather I messed
Up the living room couch
Watching people get shot
On TV?

(Lolita exits)

Why can't she say

Just once a day

Yes-mother-dear

In the familiar

Human way?

continued . . .

HUMBERT
(Sings, as an aside)
Rumbling upstairs
Like a truck on the street,
Bursting into my room
Like a walrus in heat,
That unspeakable blight,
Driving out of my sight
My Lolita, the light
Of my life!

CHARLOTTE
I'll slap her face!

HUMBERT
Hag, don't you dare.

CHARLOTTE
Look how she's coiffed.

HUMBERT
Don't change a hair.

CHARLOTTE
Anything she
Picks out to wear
Needs turpentine.
That shiny nose!

HUMBERT
Long may it shine.

CHARLOTTE
Filthy old socks!

HUMBERT
Let them be mine.

CHARLOTTE
Sitting as if
She has no spine.

HUMBERT
O spine divine!

CHARLOTTE
(Suddenly remembering)
Oh!

(The music stops abruptly)

Saturday

LOLITA

I'm...
On vacation
From teacher-child communication.
Education
Can really be a mental strain.
Vous êtes, nous sommes
Today are nothing short of gruesome.
We can do some
When I have rested up my brain.

This is Saturday;
My one day for lying
Out and frying;
And not even think about how to pay
For all I've been buying...
Saturday.

I got stuff to do;
Like something or other
For my mother.
I did something once that she asked me to;
I can't do another...
Saturday.

I feel scratchy; twitchy;
Places out of reach are itchy.
I get numblike; thumblike...
Saturday.

Why can't Saturday
Come right after Sunday
'Stead of Monday?
The weeks would be better in fact if they
Were cut down to one day:
Saturday.

Farewell Little Dream

Twenty days of total hell
In that water-logged motel!
Every germ and every stain
Well-preserved in cellophane!
Twenty days she talked and talked!
Twenty days we walked and walked
In the rain that wouldn't ebb
Till my toes began to web . . . !
Is she grateful?
She is hateful!
My wife
For life . . . !

I would never have the heart
To shoot her with a gun.
Farewell, little dream, goodbye.
I could never stand the blood.
I'd sicken at the thud.
I'd not have the heart, not I.
Farewell, little dream, goodbye.

That polluter of my life . . .
With a hatchet or a knife.
Blow her up or let her sink . . .
Line her bathing suit with zinc . . .
Broken bottle, bat or brick?
Make it slow or make it quick . . .
Let her pass on
With the gas on . . .
A club . . . !
A tub . . . !

I would never have the heart
To poison her to death.
Farewell, little dream, goodbye.
So intense would be the strain
To watch her writhe in pain
That I'd be the first to die.
Farewell, little dream, goodbye.

Bed-D-By Motel

At the busy Bed-D-By Motel . . .
There's no better place to buy and sell;
And no better place for any fell –
Ow to go to go to hell.

At convention time with all the boys . . .
There is nothing that a man enjoys
More than making money, love and noise
At the Bed-D-By Motel.

You can have your Puerto Rican cruise;
The Catskills without the Jews;
Del Ray or Fort Lauderdale . . .
They're gonna seem pale . . .

Once you jump around the Bed-D-By,
Once your feet have found the Bed-D-By,
You'll be happy just to live and die
At the Bed-D-By Motel.

You can have you San Diego Zoo;
Disneyland and Honolu-lu.
They will fade away the moment you
Hit the Bed-D-By Motel.

Tell Me, Tell Me

I'll buy you bubble gum,
Sandals and jeans;
Perfume, potato chips
And movie magazines.

I'll buy you roller skates,
Sun cream from France;
Popcorn and crackerjacks
And cotton velvet pants.

Tell me, tell me everything you crave.
Let me, let me play the game of slave.

I'll buy a tape machine
Made for the car;
Love beads, and comic books
And every candy bar.

Let me, let me, make you happy now.
Tell me, tell me, tell me how.

All You Can Do Is Tell Me You Love Me

The kids in this town –
Go out and you'll see –
They're all having fun,
Excepting for me.
And I could be, too,
Excepting for you.
'Cause all you can do
Is tell me you love me.

They go for a swim,
They're racing their cars.
They're mooning about,
Or playing guitars.
But I'm so adored
I gotta be bored.
'Cause all you can do
Is tell me you love me.

Pul up an armchair and start.
Pour out your pitiful heart.
Roll out the gloom with you love me;
And make life a tomb with you love me.

You love me, you love me . . .
I'm sick of the stuff.
To talk it is easy;
To live it is tough.
You tell me you love me;
It isn't enough.
'Cause all you can do
Is keep me in pris'n;
And tell me it's love.
I tell you it isn'.
'Cause all you can do
Is think about you, just you.

I'm not the type for l'amour.
Too young am I for toujours.
God, what a fate is you love me.
A knife on a plate is you love me.

You love me, you love me . . .
That corny refrain
You sing as you slip on
My collar and chain.
I've had it; it's over.
I'm jumping the train.
'Cause all you can do
I'm tired of doing.
I'm sick of your gloom
And all the boo hooing.
'Cause all you can do
Is think about you, just you.

How Far Is It to the Next Town?

HUMBERT
Be careful where you step;
Where you grind your heel.

(Sings)

It still is alive;
It still can feel.
But how long will it wait
To be crunched on the floor?
Not very long!
No not anymore!
Let her keep what is hers
Of my soul and my heart.
Tonight is the night
The clouds pull apart.

How far is it to the next town.
From this town where hopes end?
How long is it to the next town
From far out at rope's end?
How far, how far till it's all behind me?
To brand new highways that don't remind me?
How long, how long till the longing dwindles,
And hope awakens and life rekindles?

How far is it to the next town?
A long way! A long way!
How can I get to the next town
And not take the wrong way?
How far without getting lost without her?
Her warmth around me, my arms about her?
How long, how long will the road be winding?
The dark too dark and the pain too blinding?
How far is it to the next town?
Too far!

Toledo? Pandora?
How far is it to the next town?
Columbus? Aurora?

Dry-Run or Loveland or Marietta . . .
Since ancient Luxor there's none built betta.
Utopia, Blissfield; there's even Trenton.
The one you choose will be time well spent in.

LOLITA
How far is it to Eureka?

HUMBERT
Eureka?

LOLITA
Eureka.

HUMBERT
How wise to pick out Eureka.
It could not be chic-a.
Coshocton's grand, so is Little Hocking.
I find Long Bottom a wee bit shocking.
But there is nothing I know uniquer
Than turtle-doving in old Eureka.

ALL
How far is it to the next town?
Sandusky? Topeka?
How far is it to the next town?
Amelia? Eureka? . . .

LOLITA
(Facing front)
How far is it to the next town?

*(The Other Couples appear.
Humbert faces front)*

ALL
Monroeville? Urbana?
How far is it to the next town?
To Bloomfield or Hanna?

HUMBERT
A town without any whisp'ring chorus;
Or threatening shadows that fall before u
A town where people are few and motley
And we can dawdle persona grat'ly.

ALL
How far is it to the next town?

HUMBERT
Where no one can find us.

ALL
How far is it to the next town?

HUMBERT
There's someone behind us.

ALL

La Crosse, La Jolla, La Salle, Tarzana;
St Louis, Scranton and Santa Ana.
Tacoma, Gooserock, Blue Hole or Laski;
Fredonia, Madisonville, Pulaski.

LOLITA
(Turns. Sings)

How far is it to the next town?

HUMBERT
(Sings)

That damn red Mercedes
Will follow us if the next town
Is halfway to Hades.

He's still behind us. What is he doing?
Why is he there if he's not pursuing?
He's never farther and never nearer –
Like someone painted him on the mirror.

ALL

How far is it to the next town?
Watonga or Reno?
How far is it to the next town?
Camargo, Encino . . .

CHORUS

How far is it to the next town?
A coal town? A steel town?
How far is it to the next town?
A punk town? A real town?
How far is Pittsburgh from Pensacola?
There's no St Paul next to Mineola.
Which way is Portland? How far is Boise?
Put up the window. You're in New Joisey.
How far is it to the next town?
The next town . . . the next town . . . ?

Lolita

Lo! Lola! Lolita!
Where are you, Lolita?
You are too young;
Unseasoned, unsteady;
Too fragile, not ready to roam.
Please come home, my Lolita.
You'll have time tomorrow
To learn of the sorrow
Of love,
Lola, Lolita;
My little Lolita.
Here in my arms
I'll shelter and feed you.
Lolita, I need you –
Come home . . .

☆ THE LITTLE PRINCE ☆

The story *The Little Prince*, by Antoine de Saint-Exupéry, is one of those whimsies about children and death which will be familiar enough to anyone who has sat through *Peter Pan*. Lerner's liking for this work, with its morbid insistence that the pristine vaults of Heaven are much more pleasant than the grubby temporal world seemed to me incongruous, and it was the only one of his works which I never discussed with him. The movie which grew out of his script had a special place in his affections, and understandably so, for it was the last project on which he worked with Fritz Loewe. I recall that sitting through the production was a distinct trial, but not till the publication of Lerner's autobiography did a possible explanation come to light:

Fritz wrote the most beautiful score, filled with melody and bubbling with the innocence of youth. Alas, it never was heard on the screen as he had composed it. The director, someone named Stanley Donen, took it upon himself to change every tempo, delete musical phrases at will and distort the intention of every song until the entire score was unrecognizable. Unlike the theatre, where the author is the final authority, in motion pictures it is the director. And if one falls into the hands of some cinematic Bigfoot, the price can be high. In this case it was intolerable, because it undoubtedly was Fritz's last score.

I Need Air

I could see it wasn't worth
Spending time with them on earth.
There were fewer in the sky.
I decided I would fly.

I need air . . .
Where only stars get in my hair:
And only eagles stop and stare.
I need air.
Oh, the world is mad
And I've had my share.
I need air.
I need air.

I need air . . .
There's not a sign of life down there.
Just hats and grown-ups everywhere.
I need air.
Lots of cosy sky
That God and I can share.
I need air.
I need air.

Be Happy

If you think you're hurting me
By wickedly deserting me
And leaving me to suffer and to cry . . .
And later die –
You're very wrong.
I'll get along
And so goodbye.

Go ahead, abandon me.
Let every horror land on me.
You mustn't let it spoil your holiday.
And by the way,
Before you fly
There's something I
Forgot to say:

I do love you
And want you to

Be happy. Be happy. Be happy.
Forget you ever knew me
Or loved me at all.

Be happy. Be happy. Be happy.
Forget that I am helpless
And frightened and small.

Be happy. Be happy.
Forget that I'll be crying still
And never will
Be happy . . . be happy
Without you.

Be happy. Be happy. Be happy.
Forget that I have no one,
And nowhere to go.

Be happy. Be happy. Be happy.
Don't think of me in winter
All covered with snow.

Be happy. Be happy.
Forget that I'll be crying still
And never will
Be happy . . . be happy
Without you.

I'm on Your Side

Where did you go?
Where oh where did you go?
Little man, don't you know that
I'm on your side?
Why did you go?
Why oh why did you go?
Little man, let me show you
I'm on your side.
This world is an ocean without any shore
When you're on your own.
Dawn is the end of the rope
When you're all alone.
I've been, I've seen, I've known it.
Where can you be?
Where oh where can you be?
Hurry back and you'll see that
I'm on your side.
Where did you run?
Why oh why did you run
From the one, only one who
Is on your side?
Everybody needs a friend.
Come make use of me.
God gave people hands to lend.
Mine is free.
So why stay away?
Come what may
I'm on your side.

You're a Child

How do you expect you can understand
International things and stuff?
Scissoring the earth, carving up the land
Is the business of kings and stuff.
Continentally
You are mentally a silly-billy boy of two.
How absurd of you,
It's unheard of you could ever think as grown-ups do.
Why, you...
Why, you...

You're a child! You're a child!
You're a twirp and that's putting it mild.
You're a speck! You're a fleck!
And it's just too tough
Pounding grown-up stuff
In the bean of a green little child.

Why do borderlines exist?
Well, first and foremost on the list
If all the borders were destroyed
Tomorrow I'd be unemployed.
And what would statesmen do for fun
If all at once the world was one?
And one could wander where he pleases
Flashing smiles instead of visas?
Why...
It could...
It might...
It would...

Oh, go away and grow! Come again when you're
Not a mini-brained punk like this.
You are really too undeveloped for
Philosophical junk like this.
Too adult is it,
Difficult is it to ever get your teeth into
Too bewilderin'
For the childerin is it – and that of course means you...
Means you...
Means you!

You're a child! You're a child!
And the kind that can drive grown-ups wild.
You're a wee little pea!
Any thought profound
That I might expound
Won't fit in
To a pin-headed child!

Gimme how can you gimme understand
Gimme gimme financial stuff?
Gimme your supply, gimme my demand
Mentally is gigantial stuff.
Gimme oodles of,
Gimme boodles of I don't care what but gimme more.
You're too poor to know,
Immature to know what there are gimme-gimme's for.
Why, you're... ·
Why, you're...

You're a child! You're a child!
You're too darling and dopey and mild.
You're a nit! Half a wit!
Speaking wisdom-wise,
Private enterprise
Is too big for a twig of a child!

It's a Hat

MAN 1
(Sings – The orchestra sneaking under)
It's a hat. It's a hat.
It's a sort of a kind of hat.
Painted poorly,
But it surely is a hat.

(Close-up of woman looking at drawing)

WOMAN
(Silly ass)
It's a hat. It's a hat.
There's no doubt of it, it's a hat.
Top of poppa
Is its proper habitat.

(Man looking at drawing)

MAN 2
(Thoughtfully)
My oh my. Look at that.
Why, this dummy has drawn a hat.

(Sixteen assorted types standing like a choir, all looking down at individual drawings)

HALF
(After due study)
It's a hat.

2nd HALF
(Same deduction – concurring)
It's a hat.

ALL
If it's anything it's a hat.

(Three wise, bearded professorial looking men study the drawing, looking over the shoulder of one who has the copy)

A
Every grown-up was the same.
Uniformly they'd exclaim:

WISE MEN
(Wisely)
It's a hat.

(The camera moves slowly up and away from them into the sky. Their voices grow softer and softer)

WISE MEN
It's a hat. It's a hat . . . etc.

Matters of Consequence

A
Oh yes.
More confused than you would ever guess.

LITTLE PRINCE
Oh no!

A
Oh yes.
I'm convinced they're all as mad as hatters.

LITTLE PRINCE
Hatters?

A
An expression.
Wasting precious life on all their matters
Of consequence!
Matters of consequence!
Matters that can't be more
Stupid or
Monument'lly unimpor-
Tant grown-ups think are
Matters of consequence!
Matters of consequence!
Matters so full of air
You would swear
They could use a mental pair
Of crutches.

LITTLE PRINCE
Such's?

A
The way you dress . . .

LITTLE PRINCE
You dress. . . !

A
No more and no less.

LITTLE PRINCE
Oh no!

A
Oh, yes!
But more than dress,
They bow to
Kowtow to success.

LITTLE PRINCE
Success . . . !

A
Oh, yes!
Ah, but more than success
And the way that you dress
There's a matter of consequence
Reigning high over all
Matters of consequence.
That's the one people call

Money. . . !
If you roll in money,
Even stolen money,
You're a king!
Money. . . !
Money, money, money.
That is all that
Matters of consequence.

Matters of consequence!
Matters like: Who's your pa,
Who's your ma,
Is your family la-de-da
The grown-ups call a
Matter of consequence;
Making such little sense
That I could never share
All of their
Lesser than a decimal . . .
In-a-fin-i-tessimal,
Totally inconsequential
Matters of consequence!

Little Prince

Little Prince, from who knows where –
Was it a star? Was it a prayer?
With every smile you clear the air
So I can see.
Oh, Little Prince, don't take your smile
Away from me.
When you came, my day was done
And then your laugh turned on the sun.
Oh, Little Prince, now to my won-
Der and surprise:
All the hopes and dreams I lived among
When this heart of mine was wise and young
Shine for me again, Little Prince,
In your eyes.

I Never Met a Rose

Oh, I have met a daisy;
But where we met is hazy.
And I have walked the streets
With Margherites
And clinging vines beside me.

Oh, I've met a lot of those.
But I never met a rose.

There's often been a heather –
An armful altogether.
And I have even met
A violet
Who almost satisfied me.
Yes, I've met every kind that grows
But I never met a rose.

Among the dahlias
I often dally.
I left a lily
In the valley.

But now and then I ponder
And wonder as I wander
Among the fields and shrub:
Perhaps the trouble is – who knows? –
That I never met a rose;
Never, never met a rose.

While roaming through the clover
Could I have passed her over?
When all is said and done,
Am I the one to blame – who knows? –
That I never met a rose –
Never, never met a rose?

Why is the Desert?

LITTLE PRINCE
(Sings)
Why is the desert so lovely to see?

A
(Sings)
Why is the desert so lovely to see?

LITTLE PRINCE
There is a reason
Lovely to tell
Because the desert is hiding a well.

What makes the desert so lovely at night?

A
What makes the desert so lovely at night?

LITTLE PRINCE
Millions of reasons.

A
Tell me just one.

LITTLE PRINCE
At night the desert is hiding the sun.

What makes the desert
Lovely in May?

A
What makes it lovely?

LITTLE PRINCE
June's on the way.
Oh and what music
Waits everywhere . . .
Hiding, hiding in the air.

Why am I happy I'm sleepy tonight?

A
Why are you happy you're sleepy tonight?

LITTLE PRINCE
Only one reason:
Knowing that when
The night is over I'll see you again.

(He drifts off to sleep)

A
Happy as I am
Knowing that when
The night is over I'll see you again.

PILOT AND LITTLE PRINCE
(Sing)
Why is the desert so lovely to see?
Why is the desert so lovely to see?
There is a reason
Lovely to tell –
Because the desert is hiding a well.

A
Why am I happy we're dying of thirst?
Why am I happy we're dying of thirst?

LITTLE PRINCE
Why are you happy?

A
Why do you think?

A AND THE LITTLE PRINCE
Because there's plenty of water to
Drink.

A
Glorious liquid!
Better than beer.

LITTLE PRINCE
Why is it better?

A
Beer isn't here.
Water, I love you.

LITTLE PRINCE
Water, me, too.

A AND THE LITTLE PRINCE
H_2O, oh, here's to you!
Why was the desert so lovely before?
Why was it lovely, but not anymore?
Water was hiding
No one could see.
But now the water is hiding in me.

Closer and Closer

We'll go a glance at a time,
A small advance at a time.
We'll be afraid a bit
And shy a bit,
Avoid each other's eye a bit
Less often each day.

The ice'll soften each day,
As we get closer and closer and closer.

We'll go a blush at a time,
A happy flush at a time;
Begin to laugh a bit
And stare a bit,
And walk around on air a bit;
As gaily we grow –
As night and daily we grow
A little closer and closer and closer.

And then one day . . . !
There'll come a day . . .
A Christmas Eve –
Midsummer Day . . .
A moment when,
Right there and then
We're gonna touch!

Then we'll jump miles at a time,
A million smiles at a time;
Begin to love a lot
And live a lot,
And give and give and give a lot.
Away we will go.
And every day we will grow
A little closer and closer and closer
And closer and closer and closer
And closer and closer all the time.

A Snake in the Grass

If you would like to cure the fever called life;
Get some relief from all the struggle and strife;
The grandest medicine that I can propose
Is under your nose:
A snake in the grass.

If you would like a spot where life never goes;
Where you can leave your body home in your clothes;
The finest travel agent you'll ever meet
Is right at your feet:
A snake in the grass.

One sting... !
And you can say goodbye to all of your friends.
One sting... !
And you'll be singing as your spirit ascends:
All's well that ends.

So any day or night wherever you are,
If you would like to take a trip to a star;
The quickest transportation yet known to man
Is none other than
A snake in the grass...
A snake in the grass...

If you would like to leave this inhuman race,
And take up residence out yonder in space;
When you are ready to go travelling on,
Sit right down upon
A snake in the grass.

One sting... !
Is quite enough to make you happy and free.
One sting... !
And you'll discover how relaxed you can be,
Posthumously.

And while you're wand'ring through the heavenly blue,
If you should see the Lord come strolling in view;
Go up and say you bring best wishes from
His fallen old chum,
A snake in the grass...
A snake in the grass...
A snake in the grasssssssssssss.

☆ 1600 PENNSYLVANIA AVENUE ☆

As a desirable address, 1600 Pennsylvania Avenue occupies a place in the American litany roughly comparable to a midway position between Buckingham Palace and No. 10, Downing Street in Britain. This show, staged in 1976, gave Lerner another opportunity of expressing his sense of history and his abiding affection for what used at one time to be called The American Way of Life. In the way that the action progresses down the years from the apotheosis of George Washington to the aftermath of the American Civil War, overtones are evoked of the experimental musical *Love Life*, in which Lerner and Kurt Weill had attempted to encompass all American history within the frame of a musical. This time the experiment was carried out in harness with Leonard Bernstein, and although the public rejected it, *1600 Pennsylvania Avenue* is one of the most revealing of all Lerner's works, in that it is specific about the specifics of American history.

It's Gonna be Great

PRESIDENT

Let's start looking alive
When we arrive
It's gonna be great.

WIFE

Keep that fervour ablaze
And one of these days
It's gonna be great.

SEENA

In the course of human events
There's only one event that makes sense:

LUD

Rehearse and re-
Hearse, rehearse and don't stop
And if we do and if we don't drop
It's gonna be great.

ALL

Grindstone under the nose
And up on our toes
It's gonna be great.

Keep that fervour ablaze
One of these days
It's gonna be great.

If we have plenty of grit
And if we don't fall into the pit
Of gloom and re-

Hearse, rehearse and don't stop
And if we do and if we don't drop
It's gonna be great.

ALL

Don't let go of the thread.
Way up ahead
It's gonna be great.

Stitch by stitch and you'll see
Eventually
It's gonna be great.

Pray to God as much as you please.
He'll only say: Get off your knees;
Rise and up and re-
Hearse, rehearse and don't stop.
And if we do and if we don't drop
It's gonna be great.

ALL

Let's start knockin' 'em dead
Looking ahead
It's gonna be great.

Let's make everything pop
For up at the top
It's gonna be great.

Pray to God as much as you please.
He'll only say: Get off of your knees;
Rise up and Re-

Hearse, rehearse and don't stop
And if we do and if we don't drop
It's gonna be great.

Let's start looking alive
When we arrive
It's gonna be great.

Keep that fervour ablaze
And one of these days
It's gonna be great.

In the course of human events
There's only one event that makes sense:

Rehearse and re-
Hearse, rehearse and don't stop
And if we do and if we don't drop
It's gonna be great.

ALL

Let's go back and begin
Madame, get in
It's gonna be great.

Back through time to the day
When people could say
It's gonna be great.

Fly away, dear Abigail, fly
We're going back to try and see why
We've got to re-

Hearse, rehearse and don't stop
And if we do and if we don't drop
It's gonna be great.

Gonna be great!
Gonna be great!
Gonna be great!

If we rehearse.
If we rehearse.

Rehearse! Rehearse! Rehearse!

It's gonna be great!

> *(The lights dim. Everyone exits or becomes 'forest'. A Small Boy in rags, named Lud Simmons, age 12 or 13, enters in terror. A Choir is heard.)*

CHOIR
Lud! Lud! Lud Simmons!
We're comin' fer you.

LUD
My name ain't Lud...
Or Simmons...

CHOIR
Oh, yes it is, too.
We're comin' fer you.
Lud...

LITTLE LUD
If I wuz a dove an' my feathers wuz white
I'd look fer white blossoms – white blossoms – an' slip outta sight
Den why cain't a black boy hide out in de dark?

If I wuz a snake an' my skin it wuz green
I'd live in green meadows – green meadows – an' never be seen.
Den why cain't a black boy hide out in de dark?

Dere's somewhere to hide
If you're green er you're white
But a black boy cain't hide
In de black, black night.

> *(At the conclusion of the song: upstage the coach appears in the dark. Little Lud hears the noise. It almost hits him. Abigail Adams steps out)*

Ten Square Miles on the Potomac River

MASSACHUSETTS
(Simultaneously with others below)
The Commonwealth of Massachusetts
Noble northern Massachusetts
Is the kind of citadel of
Independence we should move to
Anyone who puts his country
First and foremost must agree
Massachusetts...

NEW YORK
(Simultaneously)
New York's our Athens, Rome and Mecca
Troy, Jerusalem and Carthage.
Nowhere else should be considered
But magnificent Manhattan
How can anyone who loves his country
Not agree that New York...

NEW HAMPSHIRE
(Simultaneously)
New Hampshire, I propose New Hampshire
Eye-beholding is the wonder
Of New Hampshire's northern meadows
Northern hills and northern valleys
Anyone who loves his country
And is honest must agree it be
New Hampshire...

PENNSYLVANIA
(Simultaneously)
And why not stay in Pennsylvania
Lovely northern Pennsylvania
Why the sudden frantic rush to
Shed the state of Pennsylvania
Anyone who loves his country
Must agree that Pennsylvania...

CONNECTICUT
(Simultaneously)
Connecticut for whom I speak
Will patriotic'lly endorse
The choice of any state providing
It is not a Southern state
So let it be Connecticut...

RHODE ISLAND
(Simultaneously)

Rhode island, flow'r of New England
Miniscule in measure only
Miniscule in measure only
Rhode Island...

NEW JERSEY
(Simultaneously)
New Jersey, I propose New Jersey
Let it be New Jersey's...

MASS.: Massachusetts'
             Where the Capitol   should be!
N. Y. : New York's
             Where the Capitol   should be!
N. H. : New Hampshire's
             Where the Capitol   should be!
PENN.: Pennsylvania's
             Where the Capitol   should be!
CONN.: Connecticut's
             Where the Capitol   should be!
R. I.   : Rhode Island's
             Where the Capitol   should be!
N. J.   : New Jersey's
             Where the Capitol   should be!

WASHINGTON
Very nicely put.
     (To the South)
Gentlemen of the South,
Can you be equally succinct?

VIRGINIA
(Simultaneously with others below)
Virginia, Sir, your own Virginia
Is there any doubt it should be
In that lovely seventh heaven
Known as our belov'd Virginia
Anyone who puts his country
First and —

N. & S. CAROLINA
(Simultaneously)
In Carolina, North or South, con-
Tiguous to both or either
Carolina North or South is just as
South as Carolina —

continued ...

DELAWARE
(Simultaneously)
In Delaware in Delaware a
Southern state that practic'lly
Is in the North –

MARYLAND
(Simultaneously)
My Maryland, my Maryland –

(Washington makes a sharp conductor's gesture of 'cut')
(Silence)

WASHINGTON
Gentlemen, I have listened as intently as unintelligibility
will allow. It is clear that compromise
must be found in the wilderness of the soul – mine.

I have been searching
And I have prayed
I have even surveyed.
And I propose
A Christian solution to our geographic woes.

On ten square miles by the Potomac River,
Potomac River...
Potomac River...
Along the shores of the Potomac River
Our Capitol will be
(If you agree)

Upon the banks of the Potomac River,
We'll hand in hand together
Unite the land together.
A Northern town built on a Southern river.
Where everyone is free.

If you agree.

TWO BLACK SERVANTS
Everyone free?

WASHINGTON
Relatively.

Beneath a Southern sky filled with Northern lights
Southern grandeur and Northern rights,
Congress there will have a home
With a magnificent dome.
(Oh I do hope
It has a dome)

And build we will on the Potomac River
A residential mansion
A Presidential mansion
Those ten square miles by the Potomac River
For ever will enshrine
The Nation's home and mine.

What shall we call it?

NEW YORK
I haven't a clue.

WASHINGTON
Federal City might easily do.

ALL
Federal City? Without any doubt.
It's simple. It's noble.

WASHINGTON
It's boring.

VIRGINIA
It's out.

NEW YORK
President Washington...

NEW JERSEY
(Overlapping)
President Washington...

VIRGINIA
(Overlapping)
President Washington...

MARYLAND
(Overlapping)
President Washington..

WASHINGTON
Washington? I am flattered. But it's hardly an honour I can bestow on myself.

MASSACHUSETTS
Let us reflect.

continued ...

CONNECTICUT

Definitely.

WASHINGTON

So shall it be.

ENSEMBLE

On ten square miles by the Potomac River
A miracle is risin'
To dazzle the horizon.
On ten square miles by the Potomac River
The Nation's home will be
Known as Washington, D.C.

*(The song comes to a conclusion. Washington exits.
The Delegates are joined by the female half of the Ensemble)*

ENSEMBLE

On ten square miles by the Potomac River
A miracle is risin'
To dazzle the horizon.
On ten square miles by the Potomac River
They say it's gonna be
Something glorious to see.

*(During the above a clothes line is strung across the
rear of the stage and sheets are thrown over it)*
(The Ensemble exits as the voice of Abigail Adams is heard)

Welcome Home

SERVANTS

Welcome home, welcome home,
Welcome home, Miz Adams.
We're glad that you is here.
De house ain't really finished
But it will be in a year.
Oh, de roof's a little leaky,
But only when it rains.
Dere's bolts fer all de winders,
All we needs is winder panes.
But if you can stand de wind, you'll love de view.
Welcome home, Miz Adams.
Welcome to you.

(Abigail looks at Adams questioningly)

ADAMS

That's only the beginning.

HENRY

You'll be mighty glad to learn
We got keresene to burn
An' de lamps is comin' in a week or more.

RACHEL

Your bedroom's jis' above,
Which we knows dat you will love;
'Cept dere ain't no stairs up to de second floor.

ADAMS

But to add a note of cheer
Only half a mile from here
There's a flight of stairs next to the kitchen door.

RACHEL

But de wood is all in stock;
An' dey start to put de front stairs up
In de mornin'.

PRESIDENT

Six o'clock.

ALL

Welcome home, welcome home,
Welcome home, Miz Adams.
De servant bells ain't in.
But holler if ya needs us
An' we'll find ya if we kin.
Oh, de cellar's full of water
But all de wells is dry
De smell o' paint's so awful
Dat de rats lay down an' die.
But dis house ain't been a house fer very long
An' things go wrong,
'Cuz things is new;
An' we is, too.
But welcome home, Miz Adams.
Welcome to you.

Take Care of This House

Here in this shell of a house
This house that is struggling to be
Hope must have been
The first to move in . . .
And waited to welcome me
But hope isn't easy to see.

> *(Adams, impressed, takes the lantern and exits)*
> *(She turns to Little Lud, as if to say goodbye – sadly)*

Lud, you will stay here after I leave and I want you to promise me something.

LITTLE LUD
(Sadly)
Yes, M'am.

ABIGAIL
Take care of this house.
Keep it from harm.
If bandits break in
Sound the alarm.
Care for this house.
Shine it by hand.
And keep it so clean
The glow can be seen
All over the land.

Be careful at night.
Check all the doors.
If someone makes off with a dream,
The dream will be yours.
Take care of this house.
Be always on call.
For this house is the hope of us all.

ADAMS
Take care of this house.

> *(Both sets of Servants enter. Some are carrying trays with food, a tablecloth, chairs, etc.)*

LITTLE LUD
Yes, Sir, I swear.

ABIGAIL
If bandits break in . . .

LITTLE LUD
I'll be right dere.

ADAMS
Care for this house.

LITTLE LUD
Shine it by hand.

ABIGAIL AND LITTLE LUD
And keep it so clean
The glow can be seen
All over the land.

ADAMS
Be careful at night.

LITTLE LUD
Check all the doors.

ABIGAIL
If someone makes off with a dream
The dream will be yours.

ADAMS, ABIGAIL, LITTLE LUD, ENSEMBLE
Take care of this house
Be always on call . . .

ADAMS, ABIGAIL, LITTLE LUD
Care for this house . . .
It's the hope of us all.

The President Jefferson March

MALE

Who is blowing on that horn
On this quiet Sabbath morn?

OTHER CITIZENS

The marine band!
The marine band!

OTHERS

Who is marching four by four
Through the Presidential door?
The marine band!
The marine band!

LADIES

Mr Jefferson today
Is having a buffet;

LITTLE LUD

And he thought the bunch
Who came to lunch
Would like to hear 'em play . . .

GUESTS

The President Jefferson March . . .
The President Jefferson Luncheon March . . .
The President Jefferson Luncheon Party March . . .
The President Jefferson Sunday Luncheon Party March . . .

(Jefferson makes his entrance)

JEFFERSON

I'm the music lover who
Added rhythm to ragout.
And I've made my share
Of culinar-
Y innovations too.

I brought waffles home from Holland;
And they're going like hotcakes ev'rywhere.

MEN

Waffles?

LADIES

Hotcakes?

JEFFERSON

I brought ice cream back from Paris;
Meringue glace et chocolat éclair.

GUESTS
Eclair?

JEFFERSON
Très légère.
And from Roma
I brought home a
Qualche cosa
Deliziosa
Called spaghetti...

GUESTS
Spaghetti!!??

JEFFERSON
But my favourite of all
Is the savoury I like to call
Brown Betty.

GUESTS
Brown Betty...?!

JEFFERSON
So let's add a bit of cheer
To the Sabbath atmosphere.
And if God at times
Gets sick of chimes
He might be pleased to hear...

JEFFERSON AND GUESTS
The President Jefferson March...
The President Jefferson Luncheon March...
The President Jefferson Luncheon Party March...
The President Jefferson Sunday Luncheon Party March...

(Jefferson and Guests dance to the music)

MEN
Oom-papa va-room-pa va-room-papa
Va-room-pa va-room

LADIES
Statuar-
Y ev'rywhere
Wearing nothing but a stony stare.

Not a Greek
In any room
Has a fig leaf on his oom-
Papa, va-room-pa

continued ...

GUESTS
Va-room-papa va-room-pa va-room

LADIES
Only Thom-
As Jefferson
Ever bargained with the French and won.

'Magnifique'
Say those with whom
He has had a little oom-

GUESTS
Papa va-room-papa

No pursuit of happiness
Ever found him aloof
Oom-pa pa

LADIES
Father of Democracy
And I'm told there is proof.

GUESTS
A master lexicographer
Violinist and geographer.

LADIES
Now we all
Are overcome
By the drumming of the

GUESTS
Dum-de-dumming of the . . .
Bum-de-bum, dum-de-dum
To the drumming of the Pres-
Ident Jefferson March.

(The music continues. The party continues choreographically)

JEFFERSON AND GUESTS
The President Jefferson March . . .
The President Jefferson Luncheon March . . .
The President Jefferson Luncheon Party March . . .
The President Jefferson Sunday Luncheon Party . . .
The President Jefferson Sunday Luncheon Party . . .
The President Jefferson Sunday Luncheon Party March . . .

LUD

Seena...
Thomaseena...
I knew her so long,
My sweet little Seena.
I knew her before she was crawlin' on the floor.
Then one day this week
Her hair brushed my cheek –
And now I don't know her no more.

I knew her so well,
My sweet little Seena.
I knew every pout, every twinkle that she wore.
Then one day her smile
Lit the sky for a mile –
And now I don't know her no more.

Oh, I used to know
If her tears were real.
But I don't know now.
All I do is feel.
And I used to know
Where her thoughts would fly;
But I don't no more.
All I do is die
Of love and want her so...
And that's all I know...
Seena... That's all I know.
Seena...

We laughed and we played,
Me and little Seena.
We ran through the years, through the trees, by the shore.
But gone is the past.
I met her at last.
And now I don't know her no more.
No, now I don't know her no more.

> (*The lights dim out on Dolley and come up on the
> dining table, set and laden with food. Three British
> Officers, Ordway, Pimms and Ross are entering.
> Each stops with astonishment when he sees the table.*)

ORDWAY

By Jove!

PIMMS

Egad!

ROSS

God's teeth!

continued ...

ORDWAY

Have I gone around the bend or
Is this appetizing splendour
Really here or just a gastronomic ghost?

PIMMS

For a leader with a talent
For conspicuous ungallant-
Ry, this Madison is quite a decent host.

(Three more British officers,
Maitland, Glieg and Barker enter)

MAITLAND

By Jove!

GLIEG

Egad!

BARKER
(Who stutters)

G-G-
What a l-l-l-libation!

(To First Three)

You'll g-get a commendation
F-f-for v-v-valour at the stove!

ORDWAY

Silly pigeon-head, we found it.

BARKER

You f-f-f-found it?

ROSS

Yes, we found it.

BARKER

You f-f-f-f-

(Admiral Cockburn strides in followed by Budgen, Pratt and Scott)

COCKBURN
(Who is slightly deaf)

By Jove!
Egad! God's teeth! I say!
What a spiffy epicurean display!

ORDWAY

It was left here, Sir, uneaten.

COCKBURN

You were once a chef at Eton?

ORDWAY
(Very loud)
Sir, uneaten, Sir; not Eton, Sir, I said.

COCKBURN
Must you mumble in your tea cup?
I will thank you, Sir, to speak up.

ORDWAY
(Loudly)
Very good, Sir.

COCKBURN
'Tis a spiffy-looking spread!

(He takes a bottle of wine from a cooler and holds it up for inspection)

I have never seen a clearer
More exuberant Madeira.
What a jolly bit of juice to leave behind them.
Pity Jamie is unable
To be with us at the table
But he's dining with his troops – if he can find them.

(He loves his 'joke' and laughs. The Rest join)

Barker, fill the beakers for a toast before we sup.

BARKER
(Taking a bottle and doing so)
V-v-very g-g-g- V-v-very g-g-g-

COCKBURN
Oh, shut up!
Where are all the fuzzies – or the darkies, as they say?
Not a servant anywhere. Ah, Pimms, and by the way . . .

Just before we landed you were certain every fuzzy
Would rise against his master and unite with us – but does he?
No! We landed and where was he;
Your fuzzy?
Ah, did he fight against them?
Fling his jungle might against them?
No! Not even one oppress-ed fuzzy.
Which obliges me to mention
That your basic comprehension
Of the fuzzy
Is fuzzy.

PIMMS
By your leave, Sir, 'twas a failure.

COCKBURN
You are leaving for Australia?

continued . . .

PIMMS
(Louder)
I agree with your contention
That my basic comprehension
Of the fuzzy
Was fuzzy . . . Sir!

COCKBURN
Failure noted. Pardon granted.
Now if the wine has been decanted . . .

(Glass up)

Gentlemen! Be upstanding!

ALL
(Glasses up)
Sir . . . !

COCKBURN
To the King!

ALL
To the King!

COCKBURN
And to Eng . . . !

(Lud and Coley enter. They are as stunned to see the British as the British are to see them)

ORDWAY
By Jove!

PIMMS
Egad!

MAITLAND
God's teeth!

COCKBURN
Mister Pimms, your calculations
Did not tot'lly miss the mark.
Just when all is lost – behold! a ray of dark!

(The British raise their glasses to Lud and Coley)

Blackie, to reward you for your laudable sedition,
You'll be serving the commander of the British expedition.

LUD
General Cockburn!

COCKBURN
(Horrified)
General 'Cockburn'?!

LUD

I was told, Sir.

COCKBURN

Stop at once!
'Tis 'Admiral' not 'General', you pre-historic dunce!
And 'Co'burn', not 'Cockburn' – though for that you are excused.
'Tis spelled c-o-c-k but only half the cock is used.

> *(Throughout the rest of the scene, whenever they can,*
> *they steal a knife here and a fork there and*
> *conceal it on their person or place it silently in the crate.*
> *If possible they do the same with glasses and plates)*

> *(A rumble is heard in the distance. All, except Cockburn,*
> *turn and look out front through an imaginary window)*

ORDWAY

Egad!

ROSS

God's teeth!

PIMMS

Hel-lo!
The building on the hill's begun to glow.

MAITLAND

The Capitol's ignited, Sir.

ORDWAY

The fire has been lighted, Sir.

BARKER

'Tis like the d-d-dawn-dawn in the sky.

COCKBURN

Barker!

LUD

It's on fire, Sir.
The Capitol's on fire, Sir!

COCKBURN

Barker, pass the wine.

LUD

But . . .

GLIEG
(To Someone)

Will someone pass the pie?

LUD

But . . . why?

continued . . .

COCKBURN
(To Lud)
Why? Simple.
Primo, I have ordered it and were it not aflame,
The officer in charge would leave here deader than he came.
Secundo, not a brighter torch could there be,
For Blackie, by tomorrow morning Washington, D. C.
Will be Washington, deceased.
(I say, this *is* a feast!)

'Tis time to make it hot for all these Yankee demagogues;
With governmental buildings being used instead of logs –
And this one saved for last.
(Egad, what a repast!)

LUD
Burn this house . . . How can you do it?

MAITLAND
How can we?

ORDWAY
How can we?

ROSS
How can we?

PIMMS
Nothing to it.
Kindling is required but there's more than one could want.

GLIEG
Chop up every bit of furniture and woodwork that you see.

ORDWAY
Second, spread a layer of rocket powder on't.

PIMMS
Third, apply the torch. And flee.

GLIEG
Hear! Hear!

BUDGEN
Bung ho!

PIMMS
By Jove!

ALL
Good Show!

COCKBURN
(Rising)

Gaze yonder through the window for the sweetest dish I know
Called Washington Flambee;
Inspired by a recipe which I learned some time ago
While visiting Pompeii.
    And fill the night with music as we British have of old
With voices harmonized;
And sing our fav'rite, drinking song which lately I am told
These Yanks have plagiarized.

ALL
(After warming up, clearing the throat, etc.)

Gather 'round by the fire
With your beaker in hand . . .
    With your beaker in hand . . .
And there let us merrily
Besot ourselves thoroughly;
Imbibe till we verily
Rupture our attire.

How blissful to gaze
Through cinder and haze . . . !
    Through cinder and haze.
    How blissful to gaze . . . !
As visions of home
Gaily dance in the blaze.
Oh, I ne'er can recall a more heart-warming sight
Than the Presidential mansion . . .
    And Senate and Congress
Burning merry and bright.

> *(There is a blink of lightning, a clap of thunder
> and the rain begins to fall)*

MAITLAND

Egad!

SCOTT

God's teeth!

COCKBURN

Oh, shit!

> *(They are all livid)*

It's raining! It's raining!

PIMMS

Unseasonably raining . . .

COCKBURN

It's treasonably raining!

continued . . .

ALL
It's raining!

COCKBURN
(Fist at heaven)
I'll never pray again to you, Sir.
There's one thing you must never, never, do, Sir:
Extinguish
The Enguish.

PRATT
If we have not destroyed their bloody house
They have the Lord to thank.

COCKBURN
(Turning on him)
Another word against the House of Lords
And, Pratt, you walk the plank.

PIMMS
(Heart-broken)
Just when the flames were climbing higher . . .

COCKBURN
(Shaking his fist at the Almighty)
How dare you pee upon my fire?!
You hear me? Stop dropping!
Enough of all this plopping!
'Tis time this slippy slopping
Was stopping.

BARKER
The flame is getting d-d-darker . . .

COCKBURN
(Exploding)
Oh, B-B-B-B-B-B-B-Barker!

PIMMS
How dare he do this monstrous thing?!

COCKBURN
As if a lord outranked a king!

BARKER
The f-f-f-f-flame's beg-g-g-g-gun to f-f-f-f-flicker

Simultaneously

ALL
The flame's begun to flicker.

COCKBURN
B-b-b-b-b-b-b-bicker!

ALL
(To Heaven)
Now stop it!

COCKBURN
Twit!

ALL
You hear, Sir!

COCKBURN
Damn!

MAITLAND
Return the night

COCKBURN
Blast!

MAITLAND (Cont'd)
To clear, Sir!

COCKBURN
God!

PIMMS
The clouds must disappear, Sir!

COCKBURN
Stop! Stop!

Lud's Wedding (I Love My Wife)

BUSHROD

Lord, please come to our weddin'.
Lord, come down from your sky.
All our windews is open
Cuz we wuz hopin'
You could drop by.

Let de weddin' bells ring out!
Where dere's love dere is life.
Take de cake from de oven,
We gotta lovin'
Husband and wife.

(Celebration, then:)

LUD

I love my wife and I love her more
Than the way I used to love her before
She became my wife but today she is
So don't call me early 'cause I'll be bus-
Y beside her waitin' for her to wake
And her eyes to open like dawn is break-
In' the whole world over for me today –
'Cause I can't believe that I heard her say
She would honour, love and obey till death
Do us – pardon me if I catch . . . (my breath) . . .
When I knew my wife was the wife for me
We went out and sat by the willow tree
And I begged and pleaded . . . Uh-huh!
Marry me, Honey – and that is what she did.

SEENA

Oh how you pleaded!
If you thought you needed
To, you sure were wrong.
You took too long.
But I kept on prayin'
One day I'd be sayin':

I love my husband I love him more
Than the way I used to love him before
He became my husband but now he is
So don't call me early 'cause I'll be bus-
Y beside him waitin' for him to wake
And his lovin' arms to reach up and take
Me for one more trip to the Milky Way
Like he did before when I heard him say
He would honour, love and obey till death
Do us – pardon me if I catch. . . . (my
breath) . . .
Oh, I never thought he'd propose to me
Till he took me out by the willow tree
And he begged and pleaded . . . Uh-huh!
Marry me, Honey – and that is what we did.

Monroviad

MONROE
Eliza, Eliza . . . Are you sleeping?

ELIZA
Yes.

MONROE
('Winningly')
Eliza, I have something to confess.
Like a child I say my prayers at night.
Imagine! A president no less
Who prays for reason to be his guiding light.

Reason, Eliza, reason . . .
How short is the supply!
Reason, the ruler of my life.

(Passion emerging)

It is not where my convictions go to die!

My tutor used to say:
In times of crisis
Do not follow
Dionysus
But Apollo!

(Looks)

Are you sleeping?
Or do you really think it wiser
Being reckless and . . . Eliza? . . . Eliza? . . .
Eliza?

ELIZA
Go to sleep, dear.
Go to sleep.
It will keep, dear.
It will keep.
The days are long, dear;
Full of cares and strains.
Sleep. Go to sleep, dear.
The staff remains . . . Dear.

MONROE
Staff? Who spoke about the staff?
Reason, Eliza . . . Reason!

Reason! It was of reason
I was speaking on behalf.
In hopes you might employ it
When we talk about the staff.

Were reason not triumphant
Thirty years ago in that Philadelphia hall
There'd be no Constitution,
No United States at all.

I was there.
Was I not?
I was there.
It was hot.
'Twas compromise and reason
That fin'lly altered the balance of the scale . . .
With a Bill of Rights

ELIZA
For whites
And for blacks a bill of sale.
Was it not?

MONROE
It was hot.
But that was thirty years ago
And there were fifty members in the hall
You could not please them all.
With fifty different minds writing laws
There were bound to be some flaws.

ELIZA
Go to sleep, James . . .

MONROE
There are flaws . . .

ELIZA
It can keep, James . . .

MONROE
In the laws.
If on occasion
Judgement went astray . . .
We can . . .

ELIZA
Sleep, go to sleep, James.
The staff will stay . . . James.

continued . . .

MONROE

Staff!? Who's speaking of the staff?
Reason, Eliza . . .

ELIZA

Reason! Reason! That wretched excuse
For ev'ry abuse!
Reason! Bah!
Was reason the name of the genius who drew
That glorious Article One, section two?
That little white lie?

MONROE

What little white lie?

ELIZA

That all men are equal except you-know-who?
Did reason supply
That little white lie?

MONROE

You have to know why.

ELIZA

Bah! Did reason or compromise help you to write
A negro shall equal three-fifths of a white?

MONROE

Three-fifths or two-thirds?

ELIZA

Stop playing with words
Or James, you will sleep on the sofa tonight.
You cannot deny
That little white lie.

MONROE

I shan't even try.
For slavery seemed to us all at the time
A minor concession and hardly a crime;
Pre-destined to die.

ELIZA

Pre-destined to die!
I'd like to know why
That little white lie
Was destined to die? Why? Why?

MONROE

You were not in that chamber
Thirty years ago and you do not know the facts.
We who framed the Constitution
Framed the loftiest of acts.

ELIZA
You who framed the Constitution
Framed the blacks.

MONROE
(Shocked)
Eliza!

ELIZA
It was wrong and, James, you knew it. You knew it.
You knew when you were Washington
How wrong it was to do it.
You knew when you were Adams, you knew it. You knew it.

MONROE
(Defensively)
Eliza!

ELIZA
As Jefferson you knew it!
As Madison you knew it!
And now that you're Monroe
You surely ought to know.

MONROE
(Pompously)
Eliza!

ELIZA
So change the law! Repeal it! Remove it!
If you believe in liberty, then prove it! Prove it!
And I will send my staff
By camel or giraffe
To Liberia or Syria or anywhere you say.
But till that blessed day
My answer will be No! No! No!
Do you hear that, James Monroe?

MONROE
Go to sleep.
It can keep, dear.
It can keep.
The days are long, dear.
Time to say amen.
Sleep. Go to sleep, dear.

MONROE AND ELIZA
We'll talk again, dear.

(Blackout)

We Must Have a Ball

Dissension, division
That Dred Scott decision
And threats that the Union will fall . . . !
There's but one
Thing to be done:
We must have a ball.

Those endless petitions
For guns and munitions
Are driving me straight up the wall.
One would think
We're on the brink . . . !
We must have a ball.

A royal soirée,
Resplendent and gay –
And lo – all of our dilemmas
Will vanish away.

We'll let it go on and on
Till early dawn.
By then every little slave
In the South will be gone.
Behaving like cultured and civilized men
Can make every mountain a molehill again.

Says Jefferson Davis:
There's nothing can save us
We'll soon be divided like Gaul.
Poo, say I,
I don't see why
We can't have a ball.
It's not fair,
Just because bugles are starting to blare,
Oh Lord, but I'm bored with it all.
We must have a ball.

Seena

Bright and black...
Oh, the future's lookin' bright.
Bright and black.
That's a fac'.

There's a load o' luck in sight
Comin' down the track...
And it's black.

Happy dreams of long ago
Comin' back.
Bright and black.
Lawdie, who'd'a' ever know
That a stovepipe hat
Could do that!

Jus' look at that land, the fields is full,
Full o' black sheep covered with kinky wool.
The magnolia tree, it's po' white trash,
Cause the bougi-villea is the latest fash-
Ion. And li'l boy black ain't blue no more
Cause there's somethin' happen never
   happen before
Today!
Hey!
Look what's come our way...!
         Look what's come to stay...!

A heabenly ebony
Rainbow black as tar.
Don't it shine
Somethin' fine?
Plus a brand new mornin' star
With a crazy light
Which ain't white.
Which is bright and black...
Bright and black...
Black and bright...
Bright and black...
Bright and black!

   (Choreographic frolic ending with)

SEENA, LUD AND ENSEMBLE
A heabenly ebony
Rainbow black as tar.
Don't it shine
Somethin' fine?
Plus a brand new mornin' star
With a crazy light
Which ain't white...
Which is bright and black,
Like is jus'
Gotta new shellac
Jus' for us.
I mean black and bright...
Bright and black...
Black and bright...
Bright and black...
Black and bright...
Bright and black...
Black and
         black!

   (Blackout)

The First Lady of the Land

ENSEMBLE
Hail! hail!
Hail! hail!
Hail to the man who . . .
          Hail!
Without whom . . .
          Hail!
Who needs no . . .
          Hail!
The man I am proud to . . .
          Hail!
It gives me . . .
          Hail!
I give U-
Lysses Simpson Grant.
Ulysses Simpson Grant.
Hail . . . once.
Hail . . . twice.
Farewell.

*(The lights come up on the wife,
as Julia Grant, who, with the
help of Seena, is getting dressed)*

JULIA GRANT
In the hist'ry of my family.
Only Grant was bottle fed.
But I'm used to heavy drinkers
I'm Missoura born and bred.

When they swear in our successor
We have got to be on hand.
I do hope that I can stand it
And that General Grant can stand.

ENSEMBLE
Hail to the man who . . .
          Hail!
Without whom . . .
          Hail!
Who needs no . . .
          Hail!
The man I am proud to . . .
          Hail!
It gives me . . .
          Hail!
I give you . . .
          Who?

JULIE GRANT
Is it Hayes or is it Tilden?
Somehow no one seems to know.
Thirteen weeks for counting ballots
I would say is rather slow.

I have packed up all the bourbon
Told them where to send the mail.
While the people march in circles
Wond'ring who the hell to hail.

(She continues dressing)

ENSEMBLE
The man I am proud to . . .
          Who?
It gives me . . .
          Who?
I give you . . .
Rutherford B. Hayes.

WIFE
Rutherford B. Hayes!!??

ENSEMBLE
Hail . . . Hayes
Praise . . . Hayes

MRS GRANT
Good God!

*(The inauguration setting is revealed.
The President, Judge, Wife and Others
get into position for the swearing-in
ceremonies. The President places his
hand on the Bible, held by the Judge)*

JUDGE
I do solemnly swear . . .

MRS GRANT
A few dozen seconds are all that remain
Until once again I am little old plain
Julia Grant.
What an anti-climax life will be
For Ulysses and me.

PRESIDENT
I do solemnly swear . . .

MRS HAYES

A few dozen seconds are all that remain
And I will no longer be ord'nary plain
Lucy Hayes.
What a blaze of glory life will be
For Ruthie and me.

(Mrs Hayes crosses)

JUDGE

... that I will faithfully execute ...

MRS GRANT

Now they'll cheer Lucy Hayes ...
That dear Lucy Hayes ...
They'll worship her matchless cucumber skin;
Her fingers like ancient bamboo.
They'll dote on her lips so enchantingly thin
That it's hard to believe there are two.

(She crosses back)

PRESIDENT

... that I will faithfully execute ...

MRS HAYES

Démodée Julia Grant ...
Passée Julia Grant ...
Her three little chins are now out of style.
Her charm has become sub-sublime.
I'm told they are planning to travel a while,
Seeing friends who are still doing time.

(She crosses)

JUDGE

... the office of the President of the United States ...

MRS GRANT

The gall of her husband, that treacherous soul,
Taking the oath of the office he stole.

(She crosses)

PRESIDENT

... the office of President of the United States ...

MRS HAYES

Thank God for our Bible, that glorious book;
Everything else Grant and Julia took.

(She crosses)

continued ...

JUDGE

... and to the best of my ability ...

MRS GRANT

He's making the oath a four-letter word
And making the eagle a hawk.
He thinks no one knows what really occurred;
But I do and I'm dying to talk.

Yah!
They counted the ballots and when they were done ...
(Oo ow!) (Oo ow!)
Far behind Tilden had Rutherford run.
(Meow!) (Meow!)
So they counted again, again one by one;
They counted and counted till Rutherford won.
And now
That cow
Is ... the ... *(She crosses quickly)*

MRS HAYES

First Lady, First Lady
Very first Lady of the Land
The bouquet of bouquets ...
I'm the whole USA's
Lucy Hayes.
Lululu ...
Cycycy ...
Hay Hay Hayes.
Lucy Hayes ...

ENSEMBLE

Lucy! Praise Lucy.
Very first Lucy of the Land.

MRS HAYES

It's too lovely to be true;
So much happiness could happen to
Lululu ...
Who-who-who
Might have never been sharing this jubilee
Had she not chosen wisely connubi'lly.
Lucy Hayes ... !
Lucy Hayes ... !
My Lucy ...

MRS GRANT *(Bitterly)*

Hayes!
Then all through the South came a call in the night:
Take Hayes! Take Hayes!
Civil is drivel and rights are not right.

Take Hayes! Take Hayes!
And those nasty black troops
Will vanish from sight;
Which made every one in the South
    who was white
Take Hayes ... Take Hayes!
And his

MRS HAYES AND ENSEMBLE
First Lady, First Lady,
Luciest Lady of the Land.

MRS HAYES
Oh, my eyes fairly glaze
When I hear people praise
Lucy Hayes.

ENSEMBLE
Lululu
Cycycy

MRS HAYES
G. O. P.

ENSEMBLE
Hay-Hay-Hayes. . . .

MRS HAYES
Lucy!

ENSEMBLE
Praise . . .

MRS HAYES
Lucy . . .

ENSEMBLE
Luciest Lucy of the Land.

MRS HAYES
Unpretentious little me . . .
Who'd imagine I would ever be
Lululu . . .

ENSEMBLE
Cycycy

MRS HAYES
Let the bells in the belfry be rung for me.
And let Santa Lucia be sung for me.
Lucy Hayes . . .
Lucy Hayes . . .
My Lucy . . .

JUDGE
. . .protect . . .

PRESIDENT
. . .protect . . .

(Mrs Grant gasps with horror)

JUDGE
. . . preserve and defend . . .

MRS GRANT
(In agony)
Three seconds more!

PRESIDENT
. . . preserve and defend . . .

MRS HAYES
(Ecstatic)
Two seconds more!

JUDGE
. . . the Constitution of the United States . . .

MRS GRANT
Oh God!

PRESIDENT
. . . the Constitution of the United States.

MRS HAYES
Oh, Ruthie! You're the President.
And I'm the
First Lady, First Lady,
Very First Lady of the Land.

Oh, one term will never do.
If you love me you will make it two . . .
For Lulu.

ENSEMBLE
Cycycy . . .

MRS HAYES
Who'd've dreamed I'd be counting my sheep at night
Where Van Buren and Polk used to sleep at night?
Lucy Hayes . . .
Lucy Hayes . . .
My Lucy Hayes . . .

American Dreaming

Mr Lincoln...
Keep your head down, Mr Lincoln,
Don't look up here today.
All the good you left behind you
They are sweeping a-away.

Presidential honour is a loser's lament.
Principle is something drawing seven percent.
And notify the meek that they are out of the will.
Just in case they are still
American dreaming.

Winning is a virtue and defeat is a crime.
(The) holocaust of living's getting worse all the time.
Ideals are put away to keep in case of a war.
I can't do any more
American dreaming.

You could drive a team of horses through my soul
Where the holy light of freedom burned a hole.

When We Were Proud

LUD

And when I drew in my breath and bowed
No bow alive ever felt as proud.
Some feelings fade
That feeling stayed.
And in this house
We lived with pride.
And in this house
One day it died.
If only once I could cry aloud
The way it was
When we were proud.

SEENA

Remember when
We all could see
The land this land
Was meant to me.

LUD AND SEENA

When Mr Lincoln walked through the hall
We saw tomorrow on every wall,
And far and wide
Men walked with pride.
Where is the dawn
That fled the sky?
Where is the land
That aimed so high?
Where are the voices to cry aloud,
The way it was
When we were proud?

The Robber-Baron Minstrel Parade

MINSTRELS

Here come the robber-baron minstrel parade!
Here comes that plunderful show.
A-pick a-plunkin'
An' a-pluckin' everywhere we go;
Pluckin' the people out of all-a their dough.
We are the pigs in the pink
Who own the whole kitchen sink;
The money-lovin'
Board o' gove'n-
Ers o' gluttony, inc.
Here come the black-
Hearted barons of the robber brigade
To say good evenin' to you and you,
Swindle and ruin you . . .

A MINSTREL
(Elegantly)

If God says money's the root of sin,
Then God is un-Amerikin.

MINSTRELS

Here comes the robber-baron minstrel parade.

ALL MINSTRELS

Oh pity the poo-er, the poo-er old poo-er
Why is it the poo-er is pooer?
Cuz dey's dum.
Cuz dey's dum dum dum,
Oh dey's dum dum de dum de dum dum . . .
Dey's jus' dum.

To say good evenin' to you and you,
Swindle and ruin you,
Here come the robber-baron minstrel parade.

The Mark of a Man

The mark of a man
Where does it show?
In the force of the sword in his hand
Defying the foe?

In firmness of mind
That burns through his eyes?
Forever secure on the throne
Of reason alone,
Is that where it lies?
The mark of a man . . .
The mark of a man . . .

But what of the man
Who paces the night,
Fumbling and stumbling
And groping and hoping
To do what is right.

To do the right thing
Whatever the toll . . .
Not heeding the cries
Of the clever and wise
But only his soul?
But only his soul . . . !

To do the right thing
With all of his might
Hoping to God he's right . . . !

Red, White and Blues

You'll get those
Red, white and blues,
The red, white and blues . . .
Cuz you'll be outta the green.
Let's see how far you can go
Without our dough dough dough de oh dough
And gotta pass the tambourine.

We'll pull your dignity down
And take off your crown,
Put someone else in your shoes . . .
Outta the green,
Outta the pink,
You'll be alone with those stinkin'
Red, white and blues.

MINSTREL AND ALL

You'll get those
Red, white and blues,
The red, white and blues . . .
Cuz you'll be outta the green.
Let's see how far you can go
Without our dough dough dough de oh dough
And gotta pass the tambourine.

We'll strip away your prestige,
Unless your oblige,
And wrap you up in old news.
Outta the green,
Outta the pink,
You'll be alone with those stinkin'
Red, white and blues.

You'll get those
Red, white and blues,
The red, white and blues . . .
Cuz you'll be out of the green.
Let's see how far you can go
Without our dough dough dough de oh dough
And gotta pass the tambourine.

We'll cut your patronage short,
Unhook your support,
And flatten out your tattoos.
Outta the green,
Outta the pink,
You'll be alone with those stinkin'
Red, white and blues.

Lonely Men of Harvard

Lonely, lonely men of Harvard
Set apart from all the rest,
Isolated men of Harvard,
All because we are the best.
The best,
The very best,
We are indubitably the best!

We're the lonely men of Harvard,
Alone, alas, alone, alack are we!
And that's the way we'll stay,
It's the price we've got to pay
For our indubitable superiority!

Solitary men of Harvard,
Unmistakably supreme,
Doomed and blighted men of Harvard,
All because we are the cream.
Cream,
The very cream,
We are irrefutably the cream!

We're the lonely men of Harvard.
Alone, alas, alone, alack, are we!
And that's the cause we share;
It's the cross we've got to bear
For our irrefutable superiority!

And that's the curse
We share;
It's the cross
We've got to bear,
For our indubitable,
Irrefutable,
Inimitable,
Indomitable,
Incalculable superiority!

☆ CARMELINA ☆

In 1969 the Italian actress Gina Lollobrigida starred in an American film called *Buona Sera, Mrs Campbell*, the story of an Italian widow whose teenaged daughter believes, with the rest of the locals, that her mother is the widow of an American soldier killed in a World War Two battle. Eighteen years after the end of the war the American battalion which once liberated the village returns for a reunion, which delights the villagers but not Carmelina, who had been involved with three GIs at the same time. After the party to celebrate the arrival of the Americans, the three ex-lovers arrive in Carmelina's house and discover the truth. Each of the three is convinced that the daughter looks like him, but the daughter is so shamed by the discovery that she attempts to elope with a local fisherman, a plan nipped in the bud by the Americans and Carmelina's local suitor. The three Americans acknowledge that Carmelina's motives for the deception were to give her daughter some creature comforts. At last the Americans depart and Carmelina is free to marry her local beau.

Ten years after the event, Lerner and Burton Lane set to work to convert this oddly unattractive tale into a musical, with Georgia Brown as the heroine. It enjoyed only a short run, but both the partners remained convinced there was much more to it than critics and public had given credit for. Indeed, at the time of his death Lerner had agreed with Lane that a London opening should take place of a revised verson of the show, with additional lyrics by an unspecified third party nominated by Lane. The plan never seems to have come to fruition, but I recall that when I discussed the show with Lerner, he felt that it had not been given a fair chance by backers who were far too hasty in withdrawing their support. He seemed to feel that *Carmelina* was one of his better pieces of work and was clearly disappointed at its failure. In 1985 Lane arrived in London with a view to laying the ground for the London opening, but to this day nothing has been heard of the plan.

Prologue

MANZONI

My friends . . . !
Allow me to introduce myself.
My name is Numzio Manzoni.
My occupation?

May'r of a town that no one ever heard of.
Not even Naples knows that we are near.
Being the may'r of somewhere no one knows or goes
Is why I'm here.

Reading about your life has made me wonder:
Why is it so much courtship ends in court?
Why has dividing furniture become the fav'rite
Indoor sport?

Maybe you might need a brief
Moment of relief
From it all.

Leave all your troubles and trials,
Come where there are smiles
Wall to wall . . .

Far from the beds you have made,
Where a serenade
Fills the air . . .

Then I suggest
Come be my guest,
And I will lead you there.

Come with me to San Forino,
High on a far-off hill.
To the town of San Forino,
So small it's almost nil.
Hard to find is San Forino,
How every dawn does it is more than we know.

If the stars can find it, too,
Which they regularly do,
So can I and so can you.

TRIO
Come with me to San Forino,
High on a far-off hill.

To the town of San Forino,
So small it's almost nil.
Hard to find is San Forino,
How every dawn does it is more than we know.

MANZONI

By the way, before we go,
There is something à propos
I believe you ought to know...

That you will find
The sad goodbyes
And blackened eyes
You left behind.
What's more,
The sun is nice and hot,
But love is often not,
Behind the bedroom door.

To make it clear
The same distress
And lovely mess
Is over here,
It's true.
But think of the great relief
In knowing that all the grief
Does not belong to you.

So come with me to San Forino,
Where there is nothing new.
To the town of San Forino,
Where we are human, too.
Where despair is having a field day;
Ah, but for you it'll be like Bastille Day.
Watching others pace the floors.

TWO MEN

Watching others up a tree...

MANZONI

On the warm Italian shores...

TWO MEN

Oh, how restful it can be...

MANZONI

And to know that for a spell

TRIO

All the old familiar hell
Is ours, not yours.

It's Time for a Love Song

It's time for a love song.
It's time to remember
The songs that in days gone by
Could warm the sky
In December.
It's time that a love song
Came back from the past;
And all the glory of passion
Came back into fashion
At last.
And I have a love song;
A song for the season,
That's filled with the fervour of
A man in love
Beyond reason.
It's time that a love song
Returned to remind us how
The world may forget
But the time for a love song is now.

Why cling to yesterday's sorrow?
What of tomorrow?
What of tonight?
When will my masculine power
Blossom and flower
For your delight?

You'll see your husband soon enough.
Pray his goodbye.
You've been in your cocoon enough.
Butterfly, fly.
Don't let me end unhappily,
Floating in the Bay of Napoli.
Take me, my love, or I'll die.

It's time for a love song.
It's time to remember
The songs that in days gone by
Could warm the sky
In December . . .

And I have a love song;
A song for the season,
That's filled with the fervour of
A man in love
Beyond reason.
It's time that a love song
Returned to remind us how
The world may forget;
But the time for a love song is now.
The time for a love song is now.

Why Him?

What can I say about his face
Except the features are in place?
He doesn't even look in trim.
Why him? Why him?

A million stars are in the skies.
Not one is ever in his eyes.
When I'm alone at night
I groan at night
Why him!

Why do I dress for him?
Why the pain of eating less for him?
Who do I itch for him?
Why an eyelid with a twitch for him?

But when I see him coming near me
And my head begins to swim,
I keep on thinking as I nod,
My God! Why him?

There's nothing bulging in his arm.
I'm not bewildered by his charm.
Where he should be he isn't slim.
Why him? Why him?

He doesn't know I am alive.
I might as well be eighty-five.
I rack my brain at night
In vain at night –
Why him?

Why do I primp for him?
Exercise until I limp for him?
Read all those books for him –
What to do about my looks for him?

Is he a knight in shining armour –
Is my vision growing dim?
I know I prayed there'd be a man
Somewhere
Who'd hear my prayer,
But, Lord, be fair –
Why him? Why him?
Why him? Why him?

Reprise

CARMELINA
At any age not counting his . . .
VITTORIO
Some people know what suffering is . . .
CARMELINA
My secret hopes are growing dim . . .
VITTORIO
Why me?
CARMELINA
Why him?
Not one encouraging advance . . .
VITTORIO
Not one seductive little glance . . .
CARMELINA
No wicked glint at all.
VITTORIO
No hint at all.
CARMELINA
Why him?
VITTORIO
How can I waken her
Or has ecstasy forsaken her?
CARMELINA
I'd put this knife in him
Just to see if there is life in him.
VITTORIO
Has she forgotten how to tremble?
CARMELINA
I feel shaky in the limb.
VITTORIO
To fall in love with someone cold
As she –
CARMELINA
Pure ice is he –
VITTORIO
Oh god, why me?
CARMELINA
Why him?
VITTORIO
Why me?
CARMELINA
Why him?

I Must Have Her

Farewell, goodbye.
No other course have I
But leave before
I suffer even more.

That skin I love
And seen so little of
Those eyes . . . that voice . . .
God help me but I have no choice:

I must have her.
I must have her.
If I must I will seduce 'er.
And be sent to hell with Luci-
Fer a sinner
But a winner!
I must have her.

I must have her.
I must have her.
I am done with self-denying –
Come tonight she will be lying
On a bed 'n
Armegeddon.
I must have her.

Am I mad? Could I vi'lently mistreat her?
Yes, I could. Indeed I could.
Would I crush one delicious centimetre?
Oh my God! Of course I would.

I must have her.
I must have her.
Could I act without discretion?
Climb the wall and take possession
Of her brut'lly?
Absolutely!
I must have her.

Oh no! Hold on!
Am I some Genghis Khan?
A beast? A swine?
Such thoughts could not be mine.

Tonight, tonight,
I'll disappear from sight.
What's done is done.
There is no other way – but one . . .

I must have her.
I must have her.
I am still a man of honour
And to force myself upon her . . . !
I would rue it.
But I'll do it.
I must have her.

I must have her.
I must have her.
If tonight there is a riot
And I cause a hue and cry it
Doesn't matter.
Let me at her.
I must have her.

If I stay there's a chance she'll be molested.
Let us pray I do not fail.
But suppose, ah, suppose I am arrested.
I will dance my way to jail.

I must have her.
I must leave her.
I will move to Portofino.
I will stay in San Forino.
I'll regret it.
I'll forget it.
I must have her.
No, never.
I'm leaving
For ever.
I will! I won't! Oh yes! Oh no!
I can't! I can! Goodbye! Hello!
I must have her.

Someone in April

All alone . . . seventeen;
The type that De Sica has in ev'ry scene;
A poor little sparrow in the human storm,
My hands with no other hands to keep them warm . . .
And then, in a way you couldn't plan,
I looked and saw a man.
And my life began . . . when

Someone in April –
A stranger in April –
Said could he come in for a while:
Somehow I knew from his smile
That he would be
Gentle with me.
Little by little my heart
Began to fill.
Soon we were never apart –
Until . . .

Someone in April,
One morning in April,
Before he went out of the door
Said: Thank you for April –
And I was all alone once more.
All alone. Just sixteen.

I was Mimi in the final scene.
I wept – I don't know – till almost four o'clock;
And then, very faintly, I heard someone knock.
Come in, I suppose, I must have said.
And when I turned my head,
All my sorrow fled . . . for

Someone in April
Was lonesome in April,
As lonesome and helpless as I;
Oh, but how bashful and shy!
Could I . . .? said he . . .
That is, could we . . . ?
Holding him close for dear life,
I lived again.
Mother and sister and wife . . .
But then –
One day in April
My someone in April
Left roses with love at the door;
That faded in April
And left me all alone once more.

All alone. Blue with cold.
My hands with no other hands for me to hold;
A child with a woman lurking in her breast;
A poor little pigeon in an empty nest.
And then out of nowhere I was blessed . . . with

Someone in April
My life became April
The moment he kneeled at my side.
Something about him implied
He hoped he might
Stay for the night.
Soon all the room in my heart
Was filled again.
Soon we were never apart . . .
But then –

Someone in April
One evening in April
Went out to the neighbourhood store –
Leaving the soup to get colder;
Leaving the wine to grow older;
Leaving me all alone once more.

Someone in April –
It had to be April –
That one little month I was with
Braddock, Karzinski and Smith.
It had to be
One of the three.
All of them came through the door
Like cavaliers.
One of them left me with more
Than tears.

Someone in April –
It happened in April
That one of those generous men
Made certain in April
I'd never be alone again.

Signora Campbell

ROSA

I look at you.
You look at you.
I see a lot more
Than you're able to.
I see a face
Fit for a crown,
The finest lady in town:
Signora Campbell.

You're standing there.
I'm standing here.
You cannot see, you
Are standing too near.
If you were me,
You would be sure
That positiv-a-ly you're
Signora Campbell.

More than a queen,
You are a saint;
Like those Madonnas
They all used to paint.
I see the tears
You never show,
The bravest widow I know:
Signora Campbell.

Always a wife,
You are the kind
That every man dreams
Of leaving behind.
Year after year,
Faithful and true;
The greatest widow are you,
Signora Campbell.

Who is the most respected lady in
    San Forino?
You are!

CARMELINA

I am?

ROSA

You are.

CARMELINA

You think so?

ROSA

In San Forino.
Open the door.
March down the street.
There's not a soul
Who is not at your feet.
They go to church.
What do they do?
They light a candle for you,
Signora Campbell.

FATHER TOMASSO

You'll have a glowing epitaph, Signora Campbell.

SHOPKEEPER

You can buy anything for half, Signora Campbell.

GIRL

Please may I have your autograph, Signora Campbell?

MAYOR

I am the may'r
And I can say
You are adored
More ev'ry day.

ALL AND ROSA

We look at you.
You look at you.
We see a lot more
Than you're able to.
We see a face
Fit for a crown,
The finest lady in town:
Signora Campbell.

More than a queen
You are a saint.
Like those Madonnas
They all used to paint.
We see the tears
You never show,
The bravest widow we know:
Signora Campbell.

Who is the most respected lady
    in San Forino?

CARMELINA

I am!

ROSA

You are.

CARMELINA

I am!

ALL

The goddess of San Forino.

CARMELINA, ROSA AND ALL

March through the town,
Down every street.
Ask everyone
You may happen to meet.
Ask for the name
They would proclaim
The most magnificent widow about?

CARMELINA

Really now, how could there be any doubt?

ALL

One and all they will shout
Signora Campbell!

CARMELINA

I am the most respected lady in San Forino.
I am . . .
I think I am . . .
I wonder . . . in San Forino . . .
They look at me . . .
I look at me . . .
I see the someone . . .
That no one can see . . .
I see the . . .

Love Before Breakfast

Love before breakfast –
Arms that I slept in,
Tingle and tell me
That morning has crept in.
No hurried goodbye,
Too long have I
Wakened without you.

Love before breakfast
Is a cloud we'll go sailing away on;
It's the air we'll be walking all day on
And the smile only we
Can see.

Love before breakfast
Morning comes stealing.
You on my pillow,
Joy with no ceiling.
Only a sunbeam could feel as I do
When love before breakfast is you.

Yankee Doodles

LADY
Tra la la la sis boom bah hip horray!
Yankee Doodles are coming to town!

LADY AND OTHERS
Hallelujah hot dogs and anchors aweigh!
Yankee Doodles are coming to town!

LADY
Six hundred lira equal a dollar.
Doll la la la la la la la lala . . .

Santa Claus is coming TWA
Yankee Doodles are coming today.

YOUNG MEN
Here we come the soldier boys of Uncle Sam,
With our pockets full of chocolate and spam.
And if there is any Nazi left in town,
Will he raise his hand so we can shoot him down!

MANZONI
What about that clock?
They are almost here.

BELLINI
Maybe in an hour.

MANZONI
Maybe in a year.

BELLINI
Maybe you shut up or we tear it all down.

MANZONI
Yankee Doodles are coming to town . . . !

ALL
Give a cheer for Kilroy and all of his men.
Yankee Doodles are coming to town.

Uncle Sam is coming to save us again.
Yankee Doodles are coming to town.

SALVATORE
One regiment is how much in money?

LADY
It's enough to make Italy sunny . . .

ALL
Chiri biri bi!
What a lovely day.
Tra-la-laverers checks
Coming our way.
Everybody sing yippi-i yippi-ay.
Four hundred wonderful, beautiful, sociable
Lovable, huggable, happy, negotiable
Yankees are coming today.
Yankee Doodles are coming . . .
Yankee Doodles are coming to town!

I Wonder How She Looks

BRADDOCK
Man, San Forino was not any picnic to take . . .

LEWIS
We were bombed by those son of a B seventeens by mistake . . .

KARZINSKI
We rolled in at dawn

BRADDOCK
And you never heard so many cheers . . .

SMITH
I wonder how she looks after all these years.

LEWIS
No men in town . . .

SMITH
The army had all taken flight.

BRADDOCK
Four hundred women . . .

FLO BRADDOCK
It must have been lonely at night.

LEWIS
What the Germans had done to the town was a God-awful crime . . .

KARZINSKI
I wonder how she looks after all this time.

BRADDOCK
She must have put on weight.
Who wouldn't with all that pasta.

KARZINSKI
Sad how we men don't change
And women get old so much faster . . .

THE THREE
Where is her house?
Where can I phone?
Why don't they all go
And leave me alone?
How does she look?
How can I wait?

VITTORIO
That is the house of the great
Signora Campbell.

LADIES
Signora Campbell.

One More Walk Around the Garden

That old April yearning
Once more is returning
And I have a longing to wander.

The leaves may be falling
But April is calling
And the primroses beckon me yonder . . .

For one more walk around the garden,
One more stroll along the shore;
One more mem'ry I can dream upon
Until I dream no more.

For one more time perhaps the dawn will wait –
And one more prayer, it's not too late
To gather one more rose
Before I say goodbye and close
The garden gate.

That old urge is saying
It's time to go straying
Where no one but April can find me . . .

To try and recover
The heart of a lover
That I left lying somewhere behind me.

Just one more walk around the garden,
One more stroll along the shore;
One more mem'ry I can dream upon
Until I dream no more.

For one more time perhaps the dawn will wait –
And one more prayer, it's not too late
To gather one more rose
Before I say goodbye and close
The garden gate.

One more rose
Before I close
The garden gate.

All That He Wants Me To Be

Those men, they were so darling and so dear with me
I don't know why but somehow deep inside
I almost have the feeling Papa's here with me.
How I hope he will be satisfied.

I will smile at everybody sweetly;
Be a bit flirtatious but discreetly.
Top to bottom I will be completely
All that he wants me to be.

Everyone will notice how polite I'm;
Down to earth considering how bright I'm;
Life will have been worth it if tonight I'm
All that he wants me to be.

I will dance
Every dance;
I will whirl until I'm woozy
Just to hear them all enthusi-
Astically
Say to me
I am all that he wants me to be.

Everybody there to whom I speak will
Say that Papa has a lovely sequel.
I'll be hitherto without an equal
All that he wants me to be.

I will laugh at things that aren't funny.
Bite my tongue at sweetie pie and honey.
I'm determined I will be the one he
Wanted me always to be.

I'll enthrall
One and all;
Be so elegant and proper
That I hope wherever Papa
Is that he
Will agree
I am all that he wants me to be.

Carmelina

She stood there with my arms about her,
Didn't she? Didn't she?
And made me swear to never doubt her,
Didn't she? Didn't she?
She swore I'd never be without her,
Didn't she? Then didn't she
Slam the window in my face?

Last night she was a raging fire,
Wasn't she? Wasn't she?
A woman oozing with desire,
Wasn't she? Wasn't she?
But where there's smoke was there a liar?
Possibly and probably
Leading me a merry chase!

Carmelina,
Yes or no, are you mine?
Nod your head or decline.
Raise a flag. Paint a sign.
Carmelina.
Carmelina.
On my knees
Tell me please
Carmelina.
Carmelina,
See my hand how it shakes.
Every part of me aches.

Will you wait till
It is fatal,
Carmelina?
When will you awaken and discover
What I know in my heart is true:
I'm the one and only perfect lover,
Carmelina, for you.

Evil thoughts begin to ramble
As my nerves begin to fray.
Could it be that Eddie Campbell
Died to get away?

Could it be that Carmelina
Will not rest until my heart
Is a broken concertina
She has push-pulled apart?

Hurry, hurry and make your mind up,
Or the future I can't foretell.
One more day and I may well wind up
En route to a padded cell.
Tell me stay or then say farewell.

Carmelina,
Not farewell. No, not that.
Give your heart, not my hat.
Let me know where I'm at.
Carmelina.
Carmelina,
From the floor
I implore,
Carmelina.
Carmelina,
Say this thing we began
Wasn't made in Japan:
And you think it
Just a trinket,
Carmelina.

I can hear you pleading not to leave you.
Then I'm dropped from the clouds above.
Heaven help me if this is a preview,
Carmelina, of love.

The Image of Me

BRADDOCK
There's something about that child . . .

KARZINSKI
What a surprise!

SMITH
It isn't the way she smiles . . .

BRADDOCK
It's not her eyes.

KARZINSKI
It's nothing I've seen her do.

SMITH
Her laughter is not the clue.

BRADDOCK
Why is it when we met I knew?

THE THREE
It's nothing I'm able
To pinpoint or label;
It's subtle and vague as can be;
But facing it squarely,
Unbiased and fairly,
I'd swear she's the image of me.

There's no way to hide it.
Her features have tried it;
But apples fall close to the tree.
And only a father can see
She is the image of me.
Complete from the ground up
She wound up
The image of me.

SMITH
My God, they'd be hurt if they knew.

KARZINSKI
Why add to the grief they've been through.

BRADDOCK
A friendship so loyal
I just couldn't spoyal . . .

SMITH
But when I am near her
I look in the mirror.

KARZINSKI
The fact is we're two of a kind.

BRADDOCK
She's me and my mother combined.

SMITH
I'll never confess it.

KARZINSKI
They never will guess it.

BRADDOCK
They're blind.

KARZINSKI
And yet I suppose in a way
It isn't peculiar that they
Don't even suspect it.

SMITH
How could they detect it?

THE THREE
It's nothing outsiders can see.
But somehow or other
Instead of her mother,
She grew up the image of me.

Her face is misleading:
But breeding is breeding.
And she is like me to a T.
The chances were one out of three:
And she's the image of me;

KARZINSKI
The picture . . .

BRADDOCK
The photo . . .

SMITH
In toto . . .

THE THREE
The image of me.

continued . . .

Reprise

FLO

You'll tell me I'm crazy,
My eyesight is hazy,
You'll never believe it is true,
But sometimes I see a . . .
Expression on Gia
When she is the image of you.

BRADDOCK

You're balmy.

FLO

I mean it.

BRADDOCK

Hung over.

FLO

I've seen it.
It's funny you don't see it too.
It's nothing you did or can do,
But she is the image of you.

BRADDOCK

You think so?

FLO

Sincerely
She's really the image of you.

I'm a Woman

I'm a woman.
And I'm not a bit ashamed.
I'm a woman.
Does it matter if I'm named
Eleanora
Or signora?
They would look at me and know
In Bora-Bora
I'm a woman.

I'm a woman.
I am no one's little dear.
I'm a woman.
If they think I'm only here
To surrender
And be tender,
Then signor had better find
Another gender.
I'm a woman.

For who went off and left me in a mess?
Take a guess.
Start it with an 'M'.
Men!
M-E-N!
It was men
Three of them!
And what am I so broken up about?
Spell it out:
Start it with an 'L'.
Love!
With an 'L'!
As in hell!
And farewell!

I'm a woman.
I don't need to be a wife.
I'm a woman.
Let the others live a life
In a prison
Till they wizzen,
And be nothing but a mama,
This one isn'.
Let another
Be a mother . . .
I'm a woman . . .

Gia, Gia! Oh, my sweet Gia,
How can I leave you here on your own?
When I know that once you are married,
That you will never be more alone?
Men expect so much looking after.
Will he forget to look after you . . . ?

Carmelina, no!
Carmelina, go!
And keep thinking as you face
Every so-and-so:

I'm a woman.
Not a pinch on the behind.
I'm a woman.
I don't need to go and find
Some gorilla
With a villa
And live happ'ly ever after
With a killer.
I'm a woman.

I'm a woman.
Through with solitary grief.
I'm a woman.
And entitled to a brief
Indiscretion
Just to freshen
The monotony of Sunday
At confession.
I'm a woman.

continued . . .

And who will soon be freer than a bird?
Say the word.
Start it with an 'M'.
Me!
M-E. Me!
Free of men!
All of them!

And who can hear the music in the air,
Everywhere?
Here is how it goes:

World,
Here I come
With my thumb
To my nose!
I'm a woman.
And I've lost a lot of time.
I'm a woman.
You can tell them all that I'm
Starting over –
And, Jehovah,
I demand a bigger share of
All the clover.
I'm a woman.

I'm a woman!
I'm a woman!
Am I!

☆ DANCE A LITTLE CLOSER ☆

Robert Emmet Sherwood was a prizewinning American playwright who detached himself from close friends of the Algonquin set to write a series of solemn plays whose windy rhetoric has not worn very well. In 1939 his stage success *Idiot's Delight* was made into a movie by MGM, starring Clark Gable as an all-singing, all-dancing newspaper reporter and Norma Shearer as an adventuress posing as a blueblood. Supported by a comprehensive selection of archetypes including a honeymoon couple, a doctor, a communist, and a selection of chorus girls, Gable and Shearer played out a melodrama in which the principals are trapped in a hotel at an Alpine ski resort on the eve of a world war. The sequences added for the screen version, in which Gable and Shearer are seen to have had an earlier encounter while in vaudeville, was written by Sherwood himself. Today the production is remembered only for the twin débâcles of Gable's impersonation of a hoofer performing 'Putting On the Ritz', and Shearer's fake Russian accent embellished by a vast cigarette-holder and a blonde, helmet-like wig.

When Lerner was first contemplating the adaptation of the property into a musical, he spent some time awaiting the arrival in London of a certain well-known songwriter whose identity astonished me for its sheer incongruity in the context of Lerner's career. His explanation for the choice was 'He's today', a defence which struck me as being invalid on two counts. First, the writer in question was not so much today as yesterday, and second it shocked me that Lerner should have bothered with such a consideration. A far maturer and more typically Lerneresque comment on the need for topicality in the theatre was the one he made to his New York audience in 1971:

The theatre is not for the young. Nor is it for the old. It's not even for everybody. It's for people who like the theatre, whatever their age.

It so happened that the songwriter who was today never showed up, and so Lerner made other arrangements. His partnership with Charles Strouse, composer of *Annie*, resulted in *Dance a Little Closer*, an updated version of Sherwood's original in which the protagonists are flung together on the eve of a *third* world war. I happened to bump into Lerner at just the time when he was completing the libretto and he told me of the coincidence attending his application of the last full stop. The day he finished this wry comedy about the imminence of a world war, his radio told him that the Russians had invaded Afghanistan, a confluence of events so startling that he wondered playfully if his writing of the text had had some malign telepathic influence over the Kremlin. In the event, the third world war did not happen and neither did *Dance a Little Closer*. After a successful off-Broadway try-out, it transferred to a large, prestigious theatre and closed after one performance, a fate so brutal as to be stupefying to one who had heard a few of the songs and found them so acceptable.

The last time I ever saw Alan was at a London junket thrown for Bob Hope, who happened to be passing through. Alan was there with his wife who, as Liz Robertson, had starred in Norma Shearer's old role in *Dance a Little Closer*. I asked her if she thought the show had deserved to close after one night. She said, after a moment's thought, 'No', and Alan, overhearing, added, 'Does any show deserve to close after one night?' Let posterity supply the answer.

It Never Would've Worked

GIRLS
Ain't it sad.

HARRY
Call the hearse.

GIRLS
Just too bad.

HARRY
Even worse.

GIRLS
Fate is fate.

HARRY
Fate's a curse.

GIRLS
'Lucidate.

HARRY
I met a girl in Tallahassee.

GIRLS
Talla – who?

HARRY
We had a whirl in Tallahassee.

GIRLS
So, what's new?

HARRY
She was as hot as pompono in a pan.
I was her man.
Yeah, but I ran.

GIRLS
Sounds insane.

HARRY
It sure does.

GIRLS
Do explain.

HARRY
She was baa-baa-bad –
Three bags full.
It never would've worked.
She was in-
Satiable.
It never would've worked.
Three days – three nights –
I thought I would die.
It never would've worked
But it would've been fun to try.

GIRLS
What a shame.

HARRY
It was rough.

GIRLS
That's the game.

HARRY
Love is tough.
I met this trick in Tuscaloosa.

GIRLS
Tusca – what?

HARRY
We made it quick in Tuscaloosa.

GIRLS
Oo – that's hot.

HARRY
She had a body that they shouldn't permit.
Man, did we fit.
Yeah, but I split.

GIRLS
Not again.

HARRY
I repeat.

GIRLS
Oh, you men.

continued . . .

HARRY
She was sweet sixteen,
Minus one.
It never would've worked.
And her pa
Had a gun.
It never would've worked.
I decided
Better say goodbye.
It never would've worked
But it would've been fun to try.

GIRLS
My poor friend.

'Sthat the end?

Is there more?

HARRY
There is more.
I met this cat in Amarillo.

GIRLS
Oh, me-ow.

HARRY
An acrobat upon the pillow.

GIRLS
Wuh-wuh-wow!

HARRY
She was wild as any cat in the zoo.
What did I do?
Man, but I flew.

GIRLS
Why did you?

HARRY
Not my sort.

GIRLS
So you flew.

HARRY
She liked short and tall,
Male and fe –
It never would've worked.
Half the town
Had her key.
It never would've worked.
Sears and Roebuck
Envied her supply.
It never would've worked
But it would've been fun to try.

GIRLS AND HARRY
Never would've worked.
Never ever would've worked.

Happy, Happy New Year

HARRY AND GIRLS
(The Guests join in half-heartedly)
Should old acquaintance be forgot
And never brought to mind.
Should old acquaintance be forgot
For Auld Lang Syne.

HARRY
Bombs are in the air.
Boom-dee-boom-dee-ay.
Hear the sirens blare
Fun times on the way.
Here's to you and me
And ev'ry bombardier.
Have a Happy, Happy New Year.

Ain't it a sight!
See all the pretty planes
Up in the sky.
Maybe tonight
We ought to kiss the New
Year, too, goodbye.

God is in his Heav'n
Keepin' free and clear.
Have a Happy, Happy New Year.

(The music continues)

THE ROOM
Should old acquaintance be forgot
And never brought to mind.
Should old acquaintance be forgot
For Auld Lang Syne.

HARRY AND THE GIRLS
Bombs are in the air.
Boom-dee-boom-dee-ay.
Hear the sirens blare
Fun times on the way.
Here's to you and me
And ev'ry bombardier.
Have a Happy, Happy New Year.

THE ROOM (cont)
For Auld Lang Syne, my dear
For Auld Lang Syne.
We'll take a cup of kindness yet
For Auld Lang Syne.

HARRY AND THE GIRLS (cont)
Ain't it a sight!
See all the pretty planes
Up in the sky.
Maybe tonight
We ought to kiss the New
Year, too, goodbye.

God is in his Heav'n
Keeping' free and clear.
Have a Happy, Happy New Year.

No Man Is Worth It

No man is worth
All the lows you get
From the highs you get
From a man.

No man is worth
All the hopes you get
From the lies you get
From a man.

The strum of guitars
Till the strings start to snap;
The flight to the moon
Till the wings start to flap;

No man is worth it,
And I mean none.
Not even . . .
Well, maybe . . .
One

    In St Paul
Who had more on the ball
Than I saw on any other.
But fool that I am
For the one in the fam-
'Ly he wanted was my brother.

And that one in St Jo
Who unravelled me so
When he covered me over with kisses
There was nothing he lacked.
I mean nothing, in fact
He had everything – plus a missus.

No man is worth
All the burns you get
From the flame you get
From a man.

No man is worth
All the fun you get
From the game you get
From a man.

The torrid hellos
And the Arctic goodbyes;
The pillow you shared
Where you cry out your eyes;

No man is worth
Letting one tear fall;
No man is worth
All the seconal;
No man is worth it
Beneath the sun.
Not even . . .
No, not even
One . . .
　　　　(So far . . .)
Well, maybe . . .
Maybe
One.
　　　　(Wherever you are . . .!)

What Are You Gonna Do About It?

HALLOWAY

Celebrations?!
Fifty thousand Russians marching through the snow...
Celebrate, he says, celebrate.
NATO forces gath'ring on the field below.
While we hold our breath and wait.

And he calls it 'Games'...
Winter 'Games'...
Of all the names.
Another sort
Of winter sport...
Winter 'Games'.
Won't someone rise up and demand
They play on someone else's land?!

HARRY

What are you gonna do about it?
What are you gonna do about it?
Stand up on an alp and shout:
'Fellers go away.
Don't wanna play.'
And they'll turn around and all go home
Exactly as you hope.
And tomorrow I will be elected Pope.

HALLOWAY

We may be headin'
For Armageddon.
And all you do is laugh it off.
Would it be so funny if this land were yours?
Think of that, my friend. Stop and think.
What if Russian troops were pounding at your doors?
Would you calmly sip your drink?

How can you forget
That any threat
Is to us all?
It's genocide.
No one can hide
Behind a wall.
Is it games or something more?
Can you see this could be war?

HARRY

What are you gonna do about it?
What are you gonna do about it?
Pal, I'd like to help you out.
Have a small libation.
An assignation.
And remember that there still is time.
So don't procrastinate!
And be sure that your Blue Cross is up to date.

HALLOWAY
(In desperation)

I have a feeling
I'm speaking Spanish.

HARRY

You're coming through fine.

HALLOWAY

This poor world could vanish.
Blow up!
End up
Just another black hole in the blue.

HARRY

Maybe you're right,
But what are you gonna do?

A Woman Who Thinks I'm Wonderful

I like a woman who thinks I'm wonderful,
Wonderful,
All the time.

I like a woman convinced a prize am I,
Wise am I,
All the time.

Someone who makes no demands on me;
Seen but seldom heard.
Eager to lavish her hands on me
When I give the word.

For I like a woman who thinks I'm wonderful,
Wonderful,
All the time.

But I don't like a woman
Who broods in the house,
Brings her moods in the house,
No, I don't like that at all.
Who annoys me with question after question
Which gives me a case of indigestion . . .
That's for lesser men,
Not a specimen
Like me.
For you see

I like a woman who thinks I'm glorious,
Glorious,
All the time.

I like a woman who feels impressed with me,
Blessed with me,
All the time.

Docile and sweet she should be with me,
That and nothing more.
Should she by chance disagreee with me;
Liebchen, there's the door.

For I like a woman who thinks I'm wonderful,
All the time.
All the time.
Not for just an hour,
Not for just a day,
Not for just a night,
But all the time.

There's Never Been Anything Like Us

CYNTHIA
I'm leaving. I'm leaving.
Don't stop me. I'm going.
I don't know why I spent the night.

HARRY
It wasn't because it
Was raining or snowing.
You know why and know I am right.
We're something rare. Something unique.
And I know well whereof I speak.

I've been around
I've had my share
Of tangled arms
And tangled hair
I've touched a cheek
That left me weak
With appetite.
But there's never been anything like us!
There's never been anything like us!
There never was anything like us last night.

I've tasted lips
Like burning sun.
Looked into eyes
And come undone.
I've been obsessed.
I've been caressed
Clear out of sight.
But there's never been anything like us!
There's never been anything like us!
There never was anything like us last night.

No fool am I.
No fool are you.
You were there
And felt it, too.
I've seen the world
And had my fill
Of every throb
And every thrill.
I've had it all
From wall to wall.
But you and I
Are something more
Than any world
I knew before.

I kissed you once
And knew it then:
That there's never been anything like us!
No, there's never been anything like us!
And there'll never be anything like us again.

CYNTHIA
I don't want to hear any of that.

HARRY
You have to.

CYNTHIA
No . . . !
The way to my heart
Is through the lobby of the Ritz,
With a diamond this big
That my finger just fits.
The way to my heart
Is on a Concorde through the sky.
Can you manage all that?

HARRY
No.

CYNTHIA
Then goodbye.

HARRY
No, stay with me.
Please stay with me.
Spend each night
And day with me.

I've seen the world
And had my fill
Of every throb
And every thrill.
I've had it all
From wall to wall.
But you and I
Are something more
Than any world
I knew before.

I kissed you once
And knew it then:
That there's never been anything like us!
No, there's never been anything like us!
And there'll never be anything like us again.

Another Life

I like you, I do, Harry.
I like you a lot.
You're what I want, Harry.
But what I need, you're not.
I know about love, Harry.
I know what it's worth.
I want the moon, Harry.
You got the earth.

The iron bed;
The noisy hall:
Where every sound
Comes through the wall.
The draughty room;
The mended clothes;
The window box
Where nothing grows...
Another life!
I want another life...

With satin sheets
Beneath my skin;
A maid who brings
My breakfast in.
And anywhere
I ever go
I'm someone who
They want to know.
Another life!
I want another life!

Someone rich may come along
And make a queen of me.
Maybe there'll be three or four,
But I don't care
As long as there

Are closets filled
With clothes to wear;
With hopes to burn
And dreams to spare.
I want to live so near the sky,
So high I'll never
Hear another train go by.
Another life!
There's got to be
Another life
Somewhere for me.

Why Can't the World?

Why can't the world go and leave us alone
To enjoy this perfect day;
Passing the carefree time away,
All on our own?

Why can't the world and its mess
Go and change its address
To a far-off star somewhere;
Leaving us here to dance on air,
Free and alone?

Let them rant and roar.
Throw a little war.
Why should you and I attend?
Why not hang a sign
Out there on the line
Saying 'Go away world'?
Hey, World,

We're the luckiest, lovingest, caringest couple
That life has ever known.
Why can't the world leave us alone?

He Always Comes Home to Me

CYNTHIA
Experience.

(Sings)

He flatters, he flatters;
Flirtation's his meat.
He struts and he glitters
Like a peacock in heat.
But somehow, whatever the reason may be,
He always comes home to me.

HARRY
You're positive?

CYNTHIA
You'll see.
He always comes home to me.

He postures, he poses,
He dallies, he baits.
He gathers his roses
But never pollinates.
And be it because of defeat or ennui,
He always comes home to me.

HARRY
You're sure of that?

CYNTHIA
Mais oui.
He always comes home to me.

It inflates his morale
To appear
'N homme fatale,
Which he does with discreet finesse.
But I think he would run
Like a deer
If someone
By mistake ever said yes.

So he'll woo her, disarm her;
His wit captivates.
A consummate charmer
Who never consummates.
For when he's exhausted his bright repartee,
He always comes home to me.

HARRY
Not a doubt?

CYNTHIA
Not a qualm.

HARRY
In the bag . . .

CYNTHIA
In my palm.
He enjoys smoke without the fire.

HARRY
Always you . . .

CYNTHIA
I can tell
Women know
Very well
Duty and guilt from desire.

So I smile at him brightly
And never complain;
And hold on so lightly
He never feels the rein.
And ergo because he believes he is free,
He always comes home to me.

From Cairo and Tel Aviv, Bonn and Bombay;
From Saigon and Moscow and even L.A.;
From Peking and Paris, Camp David and Rome,
He always comes home to me.
He always comes home to me.

>(Winkler leaves the ice with the
>Contessa on his arm and they exit
>together. Harry eyes Cynthia with
>an amused look. Cynthia never loses
>her composure)

CYNTHIA
From Florence, Milano and *old* Napoli
He always comes home to me.

I've Got a New Girl

DELIGHTS
Somethin's happened to
That old wreck
That we knew.

It just proves to you
Miracles
Do come true.

DELIGHTS
We got an old friend
That's now a new friend;
Rejuvenated
And renovated.

Love is the surgeon
That did him over;
Replaced the wrinkles
With lots of twinkles.

(Harry enters)

HARRY	DELIGHTS
I got a new girl. I got a new girl. I got a smile now That shines a mile now.	Will you look at him? Dapper Dan! Sunny Jim! Get that jaunty air, Struttin' like Fred Astaire.

HARRY
I ring the bell, the elevator
Comes up in a flash.
In every suit that I put on
I always find some cash.
When the rain begins to pour –
(click)
A taxi's at the door.
For

HARRY	DELIGHTS
She's my piece of eight, Hole in one, Tax rebate.	He's got a new girl. He's got a new girl. From feelin' no good He's feelin' so good.
She's my lucky break, Rabbit's foot, Bank mistake.	He's got a new girl. He's got a new girl. The state that he's in – She is the reason.

HARRY
I'm singin' all day through
Inka dinka dinka doo.

DELIGHTS
And so, no, thank you, Paine and Weber,
He is doin' fine.

HARRY
I even catch the waiter's eye
When I go out to dine.
Got a new inamorta . . .

ELAINE
What is that?

ALL
It means he's (I) got a
New girl!
I (he's) got a new girl!
Mine! All mine!

DELIGHTS
Never seen that feller ever dance before.
Now he's a buck and wing Baryshnikov
Upon that floor.
And tomorrow every muscle will be good and sore!

ALL
I (he's) got a new girl!
I (he's) got a new girl!
Mine! All mine!

Dance a Little Closer

Dance a little closer,
Like it used to be.
I need someone warm inside my arms,
So please don't whirl away from me.
Dance a little closer,
We don't have to speak.
I just want to feel you near
And softly hear
You breathing on my cheek.

While the music's playing,
Can't we both pretend
This is not a song for just a moment
But a song without an end?
Dance a little closer,
Till the morning light,
I don't want to feel alone tonight.

There's Always One You Can't Forget

There's always one you can't forget.
There's always one you can't forget.
One who roams around your mind . . .
One you cannot leave behind . . .

Other smiles seem painted on.
Other nights are here and gone.
Other loves become a blur.
In other arms, you think of her.

Across a room, along the street
You always hope perhaps you'll meet.
Why? Why won't it die?
You try and yet
You can't forget.
You can't forget.
You can't forget.

Other smiles seem painted on.
Other nights are here and gone.
Other loves become a blur.
In other arms, you think of her.

Across a room, along the street
You always hope perhaps you'll meet.

Why? Why won't it die?
You try and yet
You can't forget.
You can't forget.
You can't forget.

Homesick

TRIO

Homesick! Homesick!
I'm homesick as can be.
I got an ache inside
About an ocean wide
For my little home across the sea.

BEBE

Three Mile Island!
Never thought I'd miss it so.
Daddy says that half the folks
Have moved away;
And the meadow by the fact'ry that
Was green is turnin' grey.
But I sure would wake up smilin'
To be home in Three Mile Islan'
In Pennsylvan-i-ay
In the good old USA.

TRIO

I'm so homesick! Homesick!
Plain homesick as can be.
I'd give up sex for good
Gee, if I only could
See my little home across the sea.

ELAINE

Sweet Palm Desert!
On the San Andreas Fault.
Every year we get more land
And never pay,
'Cause every year the highway moves
An inch or two away.
What I'd give to be there lyin'
In the blazin' sunlight fryin'
In Californ-i-ay
In the good old USA.

TRIO

I'm so homesick! Homesick!
Real homesick as can be,
I'd give my body for
A glimpse of that old door
Of my little home across the sea.

SHIRLEY

Love Canal!
Never heard a sweeter name.
Sure the water now and then
Comes out shellac;
And a while ago the birds went south
And none of 'em come back.
But God would I be happy
Just to see my Ma and Pappy
And to hear Niagara fall
In the greatest State of all.

TRIO

Man oh man how it would feel
Just to eat a decent meal;
To be sittin' up till dawn
With a porno movie on.
Oh, I'm so homesick! Homesick!
Homesick for my Home Sweet Home!

Mad

I'm mad at this asylum that they call human life.
I'd like to storm the halls of power armed with a knife.
I'm mad at anybody who is smiling and glad.
I'm mad at you and mad at me and mad that I'm mad.

> GIRLS
> *(Sotto voce)*

He's mad about her.
He's mad about her.

> HARRY

I'm mad at every mountain and I've had it with snow.
I'm up to here with picture books of Mar'lyn Monroe.
I'm mad I'm in a data bank, a digital dot.
I'd like to see computer makers tortured and shot.

> GIRLS
> *(Sotto voce)*

He's mad about her.
He's mad about her.

> HARRY

I'm mad at Norway.
Why, I don't know.
I've never been there
And I won't go.

I'm mad at money.
Which I ain't got.
I'm mad at Frenchmen.
But who is not?

> GIRLS
> *(Sotto voce)*

He's got it bad for her.
He's really mad for her.

> HARRY

By now the German language makes my temperature soar.
I'm only ever happy when I'm slamming a door.
I'm mad, exasperated and I'm climbing the wall;
And most of all I'm mad it doesn't matter at all
That I am mad! Mad! Mad!

GIRLS
Boy, he is mad, mad, mad
. . . About her.

HARRY
I'm mad at being told I have to wait for the beep.
I'm furious that Meyer Lansky died in his sleep.
I'm mad the Japanese have made whatever I own.
I wish to hell the Romanovs were back on the throne.

GIRLS
He's mad about her.
He's mad about her.

HARRY
I'm mad at being told I have to stay home unless
I am a paid-up member of Amer'can Express.
I've had it up to here with turning on the T.V.
And finding haemorrhoidal tissue staring at me.

GIRLS
He's mad about her.
He's mad about her.

HARRY
I'm mad at places
I can't pronounce.
I'm sick of bosoms
That never bounce.
I'm mad at waiting
For every plane.
Fly Alitalia,
You go by train.

GIRLS
He's got the hots for her.
He's tied in knots for her.

HARRY
I hate the IRA, the KGB and MX.
I'm sick to death of books that take the joy out of sex.
Whoever made Atari should be hung by his thumbs.
I'm mad I have to eat so many Rolaids and Tums
From being mad! Mad! Mad!

GIRLS
Boy, he is mad, mad, mad
. . . About her.

I Don't Know

BOYLE
I don't know.
I don't know.
It's a strange predicament I'm in.
I don't know.
I don't know.
How can loving ever really be a sin?
My conscience is in a tangle can
Someone who's anglecan
Take all the rules he has
Lived by and defy them?
Yet in a world so precarious,
Someone says: Marry us,
No matter who they are
How can I deny them?

HARRY
I agree.

GIRLS
So do we.

HARRY
(To the girls)
You shut up.
No one asked for your advice.

(To Boyle)

Like I said,
Go ahead.

BOYLE
You'd proceed?

HARRY
Yes, indeed.
Let 'em wed.

BOYLE
(Face knotted)
I don't know.
I don't know.

SHIRLEY
He don't know.
There he goes with that again.

HARRY
Let him think.

ELAINE
(Sotto voce to girls)
Giv'm a drink.

BOYLE
Can a wedding be performed with only men?
Religiously I'd be vilified
Surely I will if I'd
Sanction a fruitless
And unproductive mating.

ELAINE
Hell, what's he all in a sweat about?
Can't he forget about
Sex and get on with
Champagne and celebrating?

HARRY
(To the girls)
Zip it up.
Zip it up.
This is not for your prehistoric minds.

ELAINE
(To girls)
He knows where
He can go.

BOYLE
(To Harry)
You say yes?
Acquiesce?

HARRY
I don't know.

*(The Contessa appears on the balcony
and comes down the stairs)*

Why not ask our dear Contessa?
She's no clergical professor
But I'd like to know what she would have to say.

BOYLE
(To the Contessa)
In our perilous condition . . .
Charles and Edward asked permission,
No, entreated me to marry them today.

CONTESSA
Marry?!

(She laughs).

BOYLE
If it were you,
What would you do?

CONTESSA
(Amused)
I don't know.
I don't know.
I can see it's hard to say: Of course.
Then again
They are men
And they'll stray and soon be suing for divorce.

BEBE
Let's leave it to the majority.

CONTESSA
I'm no authority.

HARRY
(To Bebe)
Neither are you.

BEBE
Harry Baby, that goes double.

CONTESSA
Poor boys, it will be a blow to them
If you say no to them.

BOYLE
But by the canon I'd
Be inviting trouble.

HARRY
That ain't good.

BOYLE
But I would.
Why must right and righteous be so far apart?

(Charles and Edward enter)

CHARLES
Reverend Boyle,
Have you thought?

continued . . .

BOYLE
I don't know.
If I can.
If I ought.

(Harry, Boyle, the girls, and the Contessa simultaneously:)

GIRLS	CONTESSA
I don't see why he's afraid to do	It's absolutely bizarre to me.
What he is paid to do!	But Yankees are to me.
Marry people.	Let them if they want to.
	Why not? Why not?

BOYLE	HARRY
Please don't believe I'm forsaking you!	I think he's caught in the middle of
I'm truly aching to	Life's common riddle of
Do what you ask but I	How can you do what you
Fear I'm not allowed.	Know you're not supposed to.

CHARLES AND EDWARD
Never mind.

ELAINE
I could cry.

CHARLES AND EDWARD
Never mind.

BEBE
So could I.

HARRY
(Seeing Cynthia, to the boys)
No, don't go. One voice has not been heard.

(The boys wait)
(To Cynthia)

Did you know . . . ?

(She restrains him with her hand and comes down the stairs)

CYNTHIA
I didn't miss a word.

HARRY
Then tell me how does it strike you? –
A well-born Londoner like you . . .
When someone isn't afraid to be
What he was made to be? –
Miss Brookfield-Bailey, what would you do?

Anyone Who Loves

Anyone who loves,
People anywhere;
Anyone who loves,
They deserve a prayer.

(Bitterly)

We're only living by the hour
While the sages with the power
Play their game of peace and war
With no shred of pity for
Anyone who lives . . .
Anyone who loves.

HARRY
Couldn't they be blessed?

GIRLS
Yeah, why couldn't they?

HARRY
(To Boyle)
Just a word or two
Maybe you could say.

We're here surrounded by the night
While God plays idiot's delight.
Why can't there be a ray of sun
That shines on anyone
Who loves?
There ought to be a ray of sun
That shines on anyone
Who loves.

Auf Wiedersehen

Auf Wiedersehen.
Auf Wiedersehen.
Perhaps one day
We'll meet again.
For all good things must end;
And so must we, sweet friend.

Auf Wiedersehen.
Auf Wiedersehen.
It's time to sing
The sad refrain
Of love that's lost the spell.
Au Revoir, Adios, Farewell.

But when we're far away,
Think well of me, I pray;
Remember all the joy I brought to you.
The places you have been;
The circles you were in . . .
All the rich
And élite
I allowed
You to meet.

Auf Wiedersehen.
Auf Wiedersehen.
Though filled with pain
Am I . . .
Goodbye. Goodbye.

She wouldn't keep her place;
Or button up her face.
I warned her not to pry but pry she would.
She wouldn't call a truce
To all her silly schmoose.
She is there
To amuse
Not annoy
Or accuse.

>   (He has finished the note and inserted a few
>   bills. He turns back to Mueller all sweetness
>   and charm and hands him the note)

So make it plain.
Auf Wiedersehen.
Though tears may stain
My tie . . .
Goodbye. Goodbye. Goodbye.

I Never Want to See You Again

If I see you coming one star-crossed day,
I'll run like hell till I'm far away.
If I close my eyes and I find you there,
I'll get out the cards and play Solitaire.

I never want to see you again,
Turn off the light and see you again.
I never want to hear you again,
Wake up at night and hear you again.

I never want to remember you
Or wonder where you are;
Or feel the ache in me lead me to
The nearest, friendly bar.

And I never want to see me again by the shore with you;
Or beside a fire finding out what living is for with you.
No, I never want to imagine me evermore with you.
Nevermore! Nevermore!
I don't ever want to see you again,
I never want to see you again.
No, I never want to see you again.
I never want to see you again.

And I never want to see you on some desert isle with me;
In a mountain lodge putting passion back into style with me;
And I nevermore want to see you sharing your smile with me;
Nevermore! Nevermore!
I don't ever want to see you again,
I never want to see you again.
No, I never want to see you again.
I never want to see you again.

Top of the World

On top of the world . . .
That's where I told them
That I wanted to be;
That's where I said one day
They'd find little me:
On top of the world . . .
On top of the world . . .
On top of the world . . .
That's where I knew
That I'd awaken one day . . .
Where all the stars
Are only inches away . . .
Gotta man –
Millionaire –
Look for me
Way up there
On the top of the world.

Feelin' fine.
Feelin' flush.
Livin' high.
Livin' lush
On the top of the world.

Plat'num clouds
Drifting by;
Diamond stars
Light the sky.
I've got it all.
I'm at the ball.

No more dives.
No more jobs.
Goodbye, losers,
Hello snobs.
There's no sight equal to
That luxurious view
On the top of the world.

See my eyes
Burning bright.
Hear me squeal
With delight:
I'm on top of the world.

Silver flakes
On my nose;
Ermine snow
'Round my toes
On the top of the world.

What is love?
All a fake.
Fools can dream,
I'm awake.
And in the mood
For altitude.

What is love?
Pork and beans
Ham on rye
Canned Sardines
Hey, Maitre d'
Make room for me.

Made my bed.
Here I lie
Watching Santa
Jingle by
My deluxe pleasure dome
That I call Home Sweet Home
On the top of the world.

On my gold crested throne . . .

Here I am . . . all alone . . .

On the top . . . on the top . . .

☆ MY MAN GODFREY ☆

At the time he died, Lerner was working on a new libretto for a musical version of the 1936 comedy produced by Universal, *My Man Godfrey*. One of the best of the satirical comedies turned out by the industry in the period, *My Man Godfrey* told the story of how a collection of rich New York nitwits organize a Scavenger Hunt, a little upper-crust foible defined by the heroine in these terms: 'A scavenger hunt is just like a treasure hunt, except in a treasure hunt you find something you want and in a scavenger hunt you find things you don't want, and the one who wins gets a prize, only there really isn't any prize, it's just the honour of winning, because all the money goes to charity if there's any money left over, but then there never is.' While the rest of the competitors bring back to the Waldorf-Ritz Hotel a succession of goldfish, goats and mangles, the heroine brings back 'a forgotten man', a prize exhibit of the Great Depression, whom she finds in a rubbish dump under the Brooklyn Bridge.

The rest of the plot is fairly predictable. The rich nitwit, played with dizzy pathos by Carole Lombard, falls for the handsome tramp, played with great sardonic charm by William Powell, and has him installed as the family butler, in which post he displays a Jeevesian insouciance which enables him to save the family fortunes by his infallible mastery of the Stock Exchange, a skill which betrays the aristocratic nature of his origins. The story, which opens with such bitter recriminations against the mindless rich, is eventually deflated by the tameness of its ending, which conforms to the Hollywood tradition by having the chastened rich open a luxurious club on the site of the rubbish dump, thus giving employment to all the butler's deadbeat friends.

Working from the original screenplay by Eric Hatch and Morrie Ryskind, Lerner had completed his groundplan for the libretto by organizing the story into fifty sequences, several of which he had broken down into sub-divisions. He had also completed a few of the lyrics, at which point he died and the project was shelved. It is hard to conceive any circumstances in which it might now be completed, let alone produced, but in view of the unique insight the surviving manuscript gives into Lerner's meticulous working methods, it seemed to the editor judicious to include all there exists of *My Man Godfrey* in a volume otherwise devoted exclusively to the words of songs.

Outline

Note: Where songs are definite, they are indicated.

As a theatrical device, Godfrey from time to time talks to the audience. One of the purposes is that in the film, a good deal of the action in the first half happens *to* Godfrey, rather than he being the instigator. Having him talk to the audience from time to time is a way of keeping his role front and centre.

1. City Dump. Meet Godfrey. Meet Irene. Cornelia gets pushed into the ashes. Godfrey agrees to go to the Waldorf-Ritz with Irene.

2. Waldorf-Ritz. Meet the father (Bullock). Meet the mother and her protégé, Carlo.

3. Kitchen. Molly the maid. Godfrey arrives.

4. The kitchen bell rings. Godfrey goes first to the mother. Cornelia does not let him in. Then to Irene.

5. Seen by father coming out of Irene's room.

6. The Process Server. Cornelia broke windows.

7. Irene and the horse in the library.

8. Living Room that evening. Meet the whole family. Run-in with Cornelia.

9. Sisters have fight over Godfrey.

10. Father complains about money.

11. Irene has crying fit.

12. Kitchen scene. Molly and Godfrey.

13. Godfrey's Room. Irene comes in.

14. The Living Room. Afternoon. Irene having a tea party.

15. Tommy Gray arrives at the tea party.

16. Irene announces her engagement to Charlie.

17. Godfrey makes a date with Tommy.

18. Breakfast next morning.

19. Godfrey and Mr Bullock. Bullock admits he has money trouble.

20. Restaurant with Godfrey and Tommy.

21. Cornelia appears in the restaurant.

22. Scene between Godfrey and Cornelia.

23. Godfrey starts to drink.

24. The Kitchen. Irene brings flowers. Scene between Irene and Molly.

25. Godfrey comes in drunk.

26. The Living Room. Carlo and the mother. Irene comes in crying.

27. Kitchen. Cornelia hiding.

28. Cornelia plants the pearls.

29. Godfrey serves dinner and drops the dishes.

30. Cornelia tells about the missing pearls.

31. Cornelia calls the police.

32. Next scene. Interrogated by police.

33. Godfrey's Room.

34. City Dump. Godfrey and Tommy.

35. Newspaper clipping. Find out Irene and Cornelia have been in Europe to get over Irene's engagement.

36. Living Room. Family all together.

37. Kitchen. Godfrey tells Irene he is leaving.

38. Living Room. Cornelia tries to make a date with Godfrey.

39. Irene faints.

40. Godfrey takes her up to the bedroom and puts her in the shower.

41. Living Room. Mr Bullock comes in very depressed.

42. Mr Bullock takes Carlo outside and knocks him through the window.

43. Cornelia enters. Mr Bullock tells the family they are broke.

44. Godfrey comes to the rescue.

45. The Kitchen. Godfrey says goodbye to Molly.

46. Living Room. Irene finds out Godfrey's gone, etc.

47. The City Dump Café.

48. Godfrey's Office.

49. Irene arrives.

50. The Mayor enters.

THE END

Scene 1
City Dump:

In the background can be seen the 59th Street Bridge and the lights of Queens across the river.

On the extreme side of the stage are two or three large containers of garbage. There are a few makeshift shacks. Behind them is the road. It is night.

The overture does not come to an end, but blends into underscoring as the curtain rises. Six to eight men in shabby clothes are on stage. Godfrey is present but he is in the shadows with his back to the audience. Two or three men are picking through the garbage containers, find nothing, turn to the others on stage and shrug their shoulders in despair. Those present sing:

Garbage isn't what it used to be.
Garbage has become a tragedy:
No discarded caviar,
Not a half-smoked good cigar;
Hardly worth the trouble
Rummaging through the rubble.

Garbage has become a sheer disgrace;
Not a tasty morsel any place.
Never see no
Drop of vino,
No bonbons from Paree;
Garbage isn't what it used to be.

When garbage used to be debris,
Not this trashy haberdashery;
Not a dented bowler hat,
Slightly worn out silk cravat;
Nothing you can use now;
Heels and soles don't have shoes now.

Since that jolly day in Twenty-nine
Garbage has been in a sad decline.
Savile Row made
Now looks home-made
Flies come down to the knee;
Garbage isn't what it used to be.

> *(The music continues. Godfrey turns and looks out at the audience for a moment and then rises and addresses them.)*

Got a job?
Got a job?
All you elegant looking people out there –
Got a job?
Any job,
Doing anything any place anywhere?

Got a job?
Got a job?
I mean you in the second row in cashmere –
Got a job?
Got a job?
You there, lady, with all the rocks in each
    ear.
Try and figure it out, dear friends, if you
    can
And you'll see that according to nature's
    plan
That the difference between an ord'nary
    man
And a slob
Is a job.

Of course you're fifty years too late.
Up here it's Nineteen-thirty-four.
But there might come a time
When you'll need one even more.

Twenty hours on the street
We're selling apples every day,
But no one wants the wretched fruit,
So we're giving them away.
Let them fall.
Take them all.

*(Small balloons in the shape of apples
fall from the ceiling all over the
audience.)*

And when they're rotten to the skin
We'll find them stinking up the bin.

GODFREY AND ALL
For
Garbage isn't what it used to be.
It's an insult to democracy;
Not a cuff-link not a stud
Just a mess of muck and mud.
One requires a strainer
To go through a container.

Garbage has become a mortal sin,
Not at all the way a bin has been.
Drop a pig in
He will dig in
With luxurious glee.
Garbage isn't what it used to be.

*(The music reaches a climax and then
continues.)*

ALL
Got a job . . .   Got a job . . .
Got a job . . .   Got a job . . .

During the above a limousine arrives on
the road behind them and Cornelia Bullock
and a vapid-looking young man, both in
evening dress, make their way through
the rubbish.

GODFREY
Got a job . . .

CORNELIA
(To Godfrey – interrupting)
Would you like to make five dollars?

She offers Godfrey $5 to go with her to
the Waldorf-Ritz where there is a
scavenger hunt in progress. The first one
to bring in a forgotten man wins. During
the dialogue Irene appears from the road
and makes her way to stage level. She is
furious with Cornelia for getting there
first. It was she who told her about this
particular City dump, but her taxi got
stuck in traffic. Cornelia's reaction is 'too
bad'. Godfrey refuses Cornelia in no
uncertain terms and backs her into an
ashpile, much to Irene's delight. Cornelia
and her friend leave in the limousine.
    Irene is deliriously happy that Godfrey
refused and that Cornelia ended up in the
ashes. She tells Godfrey that Cornelia is
her sister and always wins. Godfrey asks
exactly what is a scavenger hunt, and
Irene explains – but that she would not for
a minute ask Godfrey to come with her.
Godfrey, half amused by her and half
angry at Cornelia, agrees to go with her.
During the last bit of dialogue, the scene
changes to

Scene 2
The Ballroom at the Waldorf-Ritz:
Upstage is a platform on which stands the Master of the Hunt. Downstage, people are ballroom dancing in period style to the music of 'Dancin' My Blues Away'. There is a small bar at one side of the stage. Mr Bullock and a friend are standing there drinking. Godfrey and Irene get lost in the shuffle trying to make their way upstage.

Mrs Bullock comes on stage with a goat and her protégé, Marco.

At the end of the number, the platform with Godfrey and Irene. Irene is pronounced the winner. Godfrey is asked to say a few words. He says his few words to a reprise of 'Garbage Isn't What It Used To Be', the title being changed to 'Garbage Is Where I Would Rather Be' with appropriate lyrics.

He completes his statement and leaves the platform. Irene is horrified that she has been so insensitive. Cornelia enters with another forgotten man – too late.

Colloquy between Godfrey and Irene downstage. During the dialogue, Irene suddenly stands stockstill and stares at Godfrey. From the orchestra comes a few seconds of Max Steiner romantic background music indicating 'LOVE'. She wants to do something to make it up to Godfrey. He could use a job. Does he know how to butl'? He has never tried but is sure he would be able to. She gives him their address and some money to buy a uniform and he exits happily. Irene is delirious. The music of 'Dancin' My Blues Away' strikes up again. Someone asks her to dance. She dances a few steps then sings the refrain:

No more rain tumblin' down on me;
Not a sign of any frown on me;
I'm dancin' my blues away.

Bluebirds chirp on the sill for me;
Got no piper with a bill for me;
I'm dancin' my blues away.

Jehovah
Move ova;
Make room in the sky.
I'm ridin' so high;
My spirits soar
Right off the floor.

Hear them horns how they play for me,
Makin' life a holiday for me,
I'm dancin' my blues away.

At the end of the song, Marco appears out of the crowd dressed in ballet workout clothes. He starts leaping and practising as the scene changes to

Scene 3
The Living Room of the Bullock Mansion:
Marco continues his tour jete-ing as Molly the maid and Godfrey, in immaculate butler's attire, enter. Molly is showing him the house and pays no attention to Marco. Marco asks if breakfast is ready. Molly says it is and he leaps across the stage and exits left (or right). Molly identifies him as Mrs Bullock's protégé. Godfrey comes downstage to inform the audience that he later discovered that Marco is Mrs Bullock's third protégé in four months. One was a composer – a radical who wrote violent anti-capitalist songs which Mrs Bullock found enchanting until she discovered what they meant. Another was a painter who got drunk one night and started to paint Mr Bullock. And for the last three weeks it has been Marco, whom Mrs Bullock is convinced will be the next Pavlova.

Mr Bullock comes in on his way to the dining room for breakfast. He meets Godfrey. The doorbell is heard ringing and Molly enters to tell Mr Bullock there is a process server at the door. Cornelia got a little frisky the night before and threw rocks through some windows on Fifth Avenue. Before Mr bullock can go out to meet the process server, Molly also tells him there is a man in the kitchen who wants $50 and his horse back. Irene rode the horse up the steps the night before and left it in the library all night. Godfrey offers to get the horse, but Molly says she will take care of it.

Mrs Bullock enters on her way to the dining room. She is in a négligée. She cannot find the door to the dining room and thinks Godfrey is a dinner guest who has arrived too early. Godfrey explains who he is and aims her at the dining room.

Irene enters in a négligée, looking ravishing. Scene between Godfrey and Irene in which she tells him how exciting it is for her to have a protégé. She makes him sit on the sofa beside her. At one moment she looks at him and Max Steiner is heard again. Godfrey tries to bring a little reason into the conversation. He must not be seen sitting in the living room talking to her. Irene says she will come to his room – which he also tells her she must not do.

Cornelia enters, recognizes Godfrey and lets it be known he will regret taking this job. She and Irene start one of their fights and they fight their way into the dining room.

(It would be jolly if during this scene Molly could be seen on the other side of the arch that leads to the living room, ushering a horse through the hall.)

Molly returns when Cornelia and Irene have exited and asks Godfrey if he now would like to leave. Song by Godfrey. (Unknown.) At the end of the song, people enter one by one and take up positions in the room until there is a complete tableau of a cocktail party . . . which then comes to life.

Some People

Some people, there are some people with
    a heart of steel;
Some people never feel things that other
    people feel;
Others may long to be near them;
Some people never know;
If others told them so
They would never hear them.

Some people walk around foolishly with
    blinkers on;
Some people never care till their chance to
    care has gone;
One day they'll wake and discover
That other people
Who used to weep'll
No longer shed a tear;
And love sailed away and left them on the
    pier.

GODFREY

Some people, there are some people who
    will never learn;
Some people love to fall off the bridge of
    no return;
Let girlish passion bestir them;
There's nothing you can say
To make them go away.
It would take Attila to deter them.
Some people can't resist any time
    rejection calls;
Some people have a mad urge to bang
    their head on walls;
Others may try to persuade them
That endless moping
And hopeless hoping
Can be an awful bore;
But some people seem to love it more and
    more.

Miss Hilary Bacon of Beacon Hill

Miss Hilary Bacon of Beacon Hill
Was a Back Bay bimbo with looks to kill,
Which she did with consummate lethal skill
Till one day I picked up the marriage quill
And wed Miss Bacon of Beacon Hill.
A bloody fool, yes, a stupid pill,
I wed Miss Bacon of Beacon Hill.

In three long years I had had my fill
And stared with interest at the window sill,
My nerves spaghetti and my patience nil.
I gave her every penny in the till
And fled the Alcatraz of Beacon Hill.
I did my damndest to imbibe until
There'd be nothing left in Scotland to distill;
If you pushed me gently I was apt to spill.
Till one day it happened – God and what a
     thrill,
I forgot Miss Bacon up in Beacon Hill.

Miss Hilary Bacon of Beacon Hill;
I wish no harm and I wish no ill,
But if I heard she'd fallen off Beacon Hill,
I wouldn't be upset.

Happy Thanksgiving

Happy Thanksgiving!
Happy Thanksgiving!
But for what nobody knows
But it's Thanksgiving,
And we're still living,
And so why not say
Here's to one more day;
To keep praying
Go to sleep praying
That we'll hear a dinner bell;
Who knows, it could happen;
Ha! Ha! Ha! But what the Hell?

Happy Thanksgiving!
Happy Thanksgiving!
For this dandy year we've had;
Nothing forthcoming
But some grand slumming;
Who could ask for more
To be thankful for;
With hope reeling
We've enough feeling
For our fellow men to say,
May John D. Rockefeller, Vanderbilt
And J.P. Morgan have a
Happy, Happy Thanksgiving Day.

Happy Thanksgiving!
Happy Thanksgiving!
Turkey time is here again.
Happy Thanksgiving!
Happy Thanksgiving!
So let's hear a word
For the well-stuffed bird;
There's rum pudding,
Cake and plum pudding,
Candied yams two storeys high.
Today the sky above will have
To do without the pie.

Happy Thanksgiving!
Happy Thanksgiving!
Happy gobbler gobbling day!
It's that bulging,
Self-indulging
Day to celebrate
With a piled up plate.
Our forefathers,
Days of yore fathers,
Were they with us they would say,
Come gather round, 'tis time for grace,
To thank the Lord and fill thy face
And have a Happy Thanksgiving Day.

It Was You Again

It was you again,
It was you again;
Every face in the crowd,
Shining through ev'ry cloud,
It was you again;
From Deauville to Seville,
Rome to Capri,
Wherever I looked,
Whom did I see?

I saw you again,
It was you again;
Gondoliers sang their song,
But the voice kept belong-
Ing to you again;
Anyone I was with,
No matter who,
It was you again,
Always you.

It was you again,
It was you again,
Ev'ry dashing Don Juan
From Madrid to Milan—
O was you again;
All that Viennese charm
Oozed with your name;
Even the Pope
Somehow became

Always you again;
It was you again.
The chauffeur in the car,
Ev'ry statue in Flor-
Ence was you again;
Anyone I was with,
No matter who,
It was you again,
Always you.

I've Been Married

GODFREY
I have tied the wedding knot,
Until the blood began to clot,
For living life connubi'lly
Isn't any Jubilee.

I've seen how lovely loving starts
And slowly turns to martial arts –
I've been married.

I've tossed and turned and couldn't sleep
From counting minks instead of sheep –
I've been married.

The beautiful bower of love that began so
    volcanic
In no time at all could have easily sunk the
    Titanic.

The wonder is that I'm alive,
Considering the fact that I've
Been married . . .

You're not drying.

IRENE
Oh, I'm sorry.

GODFREY
When out the window love has flown,
Alone together means alone –
I've been married.

I practised writing epitaphs
And read the book of Job for laughs –
I've been married.

Those week-ends with Piggy and Deedee
    and Mousey and Mimsy;
Till I thought I'd tear everyone-y from
    limbsy to limbsy.

The dinosaur could not survive,
But little me, I'm here and I've
Been married.
I've been married.

I worked till five like every man,
But after five the work began –
I've been married.

GODFREY

Those hours in the bath she spent
I almost sent a bill for rent . . .

*(He is about to hand her a plate. She
has one but is staring at him in dazed
adoration. The music stops.)*

Well . . . ?

IRENE

What?

(Realizes)

Oh?

*(She takes his plate and drops hers. He
catches it in time. He smiles,
tolerantly. The music continues.)*

GODFREY

Those banquets and balls where you'd find
    me wherever the bar was,
While everyone screamed what a son of a
    bitch FDR was.

If K.O.'d boxers can revive,
Then so can I and did and I've
Been married,
Hari-karied;
I've been married
But never again.
Amen.

Outline
Scene 4: The Cocktail Party – same set

a) 'Some People'.
b) Entrance of Tommy Gray. Etc.
c) Irene announces her engagement to a
phoney Russian prince. Everybody decides
to go to El Morocco to celebrate.
d) Musical ending to the scene?

Scene 5: El Morocco

a) Song by entertainer – 'Try Love'??
b) Irene runs out.

Scene 6: The Kitchen

a) It is Godfrey's day off. Molly is sitting
sewing buttons on his clothes.
b) Irene enters with flowers for Godfrey.
c) Discovers Molly is in love with him, too.
Duet – crying.

Scene 7: Plaza – Tea Dancing

a) Tommy and Godfrey – 'Miss Hilary
Bacon'. Discover Godfrey is on the wagon
and has been since he arrived at the City
Dump and pulled himself together.
b) Cornelia asks Godfrey to dance. Reprise
of 'Hilary Bacon' with new lyrics.

Scene 8: The Living Room

a) Everybody present but Cornelia.
b) Irene says she wants to go to Europe.
Mrs Bullock thinks it would be a lovely idea
for her and Cornelia to go away.
c) Mr Bullock enters in a state – 'March of
the Dollars'.
d) Cornelia enters, her pearls are missing.
She has already called the police.

Scene 9: Godfrey's room

a) Pearls scene. Reprise of 'Dancin' My
Blues Away' by Godfrey at the end of the
scene.

Scene 10: City Dump

a) 'Happy Thanksgiving' – Men.
b) Godfrey enters (with Tommy) and four
men carrying folding tables loaded with food
and drink.
c) 'Happy Thanksgiving' – Godfrey.
d) Mention of Irene leaving for Europe that
day.
e) Reprise of 'Happy Thanksgiving' by
men. Boat siren heard in the distance.
f) Godfrey begins his first drink.

☆ SONGS ☆

Although Alan made a point not to write individual pieces with no particular dramatic context, late in his life he twice made exceptions to the rule. The first time was in 1984, when he was invited to put words to a movie title song composed by Michel Legrand, called 'The Secret Places'. Exactly one year later, unprompted by anything but affection, he reacted to a royal occasion in his adopted homeland.

Secret Places

Long ago I had secret places
That I could run to inside me.
There were sunfilled hilltops
Ablaze with flowers
Where in winter
I strolled for hours.
Far off islands with names I made up
Where gentle winds lullabied me . . .
I was safe and sound
Till one day I found
There were no more hills to climb.
The distant shores I knew
Disappeared from view
In the falling mist of time.
And now I search each day
But I've lost my way,
Lost the child who once used to guide me.
And I wonder now
What am I to do
For secret places
To help me through
The world.

Brocades and Coronets

(Prince Harry's Lullaby)

Brocades and coronets,
Horses with plumes;
Medals and uniforms
Gilding the rooms...

Hundreds of years ago
Your life began.
Brocades and coronets
Are waiting when you are a man.

Now for a fleeting hour
You're mine alone;
Mine in your tiny bower
Just my baby –
Oh my baby.
How I'll miss you when you've grown.

☆ AFTERWORD ☆

In retrospect, it is easy enough for the rest of us to realize what Alan Lerner realized at the time, that his pre-ordained partner, in terms of both style and temperament, was Frederick Loewe, and that once the partnership was broken, there would never be another. After Loewe's retirement there followed a succession of new partners, none of whom ever came close to achieving the impossible feat of filling Loewe's shoes. Of them all, it was Burton Lane, artistically speaking, who was the most notable. But after Fritz Loewe, it was never the same. This is not altogether unusual in the world of the musical stage. The career of Lerner's hero and friend, Ira Gershwin, following the death of his brother George, was markedly similar to Lerner's after the retirement of Loewe: a succession of gifted, distinguished partners who were never quite able to bridge the chasm. But so far as his own skills were concerned, Alan seems never to have lost the fine edge of that incisive mind, never to have lost the relish for seeking the unexpected rhyme in the expected situation. Having written one sublimely perfect musical, *My Fair Lady*, and one flawed masterpiece, *Camelot*, besides dozens of unforgettable individual songs, he may certainly be said to have achieved the immortality he hardly dared hope for, and which his father privately sensed would come as inevitably as the sunrise.

☆ ACKNOWLEDGEMENTS ☆

Every effort had been made to trace copyright holders and we apologise for any omissions

On The Street Where I Live extracts by permission of Hodder and Stoughton Ltd

Lyrics from **The Little Prince** © the Famous Music Corporation (USA)

Lyrics from **Brigadoon** are reproduced by permission of EMI Music Publishing Ltd (UK) and © 1947 United Artist Music Pub Co (USA)

Lyrics from **1600 Pennsylvania Avenue** © Amberson Productions (USA)

Lyrics from **Dance A Little Closer** © Warner Brothers Music Ltd (UK) and Tommy Valando Music Corp. (USA)

Lyrics from **Lolita** and **My Man Godfrey** © Alan Jay Lerner and Gerard Kenny (*Lolita*) and John Barry. *Lolita* registered with Barwin Music Co. USA.

Lyrics from **Royal Wedding** © CBS (USA)

What's Up?
'My Last Love'
Author: A J Lerner
Composer: F Loewe
© 1943 Chappell and Co Inc (USA)
British Publisher: Chappell Music Ltd

The Day Before Spring
'A Jug of Wine'
'God's Green World'
'I Love You This Morning'
'This Is My Holiday'
Author: A J Lerner
Composer: F Loewe
© 1945 Chappell & Co Inc
British Publisher: Chappell Music Ltd

Love Life
'Here I'll Stay'
'This Is The Life'
'Susan's Dream'

'Economics'
'Love Song'
'Green Up Time'
Author: A J Lerner
Composer: Kurt Weill
© 1948 Chappell & Co Inc (USA)
British Publisher: Chappell Music Ltd
'Progress'
Author: A J Lerner
Composer: Kurt Weill
© 1955 Chappell and Co Inc (USA)
British Publisher: Chappell Music Ltd
'Madrigal'
Author: A J Lerner
Composer: Frederick Loewe
© 1962 Chappell & Co Inc (USA)

Paint Your Wagon
'I'm On My Way'
'Wan'drin Star'
Author: A J Lerner
Composer: F Loewe
© 1951 Chappell Music Company (USA)
British Publisher: Chappell Music Ltd
'I Talk To The Trees'
'I Still See Elisa'
'They Call The Wind Maria'
'How Can I Wait?'
'There's A Coach Comin' In'
'Another Autumn'
Author: A J Lerner
Composer: F Loewe
© 1951 Chappell & Co Inc
British Publisher: Chappell Music Ltd
'The Gospel Of No Name City'
'Gold Fever'
'The First Thing You Know'
'A Million Miles Away'
Author: A J Lerner
Composer: Andre Previn
© 1969 Chappell & Co Inc
British Publisher: Chappell Music Ltd

My Fair Lady
'With A Little Bit Of Luck'
'Why Can't The English'
'Just You Wait'

'On The Street Where You Live'
'Ascot Gavotte'
'I Could Have Danced All Night'
'Show Me'
'Without You'
'I've Grown Accustomed To Her Face'
'A Hymn To Him'
'Get Me To The Church On Time'
'Wouldn't It Be Luverly?'
'I'm An Ordinary Man'
'You Did It'
'The Rain In Spain'
Author: A J Lerner
Composer: F Loewe
© 1956 Chappell & Co Inc
British Publisher: Chappell Music Ltd

Gigi

'She Is Not Thinking Of Me'
'I'm Glad I'm Not Young Any More'
Author: A J Lerner
Composer: F Loewe
© 1957 Chappell Music Co Inc (USA)
'Gigi'
Author: A J Lerner
Composer: F Loewe
© 1957/8 Chappell Music Company (USA)
British Publisher: Chappell Music Ltd
'Thank Heaven For Little Girls'
'I Don't Understand The Parisians'
'I Remember It Well'
'Say A Prayer'
Author: A J Lerner
Composer: F Loewe
© 1957 and 1958 Chappell Inc (USA)
British Publisher: Chappell Music Ltd
'It's A Bore'
Author: A J Lerner
Composer: F Loewe
© 1958 Chappell & Co Inc
British Publisher: Chappell Music Ltd
'The Night They Invented Champagne'
Author: A J Lerner
Composer: F Loewe
© 1957 Chappell & Co Inc

Camelot

'Fie On Goodness'
'The Jousts'
'Then You May Take Me To The Fair'
'Follow Me'
'How To Handle A Woman'
'Before I Gaze At You Again'

'If Ever I Would Leave You'
'I Wonder What The King Is Doing Tonight'
'The Simple Joys Of Maidenhood'
'Camelot'
'The Lusty Month Of May'
'The Seven Deadly Virtues'
'I Loved You Once In Silence'
'Guenevere'
'C'est Moi'
Author: A J Lerner
Composer: F Loewe
© 1960 Chappell Music Co (USA)
British Publisher: Chappell Music Ltd
'What Do The Simple Folks Do?'
Author: A J Lerner
Composer: F Loewe
© 1960 Chappell & Co Inc
British Publisher: Chappell Music Ltd

On A Clear Day You Can See Forever

'Hurry! It's Lovely Up Here'
'On A Clear Day You Can See Forever'
'On The SS Bernard Cohn'
'Melinda'
'Go To Sleep'
'Love With All The Trimmings'
'Come Back To Me'
'When I'm Being Born Again'
'What Did I Have I Don't Have?'
Author/Composer: A J Lerner/Burton Lane
© 1965 Chappell and Co Inc
British Publisher: Chappell Music Ltd

Coco

'The World Belongs To The Young'
'Let's Go Home'
'Fiasco'
'Coco'
'A Woman Is How She Loves'
'Gabrielle'
'The Money Rings Out Like Freedom'
'When Your Lover Says Goodbye'
'Ohrbach's, Bloomingdales, Best And Saks'
'Always Mademoiselle'
Author: A J Lerner
Composer: Andre Previn
© 1969 Chappell Music Co (USA)
British Publisher Chappell Music Ltd

Drawings © Al Hirschfeld reproduced by
special arrangement with Hirschfeld's
exclusive representative, The Margo Feiden
Galleries, New York.

☆ INDEX OF SONGS ☆